EXPLORING
CHIANG MAI
CITY, VALLEY & MOUNTAINS
OLIVER HARGREAVE

Odyssey Publications & Within Books

EXPLORING CHIANG MAI
City, Valley & Mountains

PUBLISHED BY ODYSSEY BOOKS & GUIDES, a division
of Airphoto International Limited, 1401 Chung Ying Building,
20 Connaught Road West, Sheung Wan, Hong Kong.
Tel: 852-2856 3896. Email: odysseyb@netvigator.com
Web: www.odysseypublications.com

Within Books is a division of
WITHIN DESIGN CO., LTD.
9 Charoenprathet Rd., Soi 9 A.Muang, Chiang Mai 50100,
Thailand Tel: (66-53) 272111 Fax: (66-53) 272666

ISBN: 962-217-717-4
First International Edition 2003
Printed in Thailand

Distribution in the United States of America by
W.W. Norton & Company, Inc.,
500 Fifth Avenue, New York, NY 10110
Tel. 800-233 4830
Web. www.wwnorton.com

Distribution in the United Kingdom and Europe by
Cordee Ltd.,
3a De Montfort Street, Leicester, LE1 7HD
Tel. 0116-254 3579
Web. www.cordee.co.uk

TEXT : Oliver Hargreave
MANAGING EDITOR: Chairat Usavangkul
ART EDITOR: Sumana Usavangkul
DESIGN & COMPOSITION: Within Design Co., Ltd.
CARTOGRAPHY & PRODUCTION FOR THIS EDITION: Oliver Hargreave
PRODUCTION CONSULTANT FOR THIS EDITION: Gordon Morton
ILLUSTRATIONS: T. Sumit
COMPUTER GRAPHICS: Saravut Sarayantanavut
TYPESETTING: Rungthiwa Boonpan
REPRODUCTION: Thung Hua Sinn Printing Co., Ltd.
PRINTING: Thung Hua Sinn Printing Co., Ltd., Bangkok.

MAIN PHOTOGRAPHER: Oliver Hargreave
CONTRIBUTING PHOTOGRAPHERS:
Hans Benziger, Ron Emmons, Stephen Elliot,
Ittipon Elajukanon, Elmer Haas, David Henley
Vicom Kittirattanachai.

The chedi of Wat Lok Moli, one of the finest in the city, had for long been hidden away behind unused land which was slated for commercial development. As the millennium turned, the land was reclaimed for use as a temple, as it had probably once been during the golden age of Lan Na.

Cover Picture: Dawn view east over the M Taeng Valley towards Doi Luang Chiang Dao d ing the cold season.

PREFACE TO THIRD EDITION

*C*hiang Mai has grown from its origins as a small northern capital to become a city representative of modern Thai culture. Yet behind its modern face Chiang Mai enjoys a traditional heritage as the capital of a region with a culture and geography distinct from that of central Thailand. Protected by mountains and by political frontiers as it is, it has remained largely sheltered from the turbulence of world events.

Making Thaphae and/or Loi Khroh permanent walking streets in the evening would capitalise on the popularity of Sunday walking streets, an innovation that first began in 2002.

Yet at first sight the city may appear bewilderingly chaotic, especially if seen from the windows of a tour coach. This book is designed to help you not only enjoy the regular tourist sights, if not to give you something to remember them by, but also to help you make your way independently. This is the best way to experience the magic that makes Chiang Mai so enjoyable.

he Imperial Hotel Group sponsored the restoration of the rea around an outlying chedi of Wat Chang Khong. Formerly idden by shanties, the chedi stands next to their property.

Many people helped in the production of this book, many have made complimentary remarks on previous editions, and a few have gone out of their way to let me know my errors. The author wishes to thank all of them, for they have helped to sustain this project. The responsibility for errors, as usual, lies with the author. Facts in guidebooks have to be checked on an all too regular basis, so if any reader can similarly help with a view to sustaining, if not improving quality of information in future editions, please feel free to e-mail your comments or suggested revisions to the author at <oliver@lanna.com>.

It is my hope that this book is easy to use and allows you to have maximum fun during your visit to Chiang Mai. The Thai word for fun is *sanuk,* and to be *sanuk* in Thailand is to guarantee yourself a wonderful time. If you can put a smile on your face when faced with little irritations, your problems should disappear for Thais will readily apply the quick fix. Truly the happy go lucky when in Thailand. May you have a pleasant stay.

The production team

TIPS FOR FIRST-TIME VISITORS

The commercial heart of the city developed between the old historical city enclosed by the moats and the river, which was the main conduit for trade. This is the very best area to stay (*Downtown Chiang Mai map 30 pp. 200-20*), but anywhere in Central Chiang Mai (*map 29 pages 184-185*) will get you close to the main attractions in the heart of Chiang Mai.

A delightful way to get around town is by bicycle — there is no reason why the walking tours should not be done on one. Using the small *sois* you can get almost anywhere in the city while avoiding the busy main routes. People going about their lives in these lanes will smile at you in the manner for which Thailand is famous. But because they are so used to being warned of an approaching vehicle by the sound of its engine, make sure your bicycle has a working bell!

You can use a bicycle to get further out of town, the grades are very gentle in the valley, or you can rent a small motorcycle. The latter are inexpensive to rent and easy to ride, but you must take care on the roads! The most pleasant routes to take out of town follow the roads that run north and south on both sides of the River Ping (*see map 6 p.80*). Within a relatively short distance, these roads will get you into pleasant valley scenery, avoiding the ribbon development along the main highways.

Public transport is readily available (*pages 196-199*) for longer journeys, but you need go no farther than Doi Suthep-Pui National Park to see the variety of plant and bird-life in the region. This is the park which covers the forested mountain directly overlooking the city from the west. *Happy Trails!*

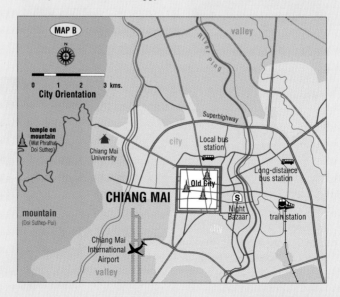

CONTENTS

THE MOUNTAIN PEOPLES

ENJOYING LIFE IN CHIANG MAI:

PRACTICAL INFORMATION:

MAP INDEX

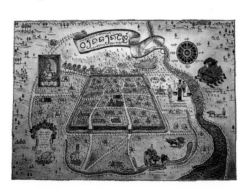

Introduction to Lan Na

Chiang Mai owes her existence to the River Ping. The river provided the route along which the power of the city could be extended beyond the wall of mountains that surrounded the valley; it was a channel for trade from China and Burma to the Gulf of Siam. The wide, fertile valley was able to support a large number of people, the basis of political power in the feudal kingdom of Lan Na.

HISTORY OF LAN NA

THE PING RIVER VALLEY was long a trading route between Yunnan and the Chao Phraya basin. Evidence from archeological remains has shown that early inhabitants used iron tools in the valley at least two thousand years ago. These early people, who came to be known as the Lawa, were later supplanted by the Mon of the Dvaravati period (6-10th centuries). Drawn by trade along the river, the Mon chose the wide, fertile valley to found Haripunchai (Lamphun), in the eighth century. It was the first city-state with a 'high culture' in the valley.

Astronomical information in the circle atop the text on the sixteenth century stela at Wat Chiang Man enabled precise dating of the founding of the city.

The fertile valley also attracted King Mangrai, a powerful Tai leader who captured Haripunchai and then founded his "new capital" — *Chiang Mai* — in 1296. He chose a site typical for a Tai city — at the foot of a mountain that provided both water and timber.

Chiang Mai became the capital of the Kingdom of Lan Na (the Kingdom of a Million Rice Fields). The kingdom reached the height of powers in the late 15th century, entering a golden age in which the

16th Century Witness

"I went from Pegu to Jamahey, which is in the country of the Langeiannes, whom we call Tangomes: it is five and twenty days' journey north-east from Pegu. In which journey I passed many fruitful and pleasant countries. The country is very low, and hath many fair rivers. The houses are very bad, made of canes and covered with straw. Here are many wild buffes and elephants. Jamahey is a very fair and great town, with fair houses of stone, well peopled, the streets are very large, the men very well set and strong, with a cloth about them, bare headed and bare footed: for in all these countries they wear no shoes. The women be much fairer than those of Pegu. Here in all these countries they have no wheat. They make some cakes of rice. Hither to Jamahey come many merchants out of China, and bring great store of musk, gold, silver, and many other things of China work. Here is great store of victuals; they have such plenty, that they will not milk the buffes, as they do in all other places. Here is great store of copper and benjamin. In these countries when the people be sick they make a vow to offer meat unto the devil, if they escape: and when they be recovered they make a banquet with many pipes and drums and other instruments, and dancing all the night, and their friends come and bring gifts, cocoes, figs, arrecaes, and other fruits, and with great dancing and rejoicing they offer to the devil, and say, they give the devil to eat, and drive him out. When they be dancing and playing they will cry and hollow very loud: and in this sort they say they drive him away. And when they be sick a tallipoie or two every night doth sit by them and sing, to please the devil that he should not hurt them. And if any die he is carried upon a great frame made like a tower, with a covering all gilded with gold made of canes, carried with fourteen or sixteen men, with drums and pipes and other instruments playing before him to a place out of the town, and there is burned..."

The Voyage of Mr Ralph Fitch to Ormus, and so to Goa in the East India; to Cambaia, Gangese, Bengala; to Bacola and Chonderi, to Pegu, to Jamahey in the Kingdom of Siam, and Back to Pegu, and from thence to Malacca, Zeilan, Cochin and all the coast of the East India. Begun in the Year of our Lord 1583, and ended 1591" in Pinkerton, John 'A General Collection of the Best and Most Interesting Voyages and Travels in All Parts of the World' (London: Longman, Hurst, Rees, Orme & Brown, 1811) Vol IX, p. 421.

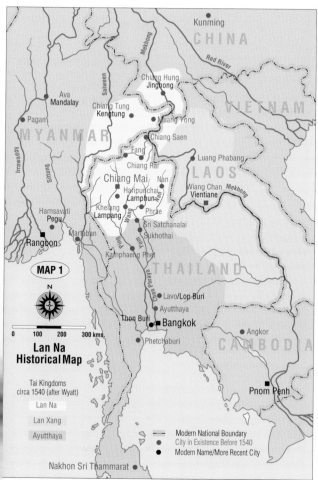

Kunming

CHINA

Red River

Mekhong

Salween

VIETNAM

Ava
Mandalay

Chiang Hung
Jinghong

Chiang Tung
Kengtung

Muang Yong

Pagan

MYANMAR

Chiang Saen

Fang

Chiang Rai

LAOS

Irrawaddy

Sittang

Chiang Mai

Nan

Luang Phabang

Haripunchai
Lamphun

Khelang
Lampang

Phrae

Wiang Chan
Vientiane

Mekhong

Hamsavati
Pegu

Sri Satchanalai

Martaban

Wang

Yom

Sukhothai

Rangoon

Ping

Kamphaeng Phet

THAILAND

MAP 1

N

Chao Phraya

Lavo/Lop-Buri

Ayutthaya

0   100   200   300 kms.

Thon Buri   Bangkok

**Lan Na
Historical Map**

Phetchaburi

Angkor

CAMBODIA

Tai Kingdoms
circa 1540 (after Wyatt)

Lan Na

Lan Xang

Ayutthaya

Pnom Penh

- - - - Modern National Boundary
○ City in Existence Before 1540
● Modern Name/More Recent City

Nakhon Sri Thammarat

---

the st
until, ̦
lack of ̦
after Kin̦
Chiang M
struggle to
of Pegu in 1

For over two centuries (1558-1774) Chiang Mai was for most of the period under Burmese control. Initially this was benign, but the Burmese wars against Ayutthaya drained the strength of the city, and revolt brought suppression. Eventually northern Thai forces allied with the Siamese to drive the Burmese out, but the remaining population was too small to defend the city and it had to be abandoned.

With Siamese help, Chao Kawila of Lampang fought against the Burmese and slowly repopulated the area, re-establishing Chiang Mai in 1796, but he was not to drive the Burmese out of their northern stronghold at Chiang Saen till 1804.

Allied in vassal status to the Siamese, the rulers of Lan Na had to make periodic displays of loyalty to Bangkok, provide military assistance if required and supply local products. The Siamese monarch appointed new rulers, but otherwise left them with control of all internal matters as well as control of relations with immediate neighbours.

With the growth of British interest in the northern Teak forests, however, the threat of Western interests forced King Chulalongkorn (Rama V) of Siam to slowly take over the administration of the north. The northern rulers were to

---

devout kings King Tilokarat and King Muang Kaeo were able to both consolidate political power and sponsor great religious works.

Tilokarat's control extended over what now constitutes northern Thailand, northwestern Laos, the eastern Shan States of Burma and Xishuangbanna Autonomous Prefecture in southern Yunnan. His sponsorship of the eighth Buddhist Council in 1477 significantly added to

the corpus of Pali scriptures, which, modified to suit local circumstances, were to form the basis of the religious system in Siam and Cambodia.

However, Lan Na was caught between the powerful maritime states of Pegu and Ayutthaya, which benefitted from trade and which could support greater populations on wet-rice cultivation. Lan Na was to fight several times against Ayutthaya in the 14th and 15th centuries, draining their powers and the independence by the end of the 19th century. Economic integration with Siam became firmer with the opening of the railway in 1921, and trade was to increase, but the timber trade declined in the depression and the economy of Chiang Mai was severely weakened. Things did not improve during the Japanese occupation in World War Two despite the Siamese invasion of Kengtung.

After the war, an influx of refugees added to the parlous state of the Siamese economy, and the communist revolution in China in 1949 marked years of poverty for Chiang Mai. Only in the late fifties and sixties, when projects to develop rural infrastructure and agriculture were initiated to prevent the area falling to communism, did Chiang Mai begin to prosper as a regional market.

Economic growth in the visible sector was accompanied by inflows of capital from immigrant Yunnanese Chinese, who developed cross border trading in the black market with Burma after the border closed to legal trade with Ne Win's socialist coup in 1962.

With the addition of the tourism boom that began in the seventies, the last twenty years of the 20th century saw unparalleled development in Chiang Mai, a growth that was encouraged by spillover from over-development in the Bangkok Metropolis. The population of the province reached a total of 1.5 million, with an estimated 250,000 living in the city area alone.

The year-long celebrations of the city's 700th anniversary in 1996-7 heralded the end of the 'bubble economy' and the economic crash that devasted the national economy. With trade links to Myanmar ever threatened by political if not military disruption, with trade with China hindered by the lack of infrastructure in Laos, and with the world economy in the shadow of recession, the city once again faces interesting times.

King Mangrai

King Mangrai was born to the ruler of Ngoen Yang (in the region of Chiang Saen) in 1239. His mother was a daughter of the Tai Leu ruler of Chiang Hung (Jinghong in Xishuangbanna Prefecture, Yunnan). The 25th in a line of Lao kings, he ascended to the throne in 1259.

A charismatic and powerful leader, he quickly established dominance over the small neighbouring principalities. As his power increased he moved his capital to Chiang Rai, which he founded in 1262, and then to Fang in 1268. In 1276, he formed an alliance with King Ngam Muang, the powerful ruler of Phayao.

King Mangrai captured the richer and more powerful city of Haripunchai (Lamphun) in 1281. He was able to do this through a conspiracy with a skilful merchant called Ai Fa, who won the confidence of the city's ruler and became chief minister. Ai Fa then undermined the king's popularity, bringing about the easy downfall of the city.

Mangrai gained further strength from his association with King Ngam Muang of Phayao, who had been tutored as a child with King Ramkamhaeng of Sukhothai. This helped Mangrai forge an alliance with the latter in 1287 securing his southern flank from attack and giving him a free hand to counter threat from the Mongol Chinese empire to the north.

At some time in the 1280's Mangrai moved his capital to Wiang Kum Kam, but the

The Nawarat bridge in 1953. The Chedi Luang (mid-left on the city sky-line against the mountain) was the tallest structure in Chiang Mai.

Courtesy of Ban Ngualai, Kat Muang, Kat Suan Kaew

Important Dates in Lanna History

site later proved to be unsuitable. In the late 1280's he made two expeditions to Burma. From the Mon kingdom of Hamsavati (Pegu) he gained an alliance and the hand of the king's daughter. From the Shan kingdom of Ava-Pagan he gained 500 families of skilled craftsmen when the area fell to the

King Mangrai

Mongols in 1287. In 1288, he took over the Mon town of Khelang (Lampang).

Mangrai founded his grandest capital, Chiang Mai, in 1296 and began to embellish it with temples. His forces successfully campaigned against the Chinese Mongols in Southern Yunnan, but after 1311 he sent tribute to the Mongols and averted further threats from the north. He died in the middle of the city, reputedly from a lightning strike, in the year 1317.

Mangrai had three sons. The second son, Chai Songkhram, was to continue the dynasty that ruled Lan Na until the death of Princess Wisutthithewi in 1578.

767   (or in the early ninth century) Haripunchai was founded by hermits who invited Princess Chamadevi of Lop Buri to rule.

1259   Mangrai (r.1259-1317) became King of Ngoen Yang. He moved his capital to Chiang Rai (1262) and then to Fang (1268).

1281   King Mangrai captured Haripunchai. He moved his capital to Wiang Kum Kam around 1288.

1296   King Mangrai founded Chiang Mai.

1345   King Pha Yu (r.1337-1355) founded Wat Phra Singh and laid the foundation for the golden age of Lan Na, which began with the reign of his son King Ku Na.

1371   King Ku Na (r.1355-1385) founded Wat Suan Dok for Phra Sumana Thera, establishing a Sinhalese Buddhist sect that became the major cultural influence in Lan Na.

1385   King Saen Muang Ma (r.1385-1401) fought off an attack from Ayutthaya, but was defeated when he attacked Sukhothai in 1387.

1405   King Sam Fang Kaen (r.1401-1441) repelled Yunnanese armies and consolidated the Kingdom of Lan Na.

1449   King Tilokarat (r.1441-1487) captured Nan, bringing Lan Na to the height of its power in the golden age. Considered the greatest of the Lanna kings after Mangrai, he supported Buddhist works and construction.

1477   The Eighth World Buddhist Council met at Wat Chet Yot to revise the Buddhist canon, bringing Lanna culture to its zenith.

1495   King Muang Kaew (r.1495-1526) patronised the arts as the last of the great kings of Lan Na. His successor, King Chettarat (r.1526-38 & 1543-45), was deposed in favour of his son, was enthroned again and then was assassinated.

1545   An earthquake damaged the Phra Chedi Luang in a year that saw unsuccessful attacks on Chiang Mai by both a Shan prince and Ayutthaya.

1546   King Setthathirat of Luang Phabang, the capital of the Kingdom of Lan Xang, ascended to the throne of Lan Na (by invitation) only to return to his Lao capital upon the death of his father in 1547. Lan Na collapsed into civil war between the chiefs of the principalities.

1551   Invited by local chiefs to rule, Phra Mekuti (r.1551-1564) began an oppressive and unpopular rule. He forbade worship of the city pillar, an act which is thought to have brought misfortune to Chiang Mai.

1558   Chiang Mai fell without struggle to the Burmese. Prince Mekuti remained in power as a vassal after swearing allegiance to King Bayinnaung and promising to pay annual tribute in elephants, horses and cloth.

1564 Mekuti repudiated his allegiance by refusing Bayinnaung's request to help when the latter defeated Ayutthaya. Bayinnaung returned to Chiang Mai to replace Mekuti with Queen Wisutthithewi (r. 1564-1578), the last of Mangrai's descendants to hold the throne of Chiang Mai.

1598 King Naresuan (r.1590-1605) captured Chiang Mai.

Elephants waiting to join the proces sion of King Rama VII and his Quee on a royal visit to Chiang Mai i 1926.

1614-15. The Burmese restored direct control of the city and took manpower with them back to Hamsavati (Pegu). This included one Thomas Samuel, who was one of two representatives of the East India Company and who had tarried in Chiang Mai after being sent there to trade cloth in 1613. He was to die in Pegu, but his partner, Thomas Driver, escaped this fate having returned to Ayutthaya earlier. These two were amongst the earliest Europeans recorded as having been in Chiang Mai.

1661 King Narai (r.1656-1688) captured and briefly held Chiang Mai. The Burmese imposed direct control on Chiang Mai, maintaining their centre of power in Chiang Saen when Chiang Mai became independent under King Oung Kham from 1727.

1763 The Burmese recaptured Chiang Mai, imposed heavy taxation and depleted the population.

1767 The Burmese destroyed Ayutthaya. King Taksin re-grouped at Chantaburi and Thon Buri.

1774 Breaking a tradition of hostility, Phraya Chaban of Chiang Mai and Chao Kawila of Lampang sided with the Siamese against the Burmese and recaptured Chiang Mai in 1775.

1776 Chiang Mai was abandoned as indefensible due to a lack of manpower to defend against Burmese attacks.

1796 Chao Kawila (r.1781-1816) re-established Chiang Mai, but the struggle against the Burmese in Lan Na was to continue.

1804 Chiang Saen, the Burmese northern stronghold, was finally taken by Kawila's forces, and the ruler of Chiang Tung became a vassal of King Rama 1. Though the struggle against the Burmese in Lan Na had ended, from 1809 the Burmese began reoccupying territories traditionally under Chiang Tung (Kengtung), paving the way for British annexation of this territory later in the century.

1855 The Bowring Treaty reduced duties on foreign trade, gave

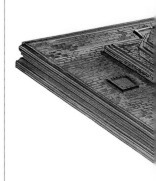

Reconstruction in 1985-1986 of the remains of Wat Ikang, Wiang Kum Kam, was based on evidence collected during archaeological excavations at the site. The pillars are those of the former viharn (20 x 13.5 m). Chronicles make no mention of the temple, but inscriptions found on bricks at the site used a style of lettering dating from the late Lanna period in the 15-16th centuries (see p.94).

British subjects extraterritorial rights and abolished royal monopolies except for opium.

1867 Daniel McGilvary was the first Presbyterian missionary to come to Chiang Mai. In 1869 two of their first five native converts were clubbed to death in the forest at the order of *Chao* Kawilorot (r.1856-70). This incident disturbed King Chulalongkorn, who was in support of the modernising (medicine and education) aspects of the American mission.

1868 King Chulalongkorn (Rama V r.1868-1910) began reforms that set the foundation for the Thai state.

1871 Chao Inthawichayanon (Inthanon r.1871—1897) was chosen to succeed to the throne of Chiang Mai by the Siamese court in Bangkok due to his more favourable disposition towards Siam.

1874 A Siamese commissioner was appointed to Chiang Mai and slowly moved to limit the prerogative of the northern *chao*

1884 Chao Thep Kraison, who had been the virtual ruler of Chiang Mai behind her weaker husband, Chao Inthawichayanon, died. The American and British established consular offices. Chinese traders started to increase in number.

1885 The telegraph reached Chiang Mai.

1892 Siam incorporated Lan Na into the administrative unit of 'Monthon Phayap'.

1893 France forced Siam to cede Laos, which included territory within the traditional domain of Lan Na.

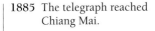

1896 The Anglo-French guaranteed a buffer area between their colonial interests in Burma and Cochin-China

1902 The Shan rebellion was the last stirring of northern independence.

1921 The railway reached Chiang Mai. Education was made compulsory.

1932 Chiang Mai became a province of Siam.

1946 King Bhumiphol Adulyadej became King Rama IX of Siam (the name of Thailand being officially recognised in 1949).

Chao Kawila

Kawila was born in 1742, the first of ten children of Prince Chai Kaew of Lampang. After he had become ruler of Lampang, Kawila joined with Prince Chaban, the ruler of Chiang Mai, in a plot to rid the cities of oppressive Burmese rule.

In 1767, they sought the help of King Taksin who had regrouped his forces at Thonburi after the destruction of Ayutthaya. Taksin sent an army under the command of Chao Phraya Chakri. With the help of Kawila, they overthrew the Burmese in Lampang in 1774 and Chiang Mai in 1776. After Burmese counter-attacks, however, Chiang Mai had to be abandoned.

In spite of an incident that resulted in imprisonment, sickness and death for Prince Chaban, and in Kawila being lashed and having the rims of his ears sliced for impudence, King Taksin gave Kawila the task of rebuilding Chiang Mai. His position as a vassal was strengthened, however, when Chao Phraya Chakri took the throne as Rama I in 1782.

The Kawila Monument

Kawila campaigned against the Burmese, building up manpower to repopulate the city. He formally reoccupied the city in March 1796. Threats to the city continued, but Kawila added to its strength by rebuilding the fortifications. He also began rebuilding the city's temples.

In 1802, King Rama I officially appointed Kawila as ruler of Chiang Mai. Kawila placed his brothers as rulers of other northern cities and continued with campaigns against the Burmese. He died of fever in 1815 at the age of 73, leaving a brother as the new *chao*. The second of Kawila's two sons eventually became the sixth ruler of Chiang Mai, Chao Kawilorot.

The results of Kawila's work may be seen in many parts of Chiang Mai. As a tribute to his military skills, his statue stands in front of Army Camp Kawila.

An artists rendition of Chao Kawila storming the city by night. (Kawila memorial, Charoenrat Rd.)

Chiang Mai, 1884

"It is a very pretty sight in the early morning to watch the women and girls from the neighbouring villages streaming over the bridge, their produce dangling from each end of a pole of bamboo over their shoulders, or accurately poised on their heads....

The ordinary costume of these graceful maidens consists of flowers in their hair...a skirt, frequently embroidered near the bottom... at times a...scarf cast carelessly over their bosom...

After passing through the gates of the outer city, we entered the market, which extends for more than half a mile to the gates of the Inner City, and beyond them for some distance towards the palace. On either side of the main road, little covered booths or stalls are set up; but most of the women spread

Chiang Mai women in the early 20th century

a mat on the ground to sit upon, and placing their baskets by their side, expose their provisions on wicker work trays or freshly cut plantain leaves."

Holt S. Hallett. *"A Thousand Miles on an Elephant"* (reprint) White Lotus, Bangkok, 1988

Trade and the loss of Northern Independence

Prior to the 19th century, foreign trade with Lan Na had come with itinerant merchants, who traded gold and luxury items like foreign cloth for forest products such as skins, horns, beeswax, benzoin (a yellowish balsamic resin used in perfumes and incense) and sticlac, items which were in strong demand in China.

At the end of the 18th century the Siamese crown generated much of its income through trade in such forest products. They also sought additional wealth by increasing manpower to expand the agricultural frontiers in a kingdom left under-populated by the wars with Burma, and so King Taksin (r. 1767-1782), himself of Teochiu Chinese descent through his father, encouraged immigration from China.

The journey upstream to Chiang Mai from Bangkok took as long as three months, thus Lan Na consisted of small, isolated muang linked to the world by difficult river and caravan routes.

While Thais could only work as slaves, or as indentured rice-farmers bound to their villages and to the land-owning aristocracy by corvée labour, the Chinese immigrants were free to move and settle as they chose. With the crown benefitting through taxation, the Chinese came to monopolise trade in the hinterland of Bangkok in the first half of the 19th century. This happened as land under cultivation started to grow along with overseas demand for agricultural products such as sugar, tobacco, pepper and, increasingly, rice.

At the same time the feudal system of corvée labour began collapsing as indentured labour evaded the system by running to the forest frontier or by paying fees in lieu of service, a process which the Siamese crown encouraged from the 1870's in order to reduce the power of landed aristocracy. State income increasingly depended on royal monopolies and trade in agricultural produce, a surplus of which was generated by extending agricultural land through the building of canals (and later railways) using immigrant Chinese labour.

At some time in the early 19th century a few pioneer Teochiu Chinese traders travelled to Chiang Mai up the river from Bangkok. Western traders, however, first came in the person of a Dr. Richardson, who started cattle exports to supply the Tennaserim state of British Burma in 1830 and who helped initiate the teak trade down the Salween to Moulmein in the 1830's. As a result of this, Burmese and Shan foresters moved into the forests of Lan Na in increasing numbers in the 1840's, helping to create a busy overland trade route to Moulmein.

Teak logs were floated down-river after the rains. Despite the exploitation by Western companies, forest cover in Thailand remained at over 65% until 1950.

The collapse of the China trade in the 1840's due to colonial intervention and then later to the Taiping rebellion encouraged the

Siamese crown to expand trade with colonial country traders. Despite the Bowring Treaty with Britain in 1855 which removed trade restrictions hitherto favouring the Chinese, the Western companies were unable to make inroads on the Chinese control of domestic distribution and supply in the rice trade and other agricultural products. However they achieved spectacular success in the teak industry due to the heavy capitalisation required, the proximity of an established industry in Burma and the demand in western controlled markets. This was to have a decisive influence on the future of Lan Na.

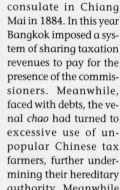

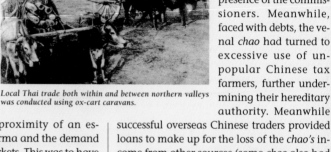

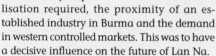

Local Thai trade both within and between northern valleys was conducted using ox-cart caravans.

By 1861 the price of one teak log had risen to 12 silver Indian rupees, and by 1775 there were more than 200 foreign foresters who in turn employed increasing numbers of Shan, Burmese and 'Lao' (northern Thai) workers as wage labourers in Lan Na. With the weakening of the corvée system and the reduction in overland trade in forest products, the teak trade along with taxation on opium and liquor monopolies provided the main source of income for the *chao*.

The *chaos* (there were five senior chiefs/royal princes lead by the *chao luang* in just Chiang Mai alone) arbitrary use of forestry leases to maximise income lead to disputes involving Shan and Burmese foresters, who enjoyed extra-territorial legal rights under the British according to the Bowring Treaty. Fearing British intervention and the potential loss of a vassal territory if he pushed too hard, King Chulalongkorn reluctantly attempted to strengthen his control of Chiang Mai, which had hitherto enjoyed considerable autonomy. Beginning with the Anglo Siamese agreement of 1874, special Siamese courts were set up to handle disputes and a royal commissioner was appointed to control lease activity. Successful legal action by teak companies against the *chao* in Bangkok put the *chao* into debt with

the Siamese crown.

Bangkok's fear of British intentions increased with the establishment of the British consulate in Chiang Mai in 1884. In this year Bangkok imposed a system of sharing taxation revenues to pay for the presence of the commissioners. Meanwhile, faced with debts, the venal *chao* had turned to excessive use of unpopular Chinese tax farmers, further undermining their hereditary authority. Meanwhile successful overseas Chinese traders provided loans to make up for the loss of the *chao's* income from other sources (some *chao* also had a propensity to gamble). These were repaid through grants of commercially valuable land near the city.

Siamese fears of the British increased with the annexation of Mandalay and Northern Burma into British Burma in 1886, prompting further reforms as Bangkok slowly took greater control of the northern administration. In 1892 thirteen northern *muang* (the territories today that lie to the east of the Salween and south of Kengtung) were ceded from Northern Siam to British Burma, whose annexations in the north ceased only with the Anglo-French agreement of 1896. This guaranteed the independence of the head-waters of the Chaophraya (Menam) basin as a buffer between French and British colonial interests, and it freed King Chulalongkorn's hand.

After the death of Chao Inthanon in 1897, the impoverished *chao* agreed to receiving salaries in return for handing over the rights to forest leases to a new Forest Department. From this time on full Siamese control was only a matter of time. The diminution of the *chao's* power was marked by their handing over highly symbolic property at the centre of the city for use by the Siamese administration in 1902, but it was not until 1908 that Bangkok no longer saw the need for the *chao* to send silver and gold trees as tribute.

PEOPLE AND CULTURE

SEVENTY PERCENT of the land in the north is mountainous and in the past was densely orested, making overland communication difficult. As a result ach valley developed slight variaions in customs and language.

People depended on the forest and wet-rice subsistence agriculture, and they were self-sustaining, making what they needed. Customs and beliefs associated with the agricultural cycle were passed down from their ancestors.

The People

THE PEOPLE of the valleys refer to themselves as the *hon muang*, and are of mixed rigin. The first inhabitants vere known as the Lawa. These people were joined by other groups moving along he trading routes of the river alleys. Notable amongst hese groups were the Mon, who originated from the reion around Thaton in Burma. The Mon founded Iaripunchai, a northern offhoot of the Dvaravati ivilisation that dominated he western part of the Chao Phraya basin before the rise f the Khmer empire to the ast. The latter, however, was never to extend its power nto the northern valleys be-

Northern Thais making merit at Wat Phra Singh early in the 20th century.

yond Si Satchanalai. By the 13th century the dominant groups throughout upper Siam were ethnic Tai, who had been migrating south into the valleys since at least the 10th century (some theories plausibly suggest the Tai may have been in the area long before this date). In the north these peoples came to be known as the Tai Yuan, or Khon Muang.

Until the European colonialism of the 19th century, the politics of the north was dominated by the struggles with the Burmese, and between the kingdoms of Ayutthaya, Lan Na and Lan Xang. Each military incursion involved forced relocation of

populations to increase manpower. Thus the wars of the region served mainly to mix ethnic Tai groups.

The Burmese wars left Chiang Mai depleted of peoples, forcing Kawila to campaign and relocate people from neighbouring *muang*. He brought in Tai Yai from Shan State, Tai Khoen from Kengtung, Tai Leu from Sipsongpanna and Tai Yong from Muang Yong, east of Kengtung. He resettled each ethnic group in defined geographical areas; the Yong, for example, were settled near Lamphun. This resulted in subtle differences between communities in the valley that persist to this day.

his abnormal tusker was unable to work and as kept by Chao Kaew Nawarat, the ninth nd last chao of Chiang Mai (r. 1911-1939). he tusks are in the National Museum.

The Tai

The Thais originate from an ethnic group known as the Tai, who were the forebears of peoples found in central Southeast Asia today. These include the Dai and Tai Leu in Yunnan, the Shan in Myanmar, the Lao, the Tai Yuan (Northern Thais) and the Siamese (Central and Southern) Thai, and total more than 90 million people.

Controversy surrounds the origin of the Tai, who spoke a language of the Sino-Tibetan group of languages. Linguistic evidence suggests that they probably originated from Kwangtung and Kwangsi in coastal south China. From there they migrated south and west.

The Tai social unit was a *muang* (the Burmese and Chinese equivalents of *muang* are *meng* and *mong*), which consisted of a group of villages protected by a central fortified town known as a *wiang*. A *muang* was physically restricted to the valley where it was located. The leader of a *muang* protected villagers from danger beyond the valley in exchange for their manpower, the main source of political strength. If the leader of the *muang* was a high ranking noble or monarch, then the fortified centre became a *chiang*.

Kingdoms were formed from alliances between semi-autonomous leaders of the *muang*. Alliances depended entirely upon personal relationships between them, so the death of a powerful king often brought political chaos.

Preparing rice seedlings for transplanting

In the mid-19th century Burmese and Shan workers began arriving to work the forests, establishing the city's Shan communities. Missionaries and Westerners were soon to follow.

While a very small number of Chinese merchants had already migrated up the Ping to Chiang Mai, larger Chinese migration came overland when Muslim Haw Chinese arrived to settle permanently after the Panthay rebellion in Yunnan in 1873. It was the overseas Chinese, however, who were to have the greatest impact when they began arriving in the 1880s in increasing numbers, following opportunities to trade or find labour.

The late 19th century also saw the beginnings of hill tribes migrating south through the uplands, but the greatest numbers were to come after the communist takeover of China in 1949. However, the full effect of the Chinese revolution was delayed until after Ne Win's socialist coup in Burma in 1962. Muslim and Kuomintang Chinese, who had fled to Burma from Yunnan in 1949, had to migrate again to escape persecution by the Burmese military and so many came to Chiang Mai, settling in particular around Fang. They helped develop Chiang Mai city with their trade links to Burma, a trade that supplied items such as medicine for the Burmese black market in exchange for jade and other, sometimes illicit, products.

Finally, the economic boom of the late 20th century brought a significant increase in Thai migration from the south, as well as a sizable influx of foreigners.

Language

THE MAIN ethnic language of the north is *kham muang*. With differences in both vocabulary and tones, Northern Thai may be considered a different language from central Thai. Though the differences are diminishing as *kham muang* borrows from the state language, a person from central Thailand cannot immediately understand the northern language.

Words of Indian origin trace their roots to Pali through the Mon civilisation, as opposed to those of central Thai which came from Sanskrit via the Khmer civilisation of Angkor. *Kham muang* has its own script used in religious texts, but most local people are unable to read it.

Religion

ALTHOUGH Mahayana Buddhism may have come to the region first via the Khmer empire and the Silk Road from China, Sinhalese Theravada Buddhism had become the dominant form of Buddhism by the end of the 14th century.

Theravada Buddhism in its essence is about the *dhamma*, the truth according to the Buddhist view. As the state religion of Lan Na, however, it became connected with Brahmanic court traditions. These came from the Indianised empires of the Khmer at Angkor and the Burmans at Pagan, which were at the height of their

'Seup Chada' — a ceremony to prolong life — at Wat Suan Dok

power in the 12th and 13th centuries.

Prior to the dominance of these beliefs, the Tai were animists with a fertility cult centred on the wet-rice cultivation cycle. The blend of this Tai spirit world with Buddhism has resulted in the variety of customs and religious practice today.

Central to the traditional Thai view of the cosmos is the cycle of rebirth. To commit sin is to be reborn into a hell world, and to make merit is to progress into a better after-life. A forest monk may explain this to a Westerner as an allegory for the laws of cause and effect known as 'karma'. To a Thai villager, the holy images in the temples are the home of powerful spirits, and the vivid depictions of heaven and hell are maps that help him find his way in the cycle of seasons and years.

The temple has long been the social centre of rural Thai communities and Buddhism is woven into the fabric of rural life. The monkhood originally provided the only education available and served to occupy males without work, especially during the rainy season. To this day folk festivals involve making merit by supporting the monkhood with food and labour.

Until quite recently the temple was the main outlet for artistic creativity, the

Northern chronicles were written in local script on palm leaves

Spirits and Mediums

The Northern Thai believe in territorial spirits for forests and fields, tutelary spirits for houses and towns, and ancestral spirits. Misfortune can be blamed on spirits not properly propitiated with such offerings as meat, liquor, areca nut, bananas, coconut, flowers and incense.

In former times the jungle beyond the *muang* was considered the abode of beasts, primitives and fearsome spirits, while the city pillar represented the heart of civilisation. Today Indic forms of worship associated with Brahmanism and Buddhism are used in ceremonies to pay respect to the highest spirits that guard the cities. Villages traditionally have a *lakban* made from a tree trunk in the center of the village, as well as a community spirit house just outside the village.

Pre-Indic practice dominates rituals that honour the lesser ancestral clan spirits. In propitiation rites female mediums following clan lineage are possessed by ancestral spirits, reflecting women's spiritual power in the traditional matriarchal structure of northern society (in rural areas men still move into the houses of their spouses).

In Buddhist cosmology the spirits possessing male or female mediums are thought to be *thewada* who dwell in heavenly realms between the cycle of rebirths, and who are sometimes identified as figures of local historical importance. By providing a beneficial link between spirit world and human realm the mediums are ensuring progress in the cycle of rebirths for all.

In propitiation rituals mediums enter trances, don bright robes, swig rice liquor, dance with abandon and offer guidance to supplicants; whether one comes across such an event is a matter of fortune.

greatest works coming as a result of sponsorship by the ruling nobility. By so doing the rulers not only gained merit, but also gained political legitimacy, as pious works were seen as a crucial part of a leader's majesty.

Buddhist values pervade the character of the Thai, who value maintaining harmony in relationships very highly. To avoid causing offence, Thais pay much attention to outward appearance. However, they also prize having a 'cool heart' — being *jai yen*. This means that you should not allow yourself to become 'hot' with desire and at the mercy of worldly passions which can lead to harmful actions.

Buddhism also teaches tolerance, and so people have been free to practice other religions. Islam first arrived with Muslim Yunnanese who have been trading in the northern valleys since the time of the Mongols (11-13th centuries), and the first permanent Christian mission was established in 1867.

Under the bo tree at Songkran, Wat Chiang Man.

A medium celebrate new year at Chaeng S Phum

Buddhism

Buddhism is based on the teachings of one Siddhartha Gautama who lived in North India in the 6th century BC. Born to the ruler of the Kingdom of the Sakyas (in modern Southern Nepal) his early life was as a prince. However, when confronted with the reality of life beyond the palace walls, he left at the age of 29 to begin the life of an ascetic in search of a solution to the suffering of mankind.

After studying many disciplines he achieved enlightenment under a bo tree (*ficus religiosis*) at the age of 35. Until his death at the age of 80, the Buddha taught the four noble truths to all who were ready to understand, regardless of caste or creed.

The first noble truth states that all existence is in a constant state of change. We are born, we become old, we get sick and we die. We are nothing more than a collection of physical and mental forces momentarily bound together as a 'human being'. This condition he described as human suffering — as *dukkha*.

We mistakenly attach a sense of self, of personal identity, to this flow of change and constantly create desires which we try to satisfy all our lives. The second noble truth is that this fundamental craving, this continuous round of desires, is the cause of *dukkha*.

The third noble truth states that if the mistaken views that give rise to *dukkha* cease, then nirvana — a "peace that passeth all understanding" and totally beyond words to describe — is revealed.

The final truth teaches that there is a way to bring *dukkha* to an end within a human being. This involves following a way of life that is 'right' in terms of the goal — the end of suffering.

Known as The Noble Eight-fold Path, the path provides explicit instruction for behaviour in eight aspects of human life. These must be pursued simultaneously. Right understanding and right thought

Lanna Image, 1465 (Wat Chiang Man)

provide a foundation for wisdom; right speech, right action and right livelihood provide a code of morality; right effort, right mindfulness and right concentration provide a practise of mental discipline.

The Buddha claimed that he was nothing more than a human being and that the ability to become a Buddha was possible for all humans. The Buddha stressed that this can only be achieved through the personal effort and intelligence of an individual following the path.

The saffron-robed community of monks — the *sangha* — are, ideally, trying to live a life that follows and supports others on this path. The general people 'make merit' by supporting the *sangha* and thereby encourage the virtue of selflessness through generosity.

Worldly attachment (panel 6 at Wat Doi Saket — see p.87)

FESTIVALS

THE CHIANG MAI valley is blessed with festivals almost the whole year round. Old festivals are based on the lunar calendar and either have their origin in Buddhist traditions or in Brahmanic and Tai beliefs associated with the rice growing cycle. Newer cultural festivals have evolved from a blend of local traditions and commercial interests.

Festivals at a Glance

Calendar / Lunar Month	Festival and location	Origin of festival
January 3rd weekend	Umbrella Festival Bo Sang village	Cultural (photo p.88)
January 4 days on weekend nearest the end of the month	Wood Carving Fair Ban Tawai, Hang Dong	Cultural
February 1st Weekend	Flower Festival Chiang Mai	Cultural (see main festivals)
February 1st or 2nd weekend	Tin Chok Festival Mae Chaem	Cultural: Celebrates local weaving traditions.
February Full moon of 3rd lunar month	Makha Bucha All temples	Buddhist: Celebrates a famous sermon given by Buddha.
March 30th-April 9th	Chiang Mai Arts & Culture Festival Chiang Mai and surrounding area	Events which include the Shan ordination at Wat Pa Pao (p.65) focus on Lanna culture (also see p.176)
April 13th-15th	Songkran All over Thailand, especially the north.	Ancient Tai-Indic: Traditional New Year (see main festivals).
May full moon of 6th lunar month	Visakha Bucha At temples all over Thailand.	Buddhist: Celebrates birth, enlightenment & death of Buddha.
May-June From 12th day of waning moon of sixth lunar month for 6 days	Inthakhin Wat Chedi Luang: Especially in the evening when crowds make offerings at the city pillar.	Ancient Tai-Indic: Pay respects to the city pillar, bring rain & encourage prosperity (see p.49).
May-June 6th-7th lunar months	Rocket Festivals Wat Pa Tung, Wat Phra Non (and several other temples).	Traditional: Bring rain (see p.91 & p.116).
June 4th day of waxing moon of 7th lunar month	Seup Jata Muang Offerings made to guardian spirits at the cardinal points of City (Gates, city pillar, etc.).	Ancient Tai-Indic: Prolong life of city.

Buddhist Festivals

Buddhist Holy Days — *wan phra* — fall on the eighth day of the rising and falling moons, on the full moon, and on first day of the new moon. Thai calendars usually have the phases of the moon and the lunar month shown under the dates. Thai years are calculated from the death of the Buddha, which is held to be 543 years before the birth of Christ. Thus 1996 is B.E (Buddhist Era) 2539.

The sangha—guardians of Thailand's Buddhist culture

If you visit a temple on a holy day, you may see people dressed in white sitting around the viharn. On holy days devout lay Buddhists traditionally stay in the temple for twenty four hours, a practice which the elderly, particularly womenfolk still observe, but it remains to be seen whether the youth of today will uphold such practices in the future.

On the three main annual Buddhist festivals — *Makha Bucha* (puja), *Visakha Bucha* and *Asalaha Bucha* — that celebrate events in the life of the Buddha, people go to the temples early in the evening for the *wien tien* ceremony. After chanting, a sermon, and some meditation, they walk mindfully three times clockwise around the chedi or viharn holding flowers, a lit candle, and burning incense. These they place nearby as an offering. The ceremony is very atmospheric and it is a good time to go to any of the temples.

Food offerings at Thai New Year, Wat Chiang Man

Parents prepare for their son's ordination.

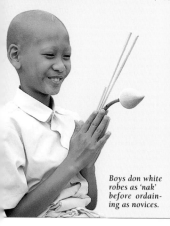
Boys don white robes as 'nak' before ordaining as novices.

'Nak' before ordination at Chiang Mai's 700th anniversary

Calendar / Lunar Month	Festival and location	Origin of festival
June 14th day of waxing moon of 7th lunar month	**Lieng Pu Sae-Ya Sae** Foot of Doi Suthep. Medium is possessed by guardian spirit.	Animist: Propitiate guardian spirits *Pu sae & Ya sae* who live on Doi Suthep (see p.85).
July Full moon and 1st day of waning moon of 8th lunar month	**Asalaha Bucha-Wan Khao Pansa** All temples	Buddhist: Marks the first sermon given by the Buddha & the beginning of the rains retreat.
August From full moon of 10th lunar month till end of September	**Salakaphat** All temples, esp. Wat Chiang Man, Wat Chedi Luang & Wat Suan Dok.	Buddhist: Lay merit making. Alms are put in baskets and given to monks by lottery.
October 1st day of waning moon of 11th lunar month	**Ok Pansa** All temples **Tak Bat Devorohana** Hill temples, esp. Wat Fai Hin by Chiang Mai University. Monks walk down and receive alms (6 a.m.).	Buddhist: End of rains retreat Buddhist: Celebrates return of Buddha to earth from heaven where he had been teaching his mother.
October Till the full moon of the 12th lunar month	**Kathin** All temples. Thais travel in groups to distant temples.	Buddhist: Lay merit making. Offerings of robes and alms.
November For three days over the full moon of the 12th lunar month	**Loi Krathong** (Yi Peng) On waterways all over Thailand.	Ancient Tai-Indic: Give thanks for water and stop the rains (*see* Main Festivals).
December Weekend nearest 5th	**Rose Festival** Suan Buak Hat/Thaphae Gate	Cultural: Beautiful flower displays honour H.M. King's birthday.
December 1st-8th in Lamphun; Dec 30th-Jan 8th in Chiang Mai	**Winter Fairs** Lamphun; esp. sports stadium beauty contests. Chiang Mai; H121 near the Provincial Hall (*sala klang*)	Cultural: A noisy mix of fun fair, freak shows, and commercial promotions (photo p.183).
December In the middle of the month	**Food Festival** Talat Choeng Doi	Cultural (*see* p.158)
December 25th-31st	Christmas & New Year	Traditional (imported)

Festival Parades

The people of the north excel at putting on parades, which are the main feature of many festivals and can last for several hours. Leading institutions sponsor a section of the procession. School marching bands (an art form for which several local schools have gained prizes in

The 'pi' — a Thai reed pipe — is commonly used in ceremonial music.

international competitions) and traditional bands accompany procession of people dressed in traditional costume or uniform. The people in the procession either hold banners or lanterns, or they perform dances.

The highlight of each section is a gorgeously decorated float with beautiful maidens. Prizes are offered for the best entries in the parade, and much effort goes into them. Good parades to see are at the Bo Sang umbrella festival, the flower festival, Song-kran, and at Loi Krathong.

Main Festivals

Rice and pulses — staples of a culture

Vicom Kittirattanachai

THE FLOWER FESTIVAL

FLOWERS IN CHIANG MAI are at their best before the end of the cool season when this festival is held. This falls on the first weekend of February. The centre of the festival is the parade held in the morning of Saturday. Floats decorated with flowers illustrate the theme chosen for the year. The beauty queens surrounded by flowers make a magical sight. The flower beds of the public gardens are bathed in colour and special displays are maintained till the end of Sunday.

The parade usually follows Thaphae Road and the outer moat road past Katam Corner to Ku Ruang Corner. The floats remain and the festival continues on the inner moat road (closed to traffic) around Ku Ruang.

Ittipon Elajukanon

The flower festival parade

Tung and Talaeo

Tung are a northern style of pennant hung from bamboo poles. They are used as offerings to Buddha images and the deceased, as well as for decorating and blessing ceremonies. The common significance of *tung* is to avert ill and secure good fortune. Their overall shape and the material from which they are made vary according to purpose.

Thalaeo above Thaphae Gate

Tung may be made of a succession of web-like forms made of threads woven round cross-shaped frames, or from single long pieces of cloth. Bamboo strips woven horizontally represent steps guiding the deceased to heaven. The longer the *tung* are, the more beneficial they are thought to be.

Talaeo are less common. Made from plaited strips of bamboo to form five or seven points, they serve as a charm against evil spirits. They are placed near entrances to houses or villages to prevent entry by the spirits of the dead. They may be seen above the city gates after the Seup Jata Muang (Seup Chada) festival as well as in rice fields beside offerings to Mae Phosop, the Goddess of rice.

Placing paper tung in sand chedi during Songkran at Wat Chiang Man

Songkran

THIS FESTIVAL marks the traditional Thai New Year, which until 1940 used to be when the Siamese new year began. The festival is the most important and traditionally occurs when the sun moves out of Pisces.

In Chiang Mai the main events take place over three days (the dates vary for other northern provinces). By custom the first day falls on April 13th and is the last day of the old year. Firecrackers are let off at dawn and people spring clean their houses.

In the afternoon a parade of Buddha images from Chiang Mai temples goes from the railway station to Wat Phra Singh. Northern people toss lustral water (water scented with perfume and flowers) to bathe the images as they pass along the streets. The Phra Sihing image leads the procession to Wat Phra Singh, where it is set in front of the temple for citizens to bathe throughout the rest of the festival.

Ceremonies are not held on the second day, which separates the new year from the old. In the afternoon sand is placed in the temple compound as a symbolic return of the sand carried out on the soles of shoes and feet of the people. The sand is made into small stupas for the next day.

The new year begins on the third day. The early morning is a particularly good time to visit the temples to watch people in traditional costume bringing offerings.

Songkran Parade 1995

"The Chief's New Year festivities on April 13 (1891)...started by parading through the streets on a highly decorated elephant, seated on a throne bearing a five-tiered umbrella and followed by other elephants carrying lesser chaos with one-tier umbrellas" (Bristowe W.S. "Louis and the King of Siam")

Ceremonies are held in the *viharn*. Outside, the people place flags in the sand chedi as well as symbolic sticks of support under bo trees to bring good fortune in the new year.

Later in the day people pay respect to seniors and heads of families in a ceremony known as *tam hua*. This is done by offering lustral water and foods (*tam hua* ceremonies may take place till the end of the month).

Bathing the Phra Sihing

In the afternoon the main government organisations hold a procession from Yupparat School to honour the governor in a *tam hua* ceremony at his residence by the river.

A winning entrant in sand-chedi competition (held on 13th) at the Phuttasathan on Thaphae Rd.

Water throwing at *Songkran*

Armed and friendly

If you suffered from a repressed childhood, then Songkran is good therapy. The young at heart arm themselves with anything that can project water and drench all but monks, the aged and mothers carrying very young children. Downtown and around the moats, traffic becomes gridlocked as revellers on sidewalks and pick-up trucks battle it out.

Ladies should be prepared for sweet words while water is poured on their necks in a traditional new year greeting. Wear clothes you can be wet and happy in, but beware of being chilled as the ice-factories do excellent business. Foreigners are particularly welcome targets so protect electronics and valuables in plastic bags.

Water throwing goes on for at least four days and longer in the countryside. It begins in the morning — start early to run errands and stay dry — and continues till sundown. If in a vehicle keep doors locked and windows closed if you don't want revellers to throw water inside. Drive very slowly, especially if on a motorcycle — going at speed into a bucketful of water thrown at you is not recommended. Regrettably, the accident rate soars during Songkran!

LOI KRATHONG

LOI KRATHONG, which is also known as Yi Peng in the north, is the most colourful festival of the year. It takes place over the three days of

Prizes are given to the best forest gates (Wat Phuak Hong).

Krathong to give thanks and blessing for water

the full moon of the twelfth lunar month, which usually falls in November. The festival may have evolved from Brahmanic rites to honour the dead as well as local rites to bring

an end to the rains. Though legends suggest it was established by the time of King Tilokarat in the late 15th century, the origins of this festival prior to the last century are uncertain.

Now people generally believe that by releasing floats and balloons they

A khom — the northern lantern

get rid of bad luck and give thanks to the water and heavenly elements. Older folks may say that it is to show gratitude to the Goddess of the River, Mae Khong Kha, for use of the water.

For the three nights of the festival people release small floats known as *krathong* — with offerings that include incense, flowers, candles and money — into the rivers and lakes. The River Ping becomes a stream of lights floating gently with the current. Small hot air balloons rise like lanterns high into the sky, complementing the floats drifting on the waters. Fireworks are let off everywhere, particularly on

At the 'giant khrathong' parade

the banks of the River Ping, and there is a parade each night in Chiang Mai.

The festival begins the day before the full moon. People decorate the entrances to their houses with coconut branches, banana trees, sugar-cane, lanterns and coloured paper. As dusk falls people light earthen lamps placed along the walls of their property and the fire-works start. The lantern parade starts on Ratchadamnoen Road, as do the other parades of Loi Krathong, and continues down Thapahe road to the Night Bazaar.

On the morning of the day

Khom loi — hot air balloons

of the full moon, people present offerings at the temples before releasing large hot air balloons from temple compounds. A competition for best balloon takes place in front of the city hall on Wang Sing Kham Road. Boat races are held on the river. At night the small *krathong* parade goes east along

Thaphae Road and ends at the City Hall.

The final round of the *Nang Noppamas* beauty contest is also held (usually at Thaphae Gate) on this night. According to legend, Lady Noppamas was a beautiful daughter of a Brahmin priest in the court of Sukhothai. The young lady impressed the king very much when she made floats of lotus flowers for the king to float down the river. Popular traditional holds that the custom dates at least from that time.

The culmination of the festival is the giant *krathong* parade held on the third night. Miss Noppamas is paraded through the streets in a very colourful procession from Ratchadamnoen

Road to the City Hall. Traditionally, one or two floats are put onto rafts and sent — *Nang Noppamas*, lights and all — down the river to the Nawarat Bridge, passing the throngs of people crowding the river banks.

Releasing krathong on the River Ping

Ittipon Elajtukanon

CHIANG MAI CITY SIGHTS

Protected by the moats, the old city is filled with monuments that mark the course of change in the city's seven hundred year history. Generations have trod the narrow lanes that link the quiet neighbourhoods to the temples and the markets. Along the main streets, trade has been the lifeblood of the city; but it is the spiritual and artistic striving focused at the temples that has given beat to the city's enduring heart.

HISTORICAL MONUMENTS

KING MANGRAI founded Chiang Mai at the location of a small Lawa settlement known as Wiang Nophaburi. The site lay between the river to the east and Doi Suthep mountain to the west. The proximity of the river was favourable to trade as well as political control of the area. Free from flooding, the site also had a good timber and water supply and enough land for rice farming to sustain the population. Finally, the omens were favourable. The city was founded on April 12 1296 with the name of *Nophabur Sri Nakhon Ping Chiang Mai*. The plan called for a square formed by moats and walls that faced the cardinal directions. Work began at the Sri Phum corner in the north-east, which is considered the most auspicious of the four corners (*central city sights map 2, pp.40-41 outlying sights, map 27 pp.168-169; inner city detail map 29 pp.184-185*).

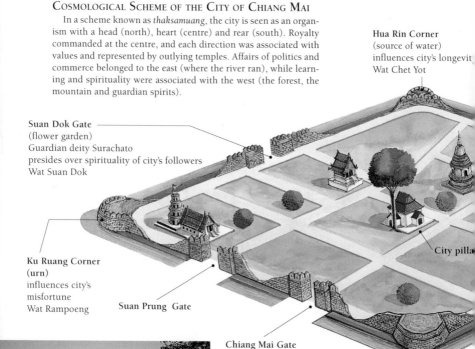

COSMOLOGICAL SCHEME OF THE CITY OF CHIANG MAI

In a scheme known as *thaksamuang*, the city is seen as an organism with a head (north), heart (centre) and rear (south). Royalty commanded at the centre, and each direction was associated with values and represented by outlying temples. Affairs of politics and commerce belonged to the east (where the river ran), while learning and spirituality were associated with the west (the forest, the mountain and guardian spirits).

Hua Rin Corner
(source of water)
influences city's longevit
Wat Chet Yot

Suan Dok Gate
(flower garden)
Guardian deity Surachato
presides over spirituality of city's followers
Wat Suan Dok

City pilla

Ku Ruang Corner
(urn)
influences city's
misfortune
Wat Rampoeng

Suan Prung Gate

Chiang Mai Gate
Guardian deity Choeyaphumo
presides over city's nobility &
administration
Wat Nantaram

Katam Corner (fishtrap)
Influences city's strength
& fortifications
Wat Chai Si Mongkhol

High-diving from Ku Ruang.

The Old City — Walls and Gates

UNLIKE earlier Thai Yuan settlements which were oval, the astrological plan for the city called for rectangular moats measuring 18 metres across, with a width of 1800 metres and a length of 2000 metres. Earth from the moats formed ramparts.

At the centre was the city pillar. In Brahmanic cosmology this represented Mount Sumeru, the upward link to heaven at the centre of the universe (this plan was also mirrored in temples, where the stupa — the *chedi* — stood at the centre). The city walls and moats were oriented to the cardinal points and symbolised the mountains and seas of the outer universe.

The fate of the city depended upon the relationship between the centre and the outer guardians at the corners and gates (the annual Seup Chada Muang ceremony propitiates these guardians to this day).

The north of the city was considered the head of the city, so royalty used Chang Phuak Gate to enter. Originally four gates were built, but King Sam Fang Kaen (r.1401-1441) added Suan Prung gate

Thippanet Bastion on the Kamphaeng Din

to let his mother travel easily from her palace to supervise construction of the Chedi Luang. This gate came to be used for funeral processions from the city.

King Muang Kaeo (r.1495-1526) is recorded as restoring the walls in the latter part of his reign and may have built the outer earthern rampart known as the *kamphaeng din*. Significant changes to the fortifications were otherwise not recorded till Chao Kawila rebuilt them, adding the corner bastions, around 1800.

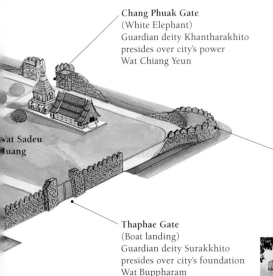

Chang Phuak Gate
(White Elephant)
Guardian deity Khantharakhito
presides over city's power
Wat Chiang Yeun

Wat Sadeu Muang

Si Phum Corner
(Light of the Land)
influences city's glory and honour
Wat Chai Si Phum

Thaphae Gate
(Boat landing)
Guardian deity Surakkhito
presides over city's foundation
Wat Buppharam

What will they make of it in 2696? Just as sections of the city walls were rebuilt in 1996, so some of Thailand's history has much less foundation in fact than the solid evidence for the existence of the city walls. Having survived threats from colonialism and communism, Thai national identity has matured to the point that some aspects of 'official' Thai history are now openly questioned. A controversy rages even upon the authenticity of the Ramkhamhaeng Inscription #1, a stela found at Sukhothai which provides the foundation for the accepted historical starting point of the Siamese-Thai nation.

Historical Development

JAMES McCARTHY'S was a suryeyor who was seconded from the government of India to the government of Siam for a period. He mapped much of SE Asia, surveying Chiang Mai in 1891 and producing a map (recreated on this page)

were set back from main thoroughfares and linked to temples by footpaths, the precursors of many of today's narrow lanes in the old city. As is typical with Asian cities, only solid religious or military structures lasted any time, however.

During his visit, Ambassador Shomburgk also wrote of

inactive and in ruins.

In former times only high ranking people and their retainers could have occupied land close to palace of the *chao*. The land belonging to Chao Inthawichayanon (Inthanon — the 'chief' in McCarthy's time)was donated by Chao Dara Rasmi for a

CHIANGMAI

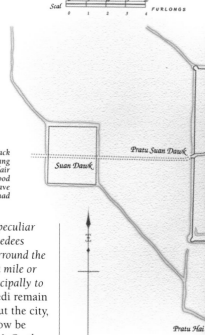

A surviving wooden house between the old city and the river that dates back to the middle of the 20th century. In his 16th century description of Chiang Mai, Ralph Fitch must have been referring to temples when he talked of 'fair houses of stone', as all other buildings would have either been made of wood or bamboo, of which there remains no trace. Such structures would have been too insubstantial or numerous for McCarthy to map in the time he had available for his survey.

which was published by the Royal Geographical Society.

Thirty years earlier (1860), visiting British Consul, Sir Robert Schomburgk, numbered the population of Chiang Mai at 50,000, but this is thought to be an overestimate. The houses of these people would have been in compounds surrounded by trees, as if in a village. These compounds

a large number of *'peculiar towerlets or phratshedees (which) not only surround the city, but extend for a mile or more beyond it, principally to the west'.* These chedi remain scattered throughout the city, and many would now be found in temples. McCarthy appears not to have recorded many of these temples, either because they were to numerous, or they were

school. The *chief's* palace by the river is now the seat of the municipality, and the Siamese Commissioner's residence became and remains the official residence of the Provincial Governor.

Western missionaries and traders were allocated land on the east side of the river, a position that accorded with their rank. The overseas Chinese first settled around Wat Ket (in the area to the

This photo (of Suan Prung or Chiang Mai Gate in 1899) was used as the basis for reconstruction of Thaphae Gate

north of the *kirk* opposite what was Dr Cheek's bridge), later taking land across the river in the Kat Luang area. The Chinese founded the commercial districts by building trading houses in close proximity to each other, with their residences on the upper floors (the precursor to than it is now) was open ground. Royal cremations took place to the north, where Kat Luang now stands, and Haw and other caravans would encamp along Thaphae (which means 'landing') Road, where they would trade until it was time to move

The former home of Chao Rachawong, now the location for the Khum Kaew khantok dinner

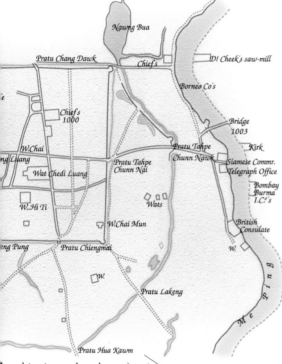

the caravan on.

Shan and Burmese traders serving the Moulmein trading route were the first to begin building houses along Thaphae Road, but they were later replaced by overseas Chinese. The Muslim Haw traders, meanwhile, established houses in nearby Ban Haw to serve as staging posts for their mule trains.

The south of the city is considered the least auspicious direction. Executions were performed in this direction, a direction which also associated with leprosy and bad spirits. Perhaps this is why much of the land today along the *kamphaeng din* is covered with shanties. The land closer to the inner city, however, was settled during the 19th century by captive ethnic groups specialising in valued crafts.

the ubiquitous shop-house). Expansion to the east along what is now Charoen Muang Road, however, was to wait until after the arrival of the railway in 1921.

The outer Thaphae Gate— *Pratu Tahpe Chunn Nawk* — marked the extent of buildings beyond the inner city walls towards the river. Prior to 1860 the area between this gate and the river (which was much wider

Records mention a pratu 'Hua Kawn' (Khua Kom = short bridge gate) which mentions a gate and a short bridge over the outer moat in 1615, suggesting the kamphaeng din predates this time.

One of a few surviving wooden trading houses on Thaphae Road

Chiang Mai's 700th Year

The Asian economic crisis of 1997 was yet distant in April 1996, and the mood in the city was buoyant. To celebrate the centenary the Phra Borromathat Chom Thong relic was brought to the city and paraded around the old city in a ceremony that had not been performed in decades. Along with sacred images usually kept under tight security in Wat Chiang Man, the relic was placed in a special shrine before Three Kings monument. On April 12 a Bhramanic ritual at nine in the morning was followed by H.M.Queen Sirikit visiting to pay respects to the city's founders in the evening.

The Three Kings Monument, April 12, 1996.

H.M. Queen Sirikit (above) and the Brahmanic ceremony (left) on April 12 , 1996.

Traditional dancers (right) paid respect prior to the arrival of the holy relic (left)

The Old City Today

BARRING minor restoration, the overall shape of the astions on the corners are much as Kawila had built hem. At some stage, perhaps by 1945, the walls and gates between the corners were demolished and the bricks used to pave roads.

The present gateways were reconstructed in the late 1960's, nd in 1996-7 the Japanese funded archaeological excavations before the walls near the bastions and gates were extensively renovated. Bricks dated Buddhist Era 539 (1996) were placed regularly in the new brickwork. At the north-east corner one of the sites in the dig has been covered and left open.

Reflecting the importance of commerce, the commonly used place for city events is the concourse in front of Thaphae Gate. The open area

haphae Gate during SEAGAMES, 1995

s used for anything from beauty contests to political allies. At each of the corners and gates, modern inscriptions in English give information about each place. These may be found facing the road on the outer side of he moats.

THE OLD CITY CENTRE

อนุสาวรีย์สามกษัตริย์

WAT SADEU MUANG — the temple of the navel of the city— used to be in the vicinity of the two old chedi's which stand near Inthawarorot Road to the south of the square containing the Three Kings Statue (40.E8).

According to legend the site was a former grove where Mangrai saw two fearless white deer drive off a pack of hunting dogs and took this as an auspicious sign. The octagonal chedi dates back to the 14th century, while the nearby Buddha images originate from the time of Kawila.

Being the symbolic centre of the city, the surrounding area was the seat of administration of former royalty. Foremost amongst these was the site now occupied by the Chiang Mai City Arts and Culture Centre หอศิลปวัฒนธรรม เมืองเชียงใหม่ (*Daily 10:00-17:00 closed Mondays. 90 Bt. adults — Thais 20 Bt.*). Once the location of the *ho kham* of Chao Kawilorot Suriyawong (r. 1856-70) and later granted to the Siamese state by Chao Dara Rasmi, the site became the symbol of Siamese domination over Lan Na when the current building was completed as the new administrative offices of Monthon Phayap (later to become Chiang Mai Province) in 1924. The front section of the centre contains 13 rooms of permanent

The area of Wat Sadeu Muang. In the background is the former Provincial Hall (now the Chiang Mai City Arts & Culture Centre). The chedi (not in the picture) to the west of the Buddha images in the foreground shows clearly how a newer chedi has been been built around a smaller, older one. The nearby area is very good for inexpensive day-time restaurants.

exhibits showing the historical and cultural development of the city, while the rear is devoted to Lanna cultural activities.

Across Prapokklao to the east, the district court is located in the former home of Chao Inthawarorot Suriyawong (r.1901-11), and to the northeast of the Prapokklao-Ratwithi intersection is Yupparat School.

The statue is a 20th century representation of an event at which the three kings (from left King Ngam Muang of Phayao, King Mangrai, King Ramkamhaeng of Sukhothai) discuss the layout of Chiang Mai on April 12, 1296. Offerings to the city founders, who are honoured as thewada, are made annually on this date.

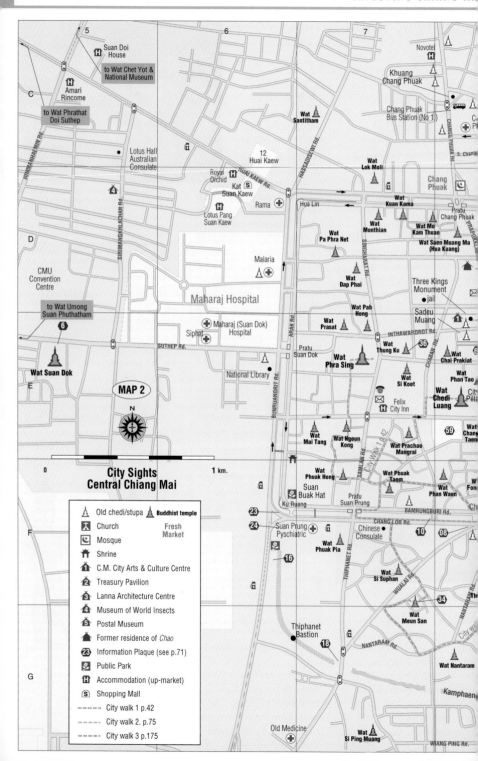

Old chedi/stupa
Buddhist temple
Church
Fresh Market
Mosque
Shrine
C.M. City Arts & Culture Centre
Treasury Pavilion
Lanna Architecture Centre
Museum of World Insects
Postal Museum
Former residence of *Chao*
Information Plaque (see p.71)
Public Park
Accommodation (up-market)
Shopping Mall
City walk 1 p.42
City walk 2. p.75
City walk 3 p.175

MAP 2
N

**City Sights
Central Chiang Mai**

0   1 km.

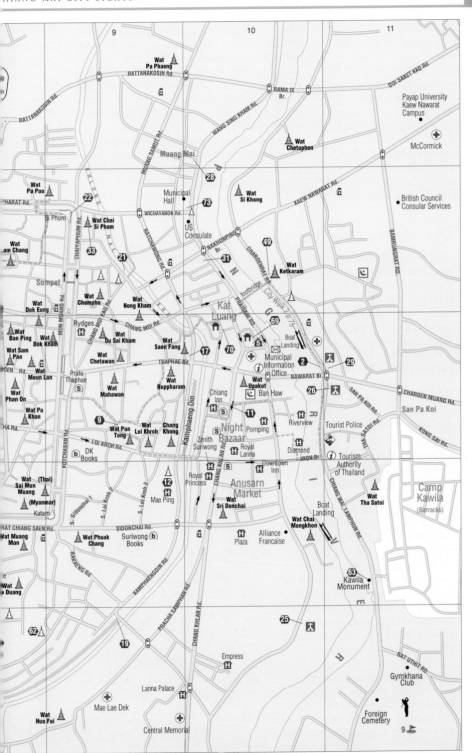

Founded as the first government school in the north in 1899, the school started using Central Thai as the language of instruction after the Shan rebellion in 1902, moving to its current location on former royal land in 1906. Apart from the old Yupparat building, which dates to the early 20th century, the school grounds contain a new dhamma hall housing a large bronze seated Buddha image (Phra Thotsaphonyanamahamuni) which, along with the nearby chedi, were once part of former Wat Nang Liao. A second old chedi and a stable specially built to present a baby white elephant to King Prajadhipok (Rama VII r. 1925-35) when he visited in 1926 are located near the main intersection.

A shrine marks where King Mangrai is thought to have been struck by lightning in a small soi east of Prapokklao about 75m. to the north of the Ratchadamnoen-Prapokklao intersection. A second shrine is located at this intersection opposite the Lanna Architecture Centre, a small museum newly established in the former home of Chao Burirat (Mon-Fri: 09:00-16:30 hrs).

Old City Walking Tour 1

(Best in the early morning when the sun strikes the east-facing temple fronts. Numbers in the text are shown on map 3 below. The walk is also shown on map 29 pp.184-185). One of the delights of Chiang Mai is to walk along the narrow lanes and through temple courtyards. Try the following route or just improvise.

Begin at Wat Pa Pao (1 p.65) or Sri Phum Corner and take Sri Phum Soi 1 to the grounds of Wat Lam Chang (2) , which is located on the site where King Mangrai used to keep his elephants. The *viharn* contains up to 200 Buddha images behind a large iron grill. These images have come from former temples in the old city that have disappeared.

From Wat Chiang Man (3 p.53), go west along Ratchaphakhinai Rd. to Wat Umong Maha Therachan (4 p.67). Walk out of Wat Umong at the back and through Wat Duang Di (5 p.63) to the Three Kings Monument (6 p.39). From there go west along Phrapokklao Rd., passing the Lanna Architecture Centre (7) to Wat Phan Tao (8 p.65) and Wat Chedi Luang (9 p.48). Leave this temple compound by the back and go to Wat Phra Singh (14 p.54) and Wat Prasat (15 p.66) for a shorter walk.

A longer route takes you to (10) Wat Phra Chao Mangrai, which has a standing Buddha image that came to its present location when the carriage transporting it from Wiang Kum Kam to Wat Chiang Man broke. The temple also has a finely decorated entrance gate. The route continues past Wat Phuak Taem (11), a temple with a workshop that makes filigree for stupa finials. The word *phuak* in a name refers to a group of people; in the case of Wat Phuak Hong (12 p.66), this probably refers to Mon people living nearby. The walk follows back lanes to Wat Phra Singh via Wat Meun Ngeun Kong (13).

For a meal, try northern Thai food at the Huan Pen restaurant (p.153). Café Chic offers air-conditioned comfort in the middle of the walk, and several good, inexpensive restaurants are found on Inthawarot Road near the Three Kings Monument (p.156).

Minor Historical Sites

CHIANG MAI has several places of historical interest that are either small or remote. You may not find them worth a visit unless you have a special interest, or happen to be nearby.

The Kamphaeng Din & Mae Kha Canal

THE KAMPHAENG DIN

กำแพงดิน

KAMPHAENG DIN (40.F6-G8-10) King Muang Kaeo (r.1495-1526) may have first constructed the outer earthen rampart— *kamphaeng din*—and the moat, which is now known as the Khlong Mae Kha, to protect the settlements that had grown outside the city walls. Though much of the rampart remains, large sections in the south are covered by shanties and the wall is best seen where lanes cross it. While the red light district that existed along the eastern section of the wall near Wat Chang Khong has disappeared, a costly attempt to clean up the Mae Kha has been less successful.

KHUANG CHANG PHUAK

ข่วงช้างเผือก

WHITE ELEPHANT TERRACE (40.C8) occupies a traffic island by Chang Phuak (no1.) bus station. The half-elephant figures inside the arched shelters are believed to protect Chiang Mai from enemies and demons.

Khuang Chang Phuak

The present structures were built by Kawila in 1800. An earlier shrine at this spot may have existed to commemorate the deeds of two retainers who carried King Saen Muang Ma to safety after his army was defeated by Sukhothai forces in 1387-8. The servants were rewarded with the titles of 'Lord Elephant of the Left Side/Right Side'.

KHUANG SINGH

ข่วงสิงห์

CHAO KAWILA built 'Lion Terrace' (169.A7) in a similar style to 'White Elephant Terrace'. Surrounded by a pond, the terrace was built in 1801. The lions symbolised

Khuang Singh

the revived power of Chiang Mai to deter the Burmese on the invasion route from the north. They were apparently successful, for the Burmese were never to occupy Chiang Mai again.

THE WHITE CHEDI

เจดีย์ขาว

THE CHEDI (41.D10) stands as a traffic island near the municipal hall on Wang Sing

The white chedi — once surrounded by water

Kham Road. It is said to contain bones; but whether the bones belong to Haw raiders, Burmese invaders, or defenders of Chiang Mai is uncertain. One story says it honours a Thai champion who contested a Burmese champion to see who would stay underwater longer. The Thai won the day by not coming back to the surface.

THE MAIN TEMPLES OF CHIANG MAI

CHIANG MAI'S TEMPLES are the cultural and historical heart of the city. The most famous have been places of pilgrimage for northern people for centuries. As traditional centres of merit making, they are the best places to see Buddhist ceremonies. Funded by noble an wealthy benefactors over a long period they have also become the repositorie of some of the finest examples of reli gious art. If you had but half a day i the city, then it is to one or two c these temples that you should go.

The Lanna Temple

THAI TEMPLES have long served as the centre of the community. While this traditional role has diminished as young people have had less time for religious observances, the temples still lie at the heart of the ritual and social life of much of Thai society.

Though earlier temples were the most durable constructions of the day, the wooden roofs and older earth filled walls have not survived the destructive forces of nature and man. Therefore most of the temple buildings seen today do not go back much before the 19th century. Only the stupas (*which shall be referred to as chedi*) and some walls and sculptured images which were built of laterite or brick covered with stucco have survived for longer periods.

THE CHEDI (*CHETIYA*)

LANNA TEMPLES originally were built round the *chedi* (stupas), which contain valuable relics of pious kings and monks. Like solid rocks in a sea of change, the old chedis mark the sites of former temples and are almost the only structures that go back to the 13th-15th centuries.

Perhaps their continued existence in some unlikely places in the city is no accident. In Brahmanic-Buddhist cosmology, the chedi 'stabilises the earth', fixing a point where heaven and earth meet. They may be likened to the rising sun at dawn, both separating and joining the earth and sky after the darkness of night. Symbolising the dhamma, they chase away the darkness of ignorance and chaos.

Though many chedi in Chiang Mai have been damaged by thieves who

The unique chedi of Wat Ku Tao. Note the Burmese style finial — 'hti'

The round chedi at Wat Rampoeng

When visiting a temple

Thais show respect for their religion by not entering temple compounds if inappropriately dressed. Inside temples they conduct themselves in an appropriate manner, not making noise. They never touch or climb religious objects like Buddha images and stupas. When Thais sit on floors, they take care not to point their feet in a direction worthy of respect, such as a Buddha image, monk, or a teacher. They consider the head as 'high' and the feet as 'low'.

ought the precious relics ontained inside, citizens ave repaired and pro-ected them. They are orshipped as sacred ymbols representing he cosmic body of the uddha and the law f the dhamma. heir shape iffers, however, ue to the articular symbolism of the hamma chosen by the uilders.

Chedis in Chiang Mai have wo basic forms; the stepped r *prasat* style, and the bell tyle. However, from these asic forms many variations n size and shape have ppeared, reflecting the

wealth of the city over the centuries. An early example of the *prasat* style is the Mahapol Chedi at Wat Chamadevi in Lamphun. Later fine examples are those of Wat Phansat near Chang Phuak bus station and Wat Lok Moli west of Chang Phuak gate.

The bell style chedi

The chedi of Wat Umong Suan Puthatham and the later chedi of Wat Phrathat Haripunchai have the bell shaped style. More recent examples are the Shan Burmese style chedis built in the late 19th century. These may be seen at the temples

on Thaphae Road.

Other variations include the octagonal form, which may best be seen at Wat Phrathat Doi Suthep and Wat Duang Di, and the round form best seen at Wat Phuak Hong. Both designs may have evolved here, or may have come with monks or traders from Ayutthaya (the octago-nal form) and Lake Erhai in Yunnan (the round form).

Chedi Chang Lom

TEMPLE BUILDINGS

THE *UBOSOT* AND VIHARN are the most ornate and important buildings in a temple compound. On the outside they are decorated with stucco motifs which are covered with lacquer, glass mosaic and gilt.

An *Ubosot*, or consecrated ceremonial hall in Lan Na, is generally small, for its religious functions involve only monks. The *ubosot* stands in consecrated ground marked by eight boundary stones and are usually kept locked. Women are generally not allowed to enter.

The viharn is a larger assembly hall where lay people and monks participate

Jewel/lotus bud symbolises supreme liberation

Spire symbolises meditation heavens

Harmika symbolises gateway to enlightenment

Round bell stupa surmounts main pile (repeat of lower *garbha*)

Image niche on external wall. In the middle of the pile a relic chamber symbolises the centre of the universe

Indented right-angled corners typical of *prasat* style

Base for bell stupa (the builder can also complete the stupa in the *prasat* style) above main pile

Garbha symbolises source of phenomenal world

Elongated (lotus) base (height varies according to builder)

Step base

The prasat style chedi — The vertical pile of any chedi represents the axis mundi, the cosmic mountain at the centre of the universe

in ceremonies. It is the main building of the temple and is usually located to the east of the chedi with the front entrance facing the auspicious direction of the sunrise.

Though many viharn in the north are characteristically Lanna in style, details in the architecture have been influenced by Ayutthaya and Rattanakosin (Bangkok) styles. Taller walls in the viharn, for example, show a distinct influence of the central (Siamese) Thai.

Both the *ubosot* and the viharn will contain the temple's most important Buddha images. During ceremonies cotton strings may be attached to these to spread the power and blessings of the image amongst devotees. Because o the value of these images an other artefacts, many viharn are also kept locked except on Buddhist holy days — *wan phra* (monks may unloc a viharn if politely requested to do so).

The viharn is often

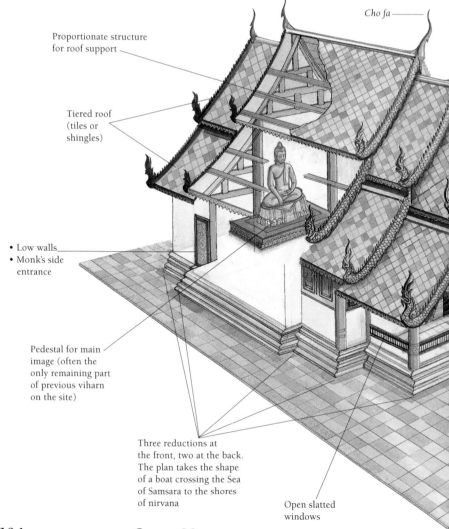

Cho fa

Proportionate structure for roof support

Tiered roof (tiles or shingles)

• Low walls
• Monk's side entrance

Pedestal for main image (often the only remaining part of previous viharn on the site)

Three reductions at the front, two at the back. The plan takes the shape of a boat crossing the Sea of Samsara to the shores of nirvana

Open slatted windows

19th CENTURY VIHARN, CHIANG MAI AREA

decorated with elaborate murals, which vary from new to old, from finely executed to roughly rendered. Scenes from the *Jataka,* the previous lives of the Buddha, may adorn the side walls. The eastern wall above the front entrance often shows the unsuccessful attack by the demons of Mara, the God of Illusion, who attempts to dissuade the Buddha from achieving enlightenment.

Many temples contain a small scripture repository raised up on a pedestal or stilts for protection. Known as *ho trai,* they are used to keep religious scripts inscribed on palm leaves. These scripts recorded Buddhist texts as well as the chronicles, which are a main source of early Thai history. The best example of a *ho trai* is at Wat Phra Singh (p.57)

Other buildings include *kuti,* the monks' living quarters, general purpose halls known as *sala,* and a bell tower which announces ritual times to monks. Temples used to be the sole source of education and compounds often contain primary schools taken over by the government.

The bo tree represents 'natural law' and the Buddha's englightenment. (Wat Mahawan)

From ancient times the temple grounds have served as a public place for festivals and fairs serving the local community. The entrances to compounds of important temples in the past would sometimes have heavily decorated entrance gates such as those at Wat Suan Dok (p.60).

Funeral rites are held in special halls, or at the homes of the deceased, from where processions will take the funeral beirs to cremation grounds at special locations set apart from communities and temples.

Bargeboard

Winged gable

Naga

• Main gable
• Carved boards fill spaces between support beams

Portico

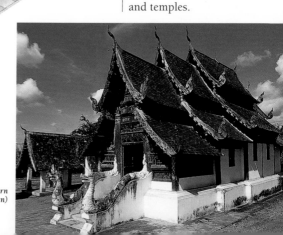

Lanna viharn (Wat Ton Khwen)

WAT CHEDI LUANG

(Prapokklao Rd. 40.E8) KING SAEN MUANG MA began construction of the Chedi Luang to enshrine the relics of his father, King Ku Na, but died before it was completed. Though King Sam Fang Kaen was an animist, his mother continued supervising construction after the King was advised that his grandfather's ghost could only rest in peace if the chedi were visible at least four kilometres from the city.

The chedi reached 24 metres during Sam Fang Kaen's reign, but it was King Tilokarat who extended it to the colossal height of 96 metres, a feat which was completed in 1481.

Though an earthquake brought the chedi down to its present height of around 42 metres in 1545, the chedi was to remain the tallest structure in Chiang Mai for over 500 years.

The Phra Chedi Luang

The City Pillar — *Inthakhin*

City pillars located at the centre of the *muang* were common to early Tai communities. The phallic looking poles are thought to represent the shoot of a rice plant, and possibly originate from an early fertility cult, and it is believed that in ancient times they may have been installed upon human sacrifices.

The main viharn during Inthakhin

The city pillar

Under Brahmanic influence, city pillars became associated with the cosmological centre of the universe. In Chiang Mai, the influence of Buddhism is clearly evident by the standing Buddha image placed upon the pedestal of the city pillar itself.

The city pillar is the home of guardian spirits for the city and must be venerated each year. The people of Chiang Mai make offerings of incense, flowers and candles during the *Inthakhin* festival to bring prosperity to themselves and the city.

The festival begins with a procession of the Phra Fon Saen Ha Buddha image around the streets. Lanna people believe that a guardian spirit resides in the image, and that bathing the image with lustral water encourages rain.

...thing the Phra Fon Saen Ha ...ring Inthakhin

One of the best times to see ...is chedi is during the *wien ...en* ceremony in the evening ...n one of the main Buddhist ...stival days (*see* p.25).

The large viharn was built in 1928. Round columns with bell shaped bases and lotus finials support the high red ceiling inside. The *Phra Chao Attarot*, a standing brass and mortar Buddha image which originates from the reign of King Saen Muang Ma (r.1385-1401), dominates the hall. Buddhist posters are placed along the walls between the windows, and cabinets with Buddha images and Bencharong ceramics line the walls.

The cross shaped hall to the south of the main viharn contains the city pillar. Statues in small shelters surrounding this building are homes of guardian spirits.

Legends say that a hermit (whose image is in a shelter on the west side of the building) went to the God Indra to ask for protection for the city from enemies. On condition that appropriate

Offerings made during Inthakhin bring prosperity.

offerings were made, Indra permitted two *kumphan* to carry the *inthakhin* pillar from the Tavatimsa heaven to the city.

Chao Kawila moved the city pillar to its present site from Wat Sadeu Muang in 1800. He built statues of the *kumphan* under shelters to the north and south of the main entrance to the temple. He also planted the three large *yang* (dipterocarp) trees. According to legend, the tree nearest the city pillar will protect the city as long

People used to consult with Phra Sangkhachai for his looks rather than for the dhamma, so he became fat.

as it is not cut down.

Other buildings in the compound include the Lanna campus of the Mahamakut Buddhist University (This is

the northern campus for monks of the *Thammayut* sect, a reformist sect founded by King Mongkut [Rama IV. r.1851-1868], who was dissatisfied with the established *Mahanikai* sect in the late 1830's). To the west of the chedi is a viharn with a reclining Buddha and the Sangkhachai image. From this area an exit leads out onto Chaban Road (go this way on city walk 1, page 42)

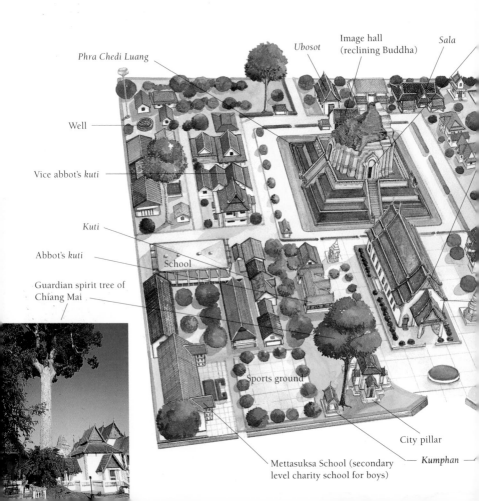

Phra Chedi Luang

Ubosot

Image hall (reclining Buddha)

Sala

Well

Vice abbot's *kuti*

Kuti

Abbot's *kuti*

School

Guardian spirit tree of Chiang Mai

Sports ground

City pillar

Kumphan

Mettasuksa School (secondary level charity school for boys)

The Phra Yok

Niche for the *Phra Yok*

The Erawan motif is an Indic feature showing Rattanakosin influence

Kuti

(restrooms)

Samakhi Wittiyathan School (secondary school for novices)

Viharn

Mahamakut Buddhist University (Lanna campus)

The Emerald and Jade Buddhas

The Phra Kaew Morakot, the 'jewel-image' better known as the Emerald Buddha, is made of a single piece of jasper and is Thailand's most revered Buddha image. It now resides in Wat Phra Kaew in Bangkok.

According to legend the image was first discovered in Chiang Rai in 1434 when a lightning strike chedi and exposed a stucco Buddha image inside. The stucco was to crack and reveal the Emerald Buddha within.

Due to a wilful elephant that would not take the road to Chiang Mai, the image first went to Lampang and stayed there for 32 years before King Tilokarat brought it to Chiang Mai and enshrined it in the eastern niche of the Chedi Luang he had just completed in 1468. In 1548 King Setthathirat, who for a short period ruled the kingdoms of Lan Na and Lan Xang, took the Phra Kaew image and other images when he returned to rule from his capital, Luang Phabang. The image was to return to Siam when Vientiane fell to the Siamese in 1778.

The Phra Yok, a solid jade Buddha 70 centimetres tall which was commissioned in 1995 for the 600th anniversary of the chedi, now resides in the eastern niche.

The Emerald Buddha

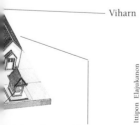

Ittipon Elajukanon

The main viharn of Wat Chedi Luang

WAT CHET YOT
วัดเจ็ดยอด

(Chiang Mai-Lampang Super Highway 168. B5) KING

Stucco deva (thewada)

TILOKARAT established this temple in 1455. The main viharn was probably copied from the design of the Mahabodhi temple in Pagan, which itself was a copy of the Indian temple at Bodhgaya. It is, consequently, quite different from anything else in the city.

It had been predicted that Buddhism would decline after 2000 years. King Tilokarat's religious works, as well as those of other Southeast Asian monarchs of the time, were therefore an attempt to prevent this decline. According to the Jinakalamali chronicle, he replanted a shoot grown from a seed from the Bodhi tree at Bodhgaya at this site. He had the temple built in 1476, one year before the Eighth World Buddhist council used the temple while revising the pali canon—*tripitaka*—of Theravadan Buddhism.

Chet yot — seven spires representing the seven hallowed spots after the Buddha's enlightenment — s atop the main rectangular viharn. A seated Buddha ima occupies an arched tunnel in the main body of the structur while the outside laterite wall are decorated with over 70 rather damaged stucco reliefs of *thewada*, beings who live i heavenly realms. These were reputed to have been fashione with faces in the likeness of King Tilokarat's relatives.

Three chedis stand in the spacious grounds, the largest of which contains the ashes o King Tilokarat. The small *ubosot* nearby has a fine carve wood gable. Several Buddha images in different attitudes may be found on the western side of the compound (signs give explanations in Englis The trees and grass in the spacious grounds have the feel of a park, creating a very pleasant atmosphere.

Wat Chet Yot

WAT CHIANG MAN
วัดเชียงมั่น

Ratchaphakhinai Rd. 41.D8)

THIS TEMPLE was built in 1297 the site of the camp King Mangrai used when he supervised the building of Chiang Mai. It was the first temple to be built in the city

The fifteen elephants at the base of the chedi are symbols of royalty, and they show Sri Lankan influence. They represent a sea of unformed matter upon which floats the cosmos in the form of the chedi.

and contains several very old artefacts. The oldest structure the Chang Lom chedi, which is in a style that could have originated from Sri Lanka via Sukhothai, or from Pagan. Nearby are a lotus pond, a raised scripture repository and an *ubosot*. The stela in front of the *ubosot* was inscribed in 1581, and is one of the oldest known records that establishes the founding of Chiang Mai *(photo p.10)*.

The temple has two Lanna style viharn. The larger one, renovated by Khru Ba Srivichai in the 1920's, contains a standing Buddha image (front right of the altar— *photo p.23*) with an inscription on its base that dates it to 1465. This makes

it the oldest dated Buddha image to be found so far in Chiang Mai. Close study shows pits and cracks that indicate the image's real age.

The smaller viharn to the north *(open 09:00-17:00)* contains two small but very important (almost to the extent of Palladia) Buddha images. The *Phra Sila* image is a bas-relief that probably came from Ceylon in about the eighth century. The image is believed to have the power to bring rain and is the focus of a festival at the temple held from April 1-5. The *Phra Sae Tang Khamani* crystal image belonged to Queen Chamadevi, who brought it from Lop Buri when she became the first ruler of Haripunchai. The image reputedly survived the

The Phra Sae Tang Khamani (front) and the Phra Sila

burning of Haripunchai when it was razed by King Mangrai. It may seem perverse, then, that it is imbued with powers to protect against disaster.

The Chang Lom Chedi

WAT PHRA SINGH
วัดพระสิงห์

Mondop in the ubosot of Wat Phra Singh

(*Singharat Rd. 40.E7*) THIS TEMPLE contains supreme examples of Lanna art. A chedi was first built by King Pha Yu (r.1337-55) to house the bones of his father King Kam Fu (r.1328-37). The original name of the temple was Wat Li Chiang Phra, but this was changed to Wat Phra Singh when the Phra Singh (Sihing) Buddha image was first housed there in 1367.

The temple was almost certainly abandoned before Kawila re-established it by building the *ubosot*, and rebuilding the chedi. Chao Thammalangka (r.1813-21) and his successor, Chao Kham Fan (r. 1821-1825) further added (or rebuilt) the *Viharn Lai Kham* and the elegant

Khru Ba Srivichai's imposing viharn from Ratchadamnoen Rd.

scripture library building.

More renovations were carried out in the mid 1920's, when Khru Ba Srivichai supervised the construction of the present main viharn and rebuilt the chedi. The *ubosot* and scripture library were renovated in 1929. Both are again under restoration in 2002, bringing the gilt and stucco work, particularly that of the porticos, back to original brightness.

The *Viharn Lai Kham* is a classic example of a Lanna style viharn and was built to house the Phra Singh image enthroned inside. *Lai Kham* refers to the elegant gold tracery used for decoration. Last restored in 1998, the building has three tiers a the front. The portico has finely carved gables as well as an ornate stucco sum above the main doors.

On the inner walls of the *Viharn Lai Kham* are some murals originally commissioned by Chao Thammalangka. These are famous for their period style and the detail depicting earthy northern Thai scenes and the ways of the Burmese court. The murals show two fables.

Haripunchai style (terracotta). Haripunchai National Museum

Standing image with ungainly proportions. Lanna school 14th C. (bronze. Standing image in Wat Phra Chao Mangrai)

'Lion style'. Lanna school before 1400 (bronze)

Image wearing royal apparel. Lanna school before 1500 (bronze)

Lanna school, 1500 (bronze)

Lanna Buddha Images and the Phra Phuttha Sihing Mystery

The Phra Singh Buddha image in the *Viharn Lai Kham* (Wat Phra Singh is the most important of a small series of 15th century 'lion-style' Buddha images cast in Lan Na. One of the most significant contributions of Lan Na to Buddhist art, these lion-style images were mostly created during the reign of King Tilokarat.

The iconography of this style is thought to be similar to that of a long lost 'Lion of Sakyas',

The Phra Singh (Sihing), Chiang Mai

which was the most sacred image in the Mahabodhi temple at Bodhgaya, India. The main features of this image, which were recorded on Pala school (11-12th C) stone slabs found near the temple, are the gem finial rising from the skull, a short shawl over the left shoulder extending to just above the nipple, the *maravijaya* hand posture (calling the earth as witness to his worthiness in the defeat of Mara) and the *vajrasana* (full-lotus) leg posture. (N.B. The majority of Lanna images have the same *maravijaya* hand-posture, but have the legs in *virasana* —half-lotus or half-crossed—posture).

Lanna versions of the lion-style image may have been created after a replica was brought to Chiang Mai from India, perhaps via Pagan, along with plans for the Mahabodhi temple, which provided the design for Wat Chet Yot. Lanna sculptors would have combined the iconography of the Pala image with the elegant form they had adopted from the Sukhothai school to make bronze images in the round.

A second theory holds that the lion-style was copied from a legendary original Sihing image, which came from Sri Lanka to Nakhon Si Thammarat. From there it travelled to Ayutthaya before coming to Chiang Mai by way of Kamphaeng Phet and Chiang Rai. Such an image was imbued with great powers and would have been coveted and copied. As a result, at some time during its travels, the

The Phra Phuttha Sihing (NMB)

original Sihing image became unidentifiable.

Three images now claim to be this Sihing image. Chiang Mai's claimant is held to be the image in the *Viharn Lai Kham*. The image leads the procession in the main parade of Songkhran (whether this was the image whose head was stolen in 1922 and replaced with a replica is uncertain).

A second lion style image claiming to be the original resides in Nakhon Si Thammarat, but features of this image suggest it may have been a peninsular or Ayutthayan copy of the lion-style. Neither this image nor the Phra Singh image in Chiang Mai have any characterics suggesting Sri Lankan origin, however.

The third claimant is the Phra Phuttha Sihing image in the Phutthasaiwan Chapel of the National Museum in Bangkok (NMB). The hand posture is in *samadhi* (meditation), a style common to most Sri Lankan images, and the leg posture is in *virasana*. Thus the NMB image is not in the lion-style, a style not associated with images from Sri Lanka. However, certain stylistic details such as the pedestal decorated with lotus petals and stamen, also appear on other images from Lan Na but not from Sri Lanka, suggesting the NMB image could have been cast in Lan Na during the golden age.

King Setthathirat took this Phra Phutta Sihing image along with the Emerald Buddha to Lan Xang in 1548, but the Sihing image returned alone to Chiang Mai, where it stayed until King Narai took it to Ayutthaya in 1661. It is assumed Lanna or Burmese troops recovered the Sihing image at the sack of Ayutthaya in 1767, and it returned to Chiang Mai again, but 28 years later a Siamese army returned with the image to Thon Buri after helping lift a Burmese siege.

* For more information see 'Buddhist Sculpture in Northern Thailand' by Carol Stratton (Silkworm Books), forthcoming.

Prince Sang Thong of the Golden Conch lies on the north wall and the Heavenly Phoenix/ Golden Swan takes up the south. The fables illustrate the long suffering of heroes fighting against the powerful forces of evil before Indra intevenes and allows good to ultimately triumph.

Recent restoration has removed the earlier restoration of the 1920's to show clearly the original syle of the work. Much of the detail has been lost, however. The north wall shows work done by a Chinese artist whose likeness is found in a small picture at the top in the middle of the wall.

Directly to the east of the main chedi, the wooden *ubosot* has ornate carvings around its doors and stucco patterns on the wooden pillars. The *ubosot* is only

The Viharn Lai Kham

opened for an hour around midday on the 15th day of the lunar month before monks enter to read the *patimoka* (the rules of behaviour for monks), when visitors may no longer enter. The *ubosot* contains a tower-like shrine known as a *mondop* (photo p.54). The shape of the shrine was said to be similar to an earlier structure that used to stand in Wat Phra Yeun, Lamphun.

Office of Religious Affairs (Chiang Mai Province)

Image hall (reclining Budd

Thammaratsuksa School (secondary level for novices)

Ubosot

Main viharn

Formerly (*photo left*) an open ground for special ceremonies, fairs & movies, the area has been divided into roadway and grass park.

etail from the Golden Conch mural
/iharn Lai Kham)

The small scripture repository — *ho trai* — in the north-east corner is the finest of its type in the north. It sits atop a raised base decorated with stucco Devas. The upper wooden structure is decorated with carvings and stucco and is covered in glass mosaic and gilded lacquer.

At the back of the compound are the temple administration buildings, monks' *kuti* and a small hall containing a reclining Buddha.

Presenting robes to newly ordained novices

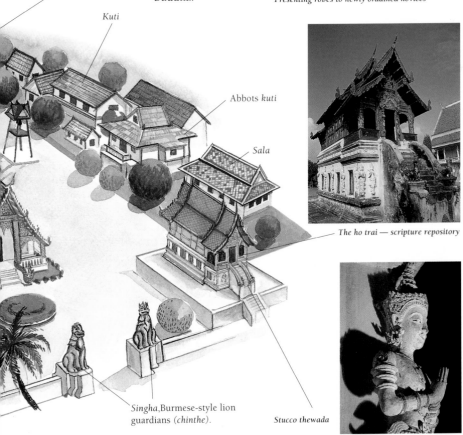

Scripture repository

Kuti

Abbots *kuti*

Sala

The ho trai — scripture repository

Singha,Burmese-style lion guardians (*chinthe*).

Stucco thewada

Khru Ba Srivichai 1878-1938

Khru Ba Srivichai is the most revered Lanna monk of the 20th century. Born in the middle of a storm, he was first given the nickname "thunder". In his childhood he showed his 'meritorious' nature by secretly releasing caged animals.

He began to study at Ban Pang temple in Lamphun province at the age of eighteen and ordained, quickly gaining a reputation as a pious monk. He had a unique ability to communicate with local people, even with the hill tribes, and he could marshal enthusiastic voluntary labour to repair or build new monastic buildings in a manner the government was simply unable to match.

Khru Ba Srivichai
(wax image at Wat Ban Pang)

Srivichai's pious asceticism was to bring him trouble with the authorities, who regarded him as a *phi bun* — a religious rebel. In 1908 Kru Ba Srivichai came into conflict with the Sangha administration, which had been centralised in 1902, over the rights to ordain. Faced with the first of several accusations that accused him of disobedience, he was seen as a threat because of his independence and popularity. The conflict culminated in 1919, when he was expelled from his monastery in Lamphun province and confined in Wat Sidonchai.

Khru Ba Srivichai never instigated civil disobedience, however, and he was reinstated in 1920 after an audience with the supreme patriarch, who found him to be gentle and to have the conscious spirit of a monk.

During his lifetime Khru Ba Srivichai was to supervise renovations at over 100 temples; these included Wat Phrathat Haripunchai, Wat Chamadevi, Wat Phra Singh and Wat Suan Dok. He also supervised construction of the road up Doi Suthep, and his car was the first to go up it. His success with communal modernisation projects and his pious independence ensured that he came to symbolise the local religious tradition as a *nak bun haeng lanna* — a Lanna saint.

Khru Ba Srivichai (standing middle) with followers (Wat Phrathat Doi Suthep, 1935)

Wat Phrathat Doi Suthep

วัดพระธาตุดอยสุเทพ

(KM. 14. Srivichai Rd. M6 p.80 Polite dress is required for the inner sanctuary. Loose clothing is available at the entrance free of charge. The inner sanctuary i open to visitors 08:00-17:00. Minibuses to Doi Suthep wait on the west corner of the Chang Phuak and Maninopharat Rd. and outside the main gate of Chiang Mai Zoo. 30 Bt. up - 20 Bt. down. min. 6 to 8 persons. The temple is planning to charg a modest entrance fee for foreigners in 2003.)

ACCORDING TO LEGEND, the temple site was chosen by an elephant carrying a holy relic. Originally the relic was to be enshrined at Wat Suan Dok in 1371, but it split in two. The second piece was placed on the back of an elephant, which proceeded to climb Doi Suthep, stopping twice. After three days the elephant finally reached a level piece of ground, circled three times, knelt down and died. A hole was dug at the site for the relic, which was then covered with a chedi seven metres high.

Until the road was built in 1935, pilgrims had to walk up the mountain and then up more than 200 steps on the long *naga* stairway to reach the temple. This stairway was originally constructed in the mid-16th century in the reign of Phra Mekuti. Like the rest of the temple, the stairway has since been renovated several times. Small tiles inscribed with the names of donors and the amounts given have been built into the walls just above each step. Nowadays, pilgrims may also use a small cable railway from the road instead of the stairway.

The inner walled sanctuary is surrounded by a lower terrace. From this level there is an excellent view over the city, weather permitting. The faithful like to ring the bells and gongs round the base of the sanctuary. A statue of the elephant commemorates the founding of the temple, and a statue adorned with a tiger-skin that sits in a niche is of Wisuthep Rishi, a hermit who gave his name to the mountain.

Phrathat Chedi Doi Suthep

The inner sanctuary is one of the Chiang Mai's classic sights. A gold plated chedi lies in the middle of a square marble tiled courtyard. The chedi reached its present height of over 16 metres (55 ft.) in 1525 in the reign of King Muang Kaew. A railing surrounding the square base of the chedi encloses a walkway for devotional rounds of the chedi (women may not enter this). Parasols, symbols of royal regalia, have been placed at the four corners of the chedi.

The courtyard took its present shape under Chao Kawila in 1805. It is lined by a cloister which contains Buddha images and murals depicting the life of the Buddha. In the middle of the east and west sides of the cloister are two ornate viharn. Murals in the eastern viharn show the

Wat Phrathat Doi Suthep and the Ping Valley

legend of the elephant and the relic, while those of the western hall show the *Vessantara Jataka* (see p.68). Devotees go to the western viharn to receive blessings and lustral water from monks sitting on a dais.

On the south and northern sides of the cloister, smaller shrines are the subject of much veneration. Thais prostrate themselves and then shake a holder with 28 sticks to see which one falls to the ground first. A fortune reading for each of the numbers may be found in a cabinet nearby.

The power of the chedi and the sanctuary attract many visitors who are invited to make merit. The sanctuary contains numerous boxes for donations to worthy causes, such as care and education of the needy.

WAT SUAN DOK

วัดสวนดอก

(Suthep Rd. 3.40.E5) THIS TEMPLE originally lay in a fortified square beyond the city walls. Legends tell that King Ku Na invited the venerable Sumana Thera, a very pious monk from Sukhothai to bring the Buddhism of Sri Lanka to Chiang Mai. The King offered him the royal flower garden (*suan dok*) as a place to build a temple. The temple was established in 1371.

When Sumana Thera was living in Sukhothai, he had a vision which showed him where to find a very holy relic that had long been buried near the city. When the relic was unearthed, miraculous illuminations took place confirming its power. These miracles did not repeat

themselves for the King of Sukhothai, who left the relic in the care of the monk. Thus

Novices release a khom filled with hot air to celebrate New Year.

when King Ku Na invited Sumana Thera to Chiang Mai, the monk brought the holy relic with him. When the relic was about to be enshrined at the temple, he found that the relic had split into two pieces. One of these pieces was kept at Wat Suan Dok, and the other was buried at Wat Phrathat Doi Suthep.

Sound and light at Wat Suan Dok as part of the 700 year centenary celebrated in 1996

The main viharn was
ebuilt in the early 1930's by
hru Ba Srivichai. A large
uddha image with a hand in
he position for holding straw
ands back to back with the
nain seated image. The
nages took on their present
hape under Khru Ba Srivichai.

A smaller viharn to the
outh contains a seated
uddha image — the *Phra
Chao Kao Tue* — cast by King
Muang Kaew in 1504. The
anna style image stands
.7 metres tall and is made
p of nine pieces. The walls
f the viharn are decorated
vith murals showing the
revious lives of the Buddha
the *Vessantara Jataka* — see
.68 — may be seen on the
pper north wall).

West of the main viharn
umerous chedi contain the
emains of the royal family of
Chiang Mai. These were
ollected from different sites
n the city and placed there at
he wish of Princess Dara
Rasmi in 1909. The com-
ound also contains the
orthern campus of the
Mahachulalongkorn Buddhist

The Phra Chao Kao Tue image

University of the *Mahanikai*
sect *(visitors are invited to join
in 'Monk Chat' 17:00-19:00 hrs.
Mons., Weds., & Fridays — an
excellent chance to learn about
Buddhism and make merit
helping monastic students to
learn English).* A wall with tall
ornamental gates surrounds
the compound, and some
remains of the earthen walls
that once surrounded the
fortified monastery are still
found on the north side of
Suthep Road.

WAT UMONG SUAN PUTTHATHAM

วัดอุโมงค์สวนพุทธธรรม

*(Suthep Rd. Soi Wat
Umong — south turn 1.5
kms. 168.F2)* LOCATED in a
grove, Wat Umong is a
practising meditation
temple. The origins of the
temple, which are traced
to the 14th century, are
obscure. The temple may
have been founded by
King Mangrai himself to
accommodate some forest
monks from Sri Lanka.

One legend relates
that King Ku Na may have
developed the temple in the
1380's to accommodate a
celebrated monk called
Therachan. The king used to

*Enlightenment from trees
(Wat Umong)*

consult the monk on various
problems when the monk
was in residence at a temple
in the old city (Wat Umong
Maha Therachan). On
occasions, however, the
monk was thought to be a
little "eccentric" because he
preferred the solitude offered
by the forest retreat to the
city temples and court ritual.

Records suggest the temple

eremonial dancing is performed as part of a ritual honouring important visitors

may have become deserted as early as the end of the reign of King Tilokarat (1487). The site only became a monastery again in 1948. A strong influence on the temple has been the Buddhist philosophy of Buddhadhasa Bhikkhu, one of Thailand's most celebrated 20th century monks. His statue stands on an islet in the lake to the south of the chedi. The Venerable favoured the natural environment of the forest over human construction. As a result the modest temple buildings are surrounded by trees.

A path from the main entrance leads up past a Buddhist museum. It continues between a *kuti* and a 'spiritual theatre' which contains murals depicting Buddhist wisdom. The path then reaches a raised area

*Untitled installation at Wat Umong
(Chiang Mai Social Installation)*

with walls of brick. Tunnels lead to meditation cells and a venerated Buddha image. Some of the oldest murals in Thailand used to be visible in these tunnels, but they have virtually disappeared. The bell shaped chedi above is reached by a stairway. From the chedi walk north above the tunnels to see a fine Buddha image cast in the

ascetic style.

The temple grounds also extend to cover an open zoo on the side of the mountain. The front entrance lies up a short lane on the south side of the temple. The zoo has an inner fenced area connected to the main temple compound by a small back gate in the west fence. This inner area contains *kuti* for monks in the classic forest tradition. Tame deer wander the park and the park sanctuary is a good site for bird watching. Sadly, the zoo lacks the proper funding to house the caged animals in a more appropriate manner.

Damaged Buddha images (Wat Umong)

CITY TEMPLES

THERE ARE more than 30 active temples in the old city alone, and many more in the greater city area. Should you be casually strolling down a narrow lane and you see a temple not listed here, take the time to walk in and look around, for every temple has something unique to offer. Many have special plaques that give a brief history at each location.

WAT BUPPHARAM

วัดบุปผาราม

Thaphae Rd. 41.E9) THIS TEMPLE was founded by King

Shutter carved by a local craftsman a design by Phra Bun Prasert (Wat Buppharam)

Muang Kaew in 1497. The Burmese-style chedi was rebuilt in 1958, and there is a sacred well nearby, which supplies holy water for bathing the King.

A small Lanna style viharn contains a large brick and stucco Buddha. Though over 500 years old, much that is seen today probably originates from a restoration at the end of the 19th century. The *mom* — the guardian beasts at the entrance — were made in 1989, however. The larger viharn (open only in the evening during chanting) goes back about

200 years and contains some mid-20th century murals that show the *Maha Chat* in a Burmese style. The carved front door panels were completed in 1983.

The newest structure is the *ho monthiantham*, the hall with the pinnacled roof. Abbot Phra Udom Kitti Mongkol had it built on the spot where an earlier wooden structure used to stand. The building took ten years to complete and was finished in 1996. With its mythical beasts, stucco reliefs, wood carvings and murals, it is an unusual demonstration of contemporary religious art.

Inside the hall on the ground floor, murals show

Viharn and ho monthientham (Wat Buppharam)

the Lanna twelve months' traditions. Local artist Pornchai Jaimon included contemporary scenes in the details when he submitted this work for his degree thesis.

The second floor is heavily decorated and contains two large seated Buddha images. The white image is solid teak and was carved after a vision by King Naresuan in the late 16th century, when he defeated the Burmese forces near Muang Ngai. This vision is depicted in the carved wood panels on the east wall.

WAT DUANG DI

วัดดวงดี

(Prapokklao Rd. 40.E8) IN A COMPOUND shaded by old longan trees, the name of this temple means 'good fortune'. A small but unusual scripture repository decorated with stucco built in 1829 is

Phra Udom Kitti Mongkol

located to the south of the tall main viharn. This Ayutthaya-style building has a very fine carved wooden gable, while inside are some crude murals between windows depicting Buddhist hells. The massive wooden doors are dated 1929, but the main building may date from the 19th century. The elegant Lanna-style *ubosot* south of the viharn is probably older.

According to an inscription

Eave support and corner of gable/ pediment (Wat Duang Di)

at the base of one of the Buddha images in the viharn, the temple was formerly known as Wat Ton Mak Nua and dates back to King Muang Kaew at the beginning of the 16th century.

WAT KU TAO
วัดกู่เต้า

(*Off Sanam Kila Rd. 40.C8*). THIS TEMPLE lies in a quiet compound containing several large trees. The main feature is an unusual chedi shaped like a series of alms bowls stacked on top of each other (*photo p.44*). The origin of the chedi is a mystery. The name *Ku* suggests a charnel ground and *Tao* a round pot shape — thus it may have been built to keep the ashes of a Burmese noble in the late 16th or early 17th century. A large new viharn is being built in place of the old one.

WAT MAHAWAN
วัดมหาวัน

(*Thaphae Rd. 41.E9*) THE ORIGINS of this temple may be traced back to at least the 17th century, making this one of the temples founded during the Burmese occupation.

Many of the temple buildings show a strong Burmese influence, particularly the viharn by the west wall. This was sponsored by a wealthy

Burmese-style image in the Viharn Lang Prachao To, Wat Mahawan

Carved doors (Wat Mahawan)

Burmese agent acting for teak companies, and was built in the late 19th century.

The compound also contains a Burmese-style chedi and large wooden scripture library that serves as the abbot's *kuti*. The small *ubosot* and large viharn next to it at the eastern end of the compound are typically Lanna. The viharn was renovated in 1957 and may have been first constructed around 1865.

Bright modern murals may be seen on its walls. Panels on the north wall show the *Vessantara Jataka* and on the south wall show scenes of the Buddha meditating as he gained enlightenment. The paintings on the wall behind the main Buddha image show a typical bo tree with an idyllic scene depicting a state of nature that has long since disappeared from the northern hills (*photo p.47*).

Crystal Sons

Many Shan people live in northern Thailand. Part of the Shan ordination ritual involves making up young boys who are to ordain and dressing them up in bright costumes. Called 'crystal sons', these boys are put on ponies or carried on shoulders and paraded to the temple where the ordination is to take place. Prior to ordination they are spoiled with little treats as if they were in heaven, and they are carried everywhere for their feet should not touch the ground.

A Crystal Son

The northern Thai ordination is less elaborate but no less important. Sons should ordain to make merit for their parents. Tradition holds that by doing so the gates of hell close for the mother and will close for the father when he becomes a monk.

In recent years Wat Pa Pao has revived the custom of having a Shan-style ordination. The festival, known as *poi san long*, lasts two days and takes place in April before the 10th of the month. During the festival the grounds of Wat Pa Pao have a carnival atmosphere.

Chedi guardians (Wat Pa Pao)

WAT PA PAO

วัดป่าเป้า

(*Maninopharat Rd. 41.D9*)
THIS is the finest example of a Shan temple in Chiang Mai. Though the Shan-style *viharn* is quite different from northern styles, the most striking feature is the sunken courtyard. It was built in 1883 by Shans who wished to have a place to practice their forms of Buddhist worship. Decorated gates tilt precariously and numerous statues of mythical beings

Shan Burmese style Chedi (Wat Pa Pao)

give the place great charm. An unusual flat-roofed *ubosot* topped with a chedi has a vaulted interior which contains three Buddha images.

WAT PHAN TAO

วัดพันเตา

Prapokklao Rd. 40.E8)
ONCE PART of Wat Chedi Luang, the temple got its name from the 'furnaces', or *tao*, that were used to cast the images for the main temple. The large viharn is a rare example of a

The viharn of Wat Phan Tao

former *ho kham* — a royal hall. Originally on stilts and used as a residence by Chao Mahawong (r.1846-54), the building was rebuilt as the viharn in 1876.

Flooding earlier this century damaged the building and concrete was used to replace some of the original structure. Though the central style dominates, the woodcarvings above the door and windows are Lanna. The gable overlooking

Prapokklao Road has fine woodcarvings. A curled sleeping dog beneath the peacock motif symbolises the birth year of the royal sponsor (animals of the northern zodiac associated with bene-factors are often found on temple buildings). At the back of the temple compound is an aviary and fish pond.

Wat Phuak Hong

WAT PHUAK HONG

วัดพวกหงษ์

(Off Samlan Rd. opposite Soi 7. 40.F7) THE GOLD ON RED

panels of the gable on the *viharn* are typical of the Lanna style. However, the most distinctive feature of this temple is the round

seven stepped chedi with 52 niches, which dates from 1517. Two other chedi in Chiang Mai, Chedi Prong and the chedi of Wat Rampoeng, have similar shapes.

WAT PRASAT

วัดประสาท

(Inthawarorot Rd. 40.E7) WAT PRASAT, to the north of Wat Pra Singh, dates back at least to the 16th century. The wooden viharn, which was built in 1823 and renovated in 1987, approaches a classic Lanna style.

The pleasing external form is matched by the artefacts inside the *viharn*. At the

Naga finial (Wat Prasat)

back of the temple the space for the main image is replaced by a highly deco-rated entrance to a short tunnel leading to the chedi. A number of metre high images with red painted robes sit on the raised pedestal on either side

Decorated gable (Wat Phan Tao)

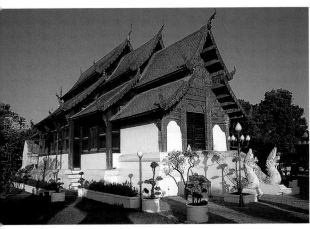

he viharn of Wat Prasat

f the entrance. The image losest to the entrance on he north side is bronze (the thers are stucco) and is ated 1590.

There is a carved wooden pulpit and the ide walls of the back of the iharn have murals in red nd gold that are thought to riginate from the 1820's.

VAT SAEN FANG

ัดแสนฝาง

Thaphae Rd. 41.E9) THE EMPLE'S ORIGINS go back to he 14th century, but the rchitecture is late 19th entury Burmese. This can learly be seen at the vestern end of the ompound, where there is chedi with lion guardians, nd an *ubosot* with small igures on the roof ridges. he elaborate carved wooden ront of the main viharn is a ater addition of what was nce the former *ho kham* of Chao Kawilorot (r.1856- 870). His successor, Chao nthanon ordered it recon- tructed for use as the viharn

in 1878. The old scripture library west of the chedi was built in 1869.

Carved panels with animal motifs on the gable of the Viharn of Wat Saen Fang

WAT UMONG MAHA THERACHAN

วัดอุโมงค์มหาเถรจันทร์

(Ratchaphakhinai Rd. 41.E8) LIKE MANY TEMPLES this one looks new, but its origins go back to 1367. The name "Maha Therachan" is said to have come from a renowned monk who was its abbot (see Wat Umong Suan Putthatham p.55). Two old Lanna-style chedis are located in the compound. The viharn contains some modern murals typical of the Rattanakosin style and show the *Vessantara Jataka*. The story begins above the main door and continues clockwise on the side walls of the viharn.

The small *ubosot* is guarded by two fierce beasts called *mom*. The same artist also did the stucco work inside and painted the side walls with bright new murals depicting scenes from the life of the Buddha. The *ubosot* also has finely carved wooden doors and windows.

The entire renovation work to the *ubosot* was completed in the early 1990's, and the whole is a good example of contemporary Lanna temple art.

Stucco mom guarding the ubosot of Wat Umong Maha Therachan. (Women may enter as long as no ritual is taking place)

The *Maha Chat* — the Great Birth

The most popular of the tales of the previous lives of the Buddha is the last one, the *Vessantara Jataka*. In this story the Buddha perfects renunciation, the last of the ten virtues of a Boddhisattva. The Thai version is divided into thirteen parts, which are often found illustrated in a set of murals on one of the side walls.

In his tenth great life, the future Buddha is born as Prince Vesantara. The prince begins his renunciation by giving away a magic white elephant that brings rain to his father's kingdom, and he is expelled. His wife, Princess Matsi, and their two children go with him. Early in his journey he gives away his horse and carriage and the family walks into the forest like hermits.

Canto 11. The Gods take care of the royal children (newer mural at Wat Umong Maha Therachan).

Meanwhile a Brahmin called Chuchok has a young wife who is scolded by other lazier wives in her village for working too hard for her husband. She begs her husband to seek out the prince and ask him for the two children as slaves. After several adventures in the jungle, Chuchok finds the prince. The children hide, but their father explains why they should go with Chuchok. Gods masquerading as wild animals prevent their mother from returning home and intervening.

Alarmed that he might also give away Princess Matsi to some unworthy person, Indra comes disguised as a Brahmin and asks for her. When Prince Vesantara gives her away, Indra reveals himself and asks the prince to look after her on his behalf.

Meanwhile Chuchok loses his way in the jungle and sleeps in a tree. The gods fear for the children and guard them during the night. Chuchok then comes upon the king and queen, who recognise their grandchildren.

Chuchok accepts a big reward for them but later dies of gluttony. The king and queen invite Prince Vesantara back to the palace in the city and he returns triumphantly.

Chuchok dies of gluttony. (older mural at Wat Phrathat Doi Suthep)

Stucco

The mythical creatures that inhabit a Thai temple are made of stucco. The sculptors who work with stucco prefer to use a traditional

Stucco decoration (ho trai at Wat Duang Di)

Vicom Kittirattanachai

mix made out of lime, sand, sugarcane juice, straw paper and animal hide glue. Once pounded into a fine mix, the ingredients have enough malleability and strength to give the artists time to create works of fine detail. A good traditional mix should last for several centuries. Though newer cement based stucco is much easier to make, it is unlikely to last nearly as long.

The Naga and Makara

The *Naga* is seen pouring out of the mouth of a *Makara*, a creature that combines the

The entwined tails above the door is an old style of representing the Naga and Makara at the small ubosot of Wat Chang Khong (41.E9).

the down pouring of rain from the sky. Thus they are powerful symbols in a culture based on wet-rice cultivation.

They may also be seen as linking the earth below to the heaven above by a celestial stairway represented by a rainbow. The colours of the rainbow represent different aspects of the unity of light at their source. The *naga* stairway, then, symbolically links opposites. It links the world of illusion, the Sea of Samsara upon which the viharn floats, to the formless world of nirvana. Thus the *naga* and *makara* symbolise the ties that bind man to the world of illusion, and the path that frees man from that illusion.

crocodile, the elephant and the serpent. They are aquatic servants of Varuna, a powerful Vedic god. In Vedic mythology Varuna controlled not only the waters, but also controlled the means that produced the cosmos.

Varuna, as the serpent king, rode upon the back of a *makara* and bound subjects who disobeyed natural law (the dhamma) in fetters which were represented as snakes. Varuna, therefore, may be closely associated with the Brahmanic notion of the universe as an illusion represented by Mara, and the Buddhist notion that man is bound to the world of illusion by sensory attachment.

The *Naga* and *Makara* live in paradises beneath the rivers, lakes and seas. They control the sources of rain and are the guardians of life-giving energy in its waters. On the balustrades to temples they represent both the rising of water to the heavens and

Naga at the Chedi Luang

PLACES OF GENERAL INTEREST

EVER SINCE KING MANGRAI founded the city, the market has been of fundamental importance. Today the commercial heart lies on what was once open ground between the old city and the rive Away from the centre of the city, th National Museum and the zoo ar some of the places of interest in th larger city area

Detail from Buddha footprint dated 1794 (Mother of pearl & glass inlay. 124 x 200cm. Chiang Mai National Museum)

CHIANG MAI NATIONAL MUSEUM

พิพิธภัณฑ์แห่งชาติเชียงใหม่

(*Chiang Mai-Lampang Super-highway. 168 A6, 09:00-16:00 except Mondays, Tuesdays and national holidays. Tel: (00 5322 1308. Adults 30 Bt.*) THE MODERN THAI-STYLE BUILDING typical of new official structures houses two floors of exhibits. The first floor contains displays showing history in chrono-logical sequence, while the second floor has displays of secular (trade, health, etc) and religious artefacts arranged by theme and by historical period. A reconstructed kiln stands in the grounds outside.

CHIANG MAI UNIVERSITY

มหาวิทยาลัยเชียงใหม่

(*KM. 3 Huay Kaew Rd. 3.B2*). THE MOST prestigious educational institution in Northern Thailand, the university was the first to be opened outside Bangkok in 1964. Competition to get a place is fierce, and there are over 14,000 students served by 5000 staff. The university includes the Maharaj Nakhon Chiang Mai Hospital (popularly known as Suan Dok Hospital). A map in English and Thai near the front entrance on Huay Kaew Road shows where things are.

The Tribal Research Institute (*see p.74*) and the Centre for the Promotion of Arts and Culture are of particular interest (*see p.178*).

CHIANG MAI ZOO

สวนสัตว์เชียงใหม่

(*168. A1- C2 Tel: (0) 5322 1179, (0) 5335 8116 Adults 30 Bht. No motorcycles/bicycles allowed but cars 30 Bht. Hrs.08:00-17:00 visitors must leave by 18:00. Suthep Road entrance closes 16:00.* FOUNDED IN 1957 the zoo is the best in Thailand. The 212 acres of lower mountain slope is a good place for exbiting the 455 species of mammal, birds, reptiles and fish in the collection. A 2.5 acre walk-ir aviary enclosing a gully is particularly fine. At week-ends around 1.30 pm. near the elephant corral, selected animals are brought out of their cages to give the public a chance to get much closer than is usually possible.

The zoo is large and allows cars inside, which is useful if you have young children. Snack bars in several places sell snacks, soft drinks and water. Outside the zoo on the opposite side of the road, the Thai-German Dairy serves home-made ice cream and locally-made cheese.

The mountain site is good for loc *species (Chiang Mai Zoo*

CHIANG MAI'S MAIN MARKET — *Kat Luang*

กาดหลวง

KAT LUANG — the main market— is bound by Chang Moi Road, Khuangmen and

The Open Museum

To celebrate H.M.King Bhumiphol Adulyadej's 72nd Birthday Anniversary on 5th December 1999, the Navaraj Damri Foundation inaugurated a project making Chiang Mai an open museum by the erection of 82 plaques at places of historical and cultural interest in and around the city.

Giving information in Thai and English, the plaques are divided into categories as follows: Auspicious sites (nos. 1-5), old communities (nos 8-12), palaces (nos. 13-15), city wall & gates (nos. 17-24), Christian sites (nos.25-31, 63), temples (nos. 32-47), former temples (nos.48-62). Additional plaques cover a miscellany of sites ranging from educational institutions to Chinese temples.

Where the author has been able to find these plaques, they are marked according to their official number as symbols (**70**) on maps, the line indicating precise location. The plaques may not warrant a special journey, but should you happen to be passing by, you will gain additional information about the city not found on these pages.

Over the years other organisations have also created plaques providing information about the city in English and Thai. Unfortunately the bleaching effect of sunlight has made some of them illegible.

According to plaque #70, the Mae Bun Ruang Gold Shop (Khuang Men Rd) was formerly Grandma Saen Kamma's Rest House, one of the earliest guest houses in Chiang Mai.

raisani Roads (41.D10 — *e City Walk 2)*

Warorot and Lam Yai markets (west and east of Vichayanon Road respectively) contain large covered alls with galleries where ried foods, clothing and many other products are old. Prices can be far lower han in the Night Bazaar.

Two Chinese shrines are ound in the narrow streets which throng with people visiting the Chinese, Sikh nd Thai traders. The bustling arrow passages, the smell of pices and the fragrance of ncense create a traditional ision of the East.

THE FOREIGN CEMETERY & GYMKHANA CLUB

สานต่างชาติและยิมคานาคลับ

Old Chiang Mai -Lamphun Road 41.G11) FROM HER PLINTH, Queen Victoria's statue surveys the piece of land where some of Chiang Mai's most notable foreign residents find their final place of rest. Bordered by the Gymkhana Club and the Chiang Mai-Lamphun Road, the land was granted by King Chulalongkorn in 1898 for the burial of foreigners only.

Notables buried here include British Consul, W.A.R.Wood. His book, *Consul in Paradise* (Trasvin Publications, 1992), is a series of amusing tales about life in the Chiang Mai in the early 20th century. More can also be found out by buying a copy of *De Mortuis: the story of the Chiang Mai Foreign Cemetery* from the cemetery's caretaker.

If things get a bit morbid, nip around the corner for a tot on the verandah of the Gymkhana Club (founded 1898, *non members welcome*) and contemplate the passing beauty of the club's giant rain tree.

"ERECTED AS A TOKEN OF DEEP REVERENCE AND AFFECTION FOR THE MEMORY OF THEIR LATE GRACIOUS QUEEN VICTORIA BY HER LOYAL SUBJECTS OF EVERY RACE RESIDING IN THE CHIENGMAI, LAKON - LAMPANG, PHRE, NAN, SAWANKALOK, AND RAHENG DISTRICTS OF NORTHERN SIAM."

After an unexpected overland journey from Moulmein instead of coming upriver from Bangkok, Queen Victoria's statue was installed in the British Consulate grounds in December 1903. She was hidden from the Japanese during World War Two, and was later propitiated by hill-tribe people who, as reported in the Sunday Times, 24 December 1972, 'sought fertility, virility and money'. At the closure of the consulate in 1978, the statue was moved to the Foreign Cemetery.

The Rev. Daniel McGilvary, D.D., LLD.

The Reverend Daniel McGilvary's unassuming grave in the Foreign Cemetery gives little indication of his importance to Chiang Mai.

Reaching Bangkok in 1858 at the age of 30, McGilvary married Sophia Bradley, daughter of Daniel Bradley of the Siam Presbyterian Mission. Fired with evangelical zeal, he became interested in the 'Lao states' and made an exploratory tour of the north in 1863-4. He eventually gained permission for a mission to Chiang Mai from Chao Kawilorot in 1866, when the latter visited Bangkok.

Arriving in 1867, the McGilvarys stayed in a three sided *sala* which was virtually open to public view. His first four converts were people of high rank and included two Buddhist abbots. This aroused the enmity of the chauvinistic Chao Kawilorot and led to his ordering the murder of two of the converts. The confrontation between McGilvary and Kawilorot came in front of his entire court after the *chao* had received a royal letter from Rama V giving protection to the missionaries in 1869. In this encounter the angered *chao* admitted to the murder and said that leaving the religion of his country was a rebellion against him, but he allowed McGilvary and his colleague and friend, the Rev. Wilson, to remain to treat the sick but not to evangelise*.

The Presbyterian missionaries had been fortunate that they had taught English and science to Crown Prince Mongkut (later to become Rama IV) when he was in the monkhood, and Prince Chulalongkorn had become familiar with their presence. Though neither monarch ever had much faith in Christian beliefs, both respected the role the mission's medical and educational work could play in modernising Siam. Thus McGilvary had the support of the Siamese monarch against the *chao*, and again in 1878, when Rama V made a proclamation of religious toleration to protect the northern missions.

Despite accusations that the missionaries offended the spirits, they enjoyed early success, particularly amongst those accused of witchcraft, a device used to relocate people or banish enemies. Methods of persuading people to accept Christianity varied. One Christian women wrote that when her sister became so angry at her conversion that she ran up and down a rice-field screaming that the devil was chasing her, "the vigorous application of her Christian hymnal on the head of her crazed sister exorcised the demon and restored the reason of her possessed relative".

The medical work began with McGilvary

Courtesy of Phayap University Archives

The Rev. & Mrs McGilvary circa their golden wedding anniversary, 1910

himself introducing the use of quinine against malaria and inoculations against smallpox. Medical doctors such as Cheek and McKean were to follow, establishing an "American" hospital in 1888 (to become the McCormick Hospital in 1925) and the leprosarium in 1908.

The mission to "enlighten the mind and enlarge the spirit" through education was to have no less significant results. What started with Mrs McGilvary teaching Siamese, sewing, bible studies, knitting and household economy to a few girls in her home grew into a more formal girls school in 1879 (to become the Dara Academy in 1910), and a boys school in 1887 (to become the Prince Royal College in 1912). McGilvary's Theological Seminary (founded 1912) and the nursing school (founded 1923) were to evolve into Phayap University, the first private college to be granted university status in 1976.

McGilvary never tired of evangelism, teaching both valley and mountain folk. Beginning in 1872 and continuing most travelling seasons till the year of his death in 1911, he went on explorations all over the Tai speaking north, sometimes travelling with Dr James McKean, who would dispense medical aid, while McGilvary sat on the floor by his touring lamp, giving reading classes from the shorter catechism while pointing to the Lao characters upside down in front of him with a sliver of bamboo. It was McGilvary who was largely responsible for the expansion of the mission and the establishment of Christian communities with schools and hospitals throughout Northern Thailand.

*This event is described in A Half Century among the Siamese and the Lao by D McGilvary (Fleming H Revell & Co, London 1912). This and other old volumes may be studied at the Phayap University Archives, Kaeo Nawarat Campus (opp. McCormick Hospital) on Kaew Nawarat Rd. Mon-Fri. Hrs: 08:00-16:30 closed for lunch 12:00-1300

Marion Alonzo Cheek M.D.

In 1874 Dr. Marion Cheek was 21 when he was recruited from a North Carolina medical school by Daniel McGilvary. Upon arriving in Bangkok, he met and married Sarah Bradley, becoming a brother-in-law of the Rev. McGilvary.

Courtesy of Phayap University Archives

After reaching Chiang Mai in 1875, he initially made slow progress and his relationship with McGilvary began to turn sour in 1877, when he was absent on unauthorised sick leave during a serious outbreak of malignant malaria. However, he became popular amongst the foreign community for his hunting skills, and amongst the Lao for his medical knowledge and interest in their culture. For healing the chao's principal wife in 1876 after the village doctors had given up on her, he was awarded a beautiful slave girl called Noja and a block of land.

By 1881 he had built up a practice treating up to 13,000 patients a year, but he was to chafe at the lack of a proper hospital. His success brought hostility from village doctors, and, as a mission physician, his professed concern for men's bodies rather than for their souls can only have made his relationship with McGilvary worse.

Using his good contacts with the Lao, Cheek's interest turned towards acquiring wealth through the teak trade, and he became the Borneo Company's Chiang Mai agent when he returned from leave in America in 1884. In return he got access to capital for leases, foresters, elephants and for log rafting.

He told the missionaries in Chiang Mai that he was resigning, but he ignored requests for clarification of status from the Presbyterian Board in New York. He only officially resigned in 1886, when, after praising his medical skills but criticising his zeal for business activities, a mission inspector withheld funds for the construction of a proper hospital that Cheek had personally raised in America.

Cheek was to keep serving as a doctor to mission families in times of crisis, and he worked successfully for the Borneo Company. However, he also borrowed company funds to operate a paddle steamer, to start a boatyard and to form a construction company that built schools, houses and a teak bridge over the Ping that would last 40 years.

Alarmed by Cheek's debts and lavish lifestyle, the Borneo Company summoned him to Bangkok in 1889, but they were unable to reach agreement. Cheek then contracted with the Siamese Commissioner to supply teak, an act which the Siamese hoped might limit British activities and weaken the links between the chao and the forests.

Bad luck and poor judgement were to lead Cheek into disaster. In 1989, with one of their sons ill, a distressed Sarah Cheek sailed for America with their five children*. In Chiang Mai, his relationship with the Chao suffered because of his new relationship to the Siamese, whose inroads the Chao resented.

His undoing came with successive failures in the rains in 1891-2, which caused bad floating seasons (and famine). At a time when the Siamese were starting to see the promotion of British activities in the north as a useful means of resisting French expansionism, Cheek failed to respond to repeated royal summons to Bangkok, claiming he could not leave his business. The commissioner issued a proclamation seizing his assets in July 1893, ruining him one month before 4000 of his logs were to arrive near Bangkok with the rainy season surge.

With the help of the American Consulate, Cheek sought redress in a famous legal case which was to save his family from poverty, but not save him from his fate. Enjoying diplomatic immunity, American Vice-Consul General Kellet helped Cheek in Chiang Mai while Cheek struggled in the jungles to exploit the (well-armed) foresters and 72 elephants that remained in his control. But Cheek was to fail against the active opposition of the Siamese commissioner and the competition from his friend, Louis Leonowens, who represented the Borneo Company. Fever and dysentery took its toll, making him so ill that he was forced to take ship for treatment in Hong Kong in June 1895. He died of an abscess of the liver as the vessel lay off the island of Si Chang.

---

* *Cheek built up a harem of about 20 local women in Chiang Mai, an action for which he achieved notoriety, and for which he is still remembered in a northern Thai folk chant advising him to "hurry up and finish". This and other aspects of this period of history are described in "Louis and the King of Siam" by W.S.Bristowe, Chatto & Windus, London 1976 (out of print).*

The Chiang Mai Christian Church was completed in 1891 on grounds given to the mission by Chao Kawilorot in 1868.

River Ping Cruises

Mae Ping Cruises runs boat trips from Wat Chaimongkol landing, Charoen Prathet Rd 08:30-17:00 Bt.300 per person min. 2 passengers includes free drink and fresh fruit. Length 8kms/90-120 min. A dinner cruise at 400 bht/head includes hotel transfer approx.19:00 hrs. reservations Tel: (0) 5327 4822. or (0) 1885 0663. The company also runs river cruises from the east bank near the Riverside Pub & Restaurant hourly departures between 10:00 through 15:00 with approx. 40 mins at Tha Luk. 100 bht return min. 2 passengers includes free drink. Return by road is possible till sunset, when the songthaeo's stop running.

The short trip upriver makes for a lazy half-day appreciating steps being taken to clean up the river banks and stop encroachment onto the river. On the east bank north of the Rim Ping Condominium, a large private property with traditional Thai buildings belonged to descendents of the Chiang Mai Royal Family, but apparently the place is haunted.

Beyond the super-highway bridge, the river goes through a tranquil reach, passing some desirable residences. Boat tours from Wat Chaimongkol go to a sala and herb garden on the west bank. Boats from the east bank go a little further upstream to Tha Luk on the east bank, so named after its waterwheels. There, a curious tambon development consisting of large wooden buildings offers a massage service amongst other things. The adjacent rustic San Phi Sua Restuarant is pleasant.

Special Museums

- **The Museum of World Insects & Natural Wonders** (40. D5. 72 Nimmanhaemin Soi 13, Sirimangkhlachan Rd. Hrs. 09:00–16:00 daily. Tel: (0)5321 1891. Ring bell if door not open. 100 Bt. adults, children 50 Bt.) Located in a new building, this museum will fascinate those interested in Thailand's insects.

- **The Postal Museum** (Praisani Rd. 41.E10 Hrs. 09:00–16:00. Closed Mondays. Free). Displays show many of Thailand's stamp issues, along with some old postal equipment. New issues are also sold.

- **The Treasury Pavilion** (52 Ratchadamneon Rd. C.M. 50200 (40.E8) Tel: (0) 5322 4237-8. Hrs. Mon-Fri 9:00– 12:00, 13:00–15:30) A well-displayed collection contains coinage dating from before the Kingdom of Lan Na, as well as medallions from the Rattanakosin period.

- **Tribal Museum and Research Institue (TRI)** (Ratchamangkhla Park, H107 KM5. Tel: (0) 5321 0872, (0) 5322 1933. Fax: (0) 5322 2494 Hrs. 09:00—16:00 Monday-Friday). A pagoda-shaped building in a lake east of the Rama IX gardens contains an extensive range of hill tribe artefacts. The library is located at the main TRI main offices in Chiang Mai University (168.C2 Hrs 08:30—12:00, 13:00—16:30 weekdays only. Tel: (0) 5322 1933)

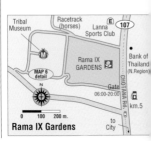

Rama IX Gardens

Thaphae & River Ping Walking Tour

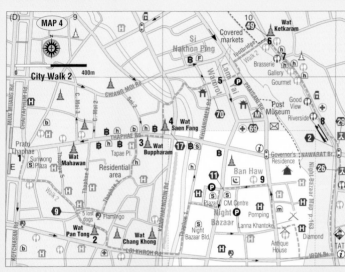

(Best in the later afternoon for a sundowner by the river— see map 30 p.200-201 for detail). Begin at (1) Thaphae Gate and follow the lane to "5 lost dogs junction". Drop into the leafy courtyard of Wat Phan Thong (2), or go straight to Wat Buppharam (3 p.63 NB. the *ho monthiantham* closes at 17:00) and Wat Saen Fang (4 p.67). Walk out of the back of Wat Saen Fang and make your way through Kat Luang (5 p.70) to the footbridge. This crosses to Tha Chang—the elephant landing—so named because elephants were used in the transhipment of logs in this area.

Cross the road to (6) Wat Ketkaram. This temple was founded in the early 15th century and has an old stela, an ubosot with unusual decoration, and a chedi which was built askew as the builders did not wish it to point directly at heaven. A temple museum (usually open mornings and afternoons) contains some valuable artefacts.

Charoenrat Road to the south goes through the old riverside mercantile community (7) whose wooden houses are the best preserved in Chiang Mai. These belonged to overseas Chinese families who first settled in this area in numbers in the 1880s.

Ban Tha Chang is now dominated by stylish shops selling handcrafted products and home decor (see p.180), and restaurants. Go into six-pole house (Oriental Style) and note the large showroom (formerly a storeroom) and the hole in the ceiling above the entrance. This was probably a spy hole monitoring the entrance, or possibly a port for lifting goods.

From the bank just south of the Riverside Pub & Restaurant, you may catch a boat for a tour up the river from just south of the Riverside

(8— see facing page). Or you can walk a short distance north along the river bank from Tha Chang. The municipality has completed this path as far as the Super-Highway Bridge, except for where access has been blocked by private interests; this despite the fact that the immediate river bank is public land by law. Sadly, the northern part of the path is only accessible from around the super-highway bridge and as yet does not go anywhere.

Cross back to the Night Bazaar area by the Nawarat or Iron bridges. The Muslim Haw Chinese community (Ban Ho) on Soi 1 of Charoen Prathet Rd.(9) grew as a staging post for the overland trade across borders north. Larger wooden houses in the area such as the Lanna Khantoke House were built by Haw families over 100 years ago.

Covered alley (Warorot Market)

Touring Valley & Mountains

The royal chedis are close to the summit of Doi Inthanon, the highest mountain in Thailand. They are easily reached by a steep, sealed road that leads right to the summit.

In past times travellers had to follow tracks up the riverbeds and torrents, braving tigers and occasionally bandits, just to pass into the next valley.

While sealed roads now make travel easy, there still remains plenty of rugged mountainous country that may only be reached on foot or by four-wheel drive.

TOURING: THE BASICS

THE TOUR ROUTES in this guide follow the main highways out of town before branching off. For the first few kilometres these highways are high-speed double roads lined with commercial developments. Small lanes lead away from these main highways into traditional villages and modern housing projects. Once away from the city, the highways become single roads that go through small towns and countryside before climbing out of the valley.

Getting Around

Four-Wheel Vehicles

Hiring a four-wheel drive (4WD) vehicle is ideal if you want to go on dirt roads, but if hiring a Suzuki Caribian, beware of stability on corners. Sedan cars offer better fuel consumption than jeeps, but they should not be taken onto unsealed roads because of low clearance and weaker suspension. Small, economical four-stroke Honda motorcycles are readily available for hire and go as far as you are prepared to sit on one.

Current rates for cars/jeeps start at 1000 baht per day depending upon time of year, length of rental and quality of car. You need a passport and a valid English language drivers license, as well as a credit card if hiring from majors (Avis, Budget). Car companies must have insurance cover by law, but check the conditions of the policy before renting (*see* p.196-9 for rental agencies).

Two-Wheel Vehicles

The narrow lanes linking traditional communities in the city or valley are ideal for mountain bicycles (or small motorcycles). A flannel and a change of clothes might be useful if on a long bicycle ride. The exercise in the tropical climate will cause you to sweat, and can create a thirst which can only be satisfied with electrolytes *ya khlua rae* (ยาเกลือแร่). These are sold as drinks (MSport, Sponsor are inexpensive local electrolyte drinks) at many roadside shops and in sachets of powder (O-Lyte) at pharmacies.

Ron Emmons

Mud, glorious mud ... a close encounter during the rainy season

Public Transport

Though this guide recommends you rent a vehicle, public transport is available on most roads. The busier routes are served by buses, while pick-ups serve minor roads. In the mountains, pick-ups from remote villages tend to bring people to the market in the morning, returning to the village in the afternoon. Go to the nearest market if you want to get up a local road. (*see* p.196-7 for public transport from Chiang Mai).

Maps

Roads in this guide are identified by their highway number (H107, for example runs between Chiang Mai and Fang). Rough, unsealed tracks are classified as 4WD (best for four-wheel drive, pick-ups, or other vehicles with robust suspension). Distances are indicated by reference to kilometre stones.

More detailed bilingual military maps (1:50,000 series with green and white covers written in Thai) are available at Suriwong and DK Bookstore in Chiang Mai. The four relevant maps for the Chiang Mai area are: Chiang Mai #4746 I, San Sai District #4846 IV, Sanpatong District 4746 II, and Lamphun #4846 III. These maps are based on survey data at least ten years old and many of the new major as well as minor roads are not marked. However proficient map readers will find these useful for orienting themselves in the valley. The best overall maps are the B&B Map "Thailand North", and the Mae Hong Son Loop by the "Golden Triangle Rider".

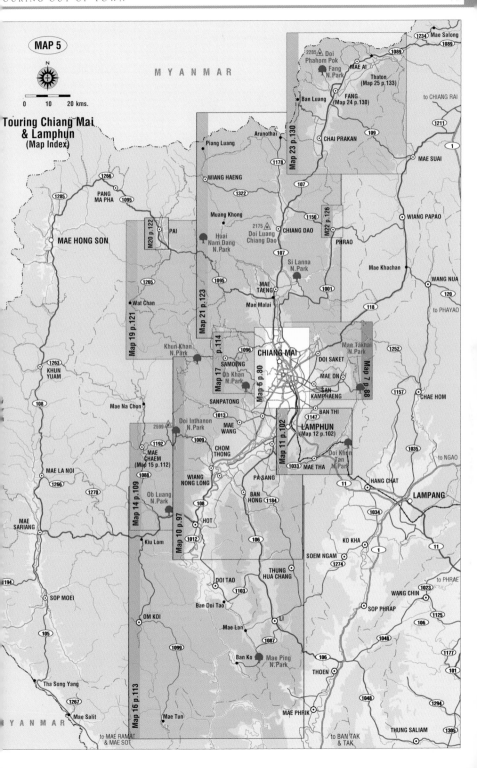

MAP 5

Touring Chiang Mai & Lamphun
(Map Index)

0 10 20 kms.

MYANMAR

Mae Salong 1234 1089

2285 Doi Phahom Pok
Fang N.Park
MAE AI
1089
to CHIANG RAI

Thaton (Map 25 p.133)

Ban Luang

FANG (Map 24 p.130)

Map 23 p.130

Piang Luang
Arunothai
CHAI PRAKAN
109
1211

1
MAE SUAI

1178

1266
PANG MA PHA
1095

1285

WIANG HAENG
107

1322

1150
WIANG PAPAO
Map 22 p.126

MAE HONG SON

Muang Khong
2175 Doi Luang Chiang Dao
CHIANG DAO
PHRAO

Map 20 p.122
PAI
Huai Nam Dang N.Park
107

1266

Wat Chan
1095
MAE TAENG
Si Lanna N.Park
Mae Khachan
WANG NUA

Map 21 p.123
Mae Malai
1001
120
to PHAYAO

1263
KHUN YUAM

1096
CHIANG MAI
Map 17 p.114
SAMOENG
DOI SAKET
Mae Takhai N.Park
1252

Map 6 p.80
Ob Khan N.Park
MAE ON
Map 7 p.88
1157
CHAE HOM

108
Mae Na Chon
SANPATONG
SAN KAMPHAENG
BAN THI
BAN THI

1013
MAE WANG
1147
LAMPHUN (Map 12 p.102)
1035
to NGAO

2599 Doi Inthanon N.Park
1009
CHOM THONG
Map 11 p.102
Doi Khun Tan N.Park
HANG CHAT

MAE LA NOI
1192
MAE CHAEM (Map 15 p.112)
1033
MAE THA
11
LAMPANG

1266
1088
WIANG NONG LONG
PA SANG

1270
Map 14 p.109
Ob Luang N.Park
108
BAN HONG 1184
1034

MAE SARIANG
HOT
KO KHA

Kiu Lom
Map 10 p.97
1012
106
SOEM NGAM
1
11

1194
THUNG HUA CHANG
1274
to PHRAE

SOP MOEI
DOI TAO
WANG CHIN
1023

1103
SOP PHRAP
1125

105
Ban Doi Tao
LI
106

OM KOI
Mae Lan
1048
1177

1099
1087
THOEN
101

Tha Song Yang
Ban Ko
Mae Ping N.Park
106

Map 16 p.113
1267

MYANMAR
Mae Salit
Mae Tun
MAE PHRIK
1048
THUNG SALIAM 1305
1294

to MAE RAMAT & MAE SOT
to BAN TAK & TAK

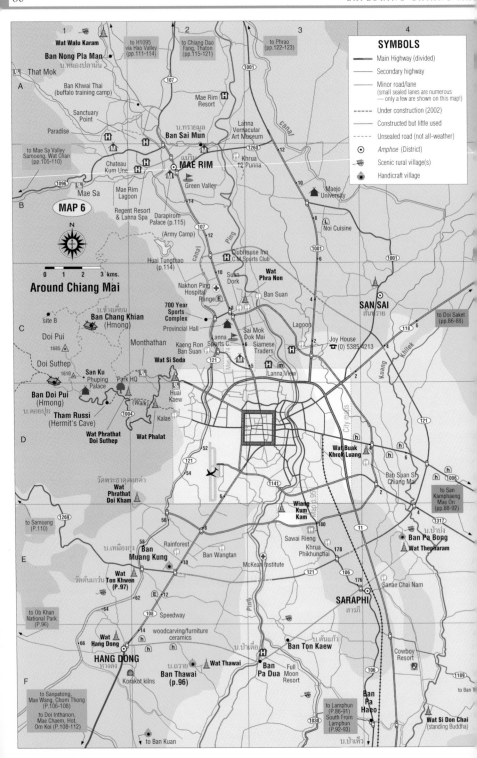

SYMBOLS

— Main Highway (divided)
— Secondary highway
— Minor road/lane
  (small sealed lanes are numerous
  — only a few are shown on this map!)
---- Under construction (2002)
— Constructed but little used
---- Unsealed road (not all-weather)
⊙ *Amphoe* (District)
🏚 Scenic rural village(s)
🏛 Handicraft village

MAP 6

Around Chiang Mai

0   1   2   3 kms.

N

1. Doi Suthep - Pui National Park (H1004)

Map 6 C & D1. Half
One Day. Round trip
summit 46 kms. Go
the market on Mani-
opharat Rd. at the
hang Phuak Gate
tersection to catch a
songthaeo" bus to Wat
hrathat Doi Suthep.
r go to the red
inibuses on Huai
aew Rd. by the front
ate of Chiang Mai
oo. A TRIP UP to Wat
hrathat Doi Suthep
a pilgrimage for
hais who visit
hiang Mai. Beyond
e temple, many
sitors like to visit
e King's mountain
treat at Phuping
d the Hmong
llage of Ban Doi Pui
an Maew).
The widened road up the
ountain handles a lot of
ses and riders and drivers
ould take care on the
umerous bends. The
ational Park offers some
easant walking that is easy
long as you stay on the
ide tracks. The upper part
the mountain will interest
ture lovers. The car parks
the main sights have lots
stalls selling souvenirs,
inks and food.

oi Suthep - Pui — Sacred
ountain & National Park

HE PEOPLE of Chiang Mai
lieve that the Doi Suthep-
i (1685m) is the domain of
ardian spirits and seek to
otect it. The mountain is
so a conservation area

Local people venerate the statue of Khru Ba Srivichai (see p.58), which is located at the start of the road up the mountain (KM3+).

(265.5 km^2) protected by its
national park status. Despite
the forested appearance of
the mountain from the city,
much of the park has been
severely disturbed by fire,
upland agriculture, construction and encroachment.
Established in 1981, the
National Park yet remains a
home to a wealth of diversity.
The seasonal tropical forest
contains 90 different species
per hectare. In addition to
more than 2100 species of
vascular plants so far
identified (by the Herbarium
at the Department of Biology
at Chiang Mai University),
birds (326 species), mammals
(61 species including bats),
reptiles (50 species),
amphibians (28 species) and
numerous types of butterfly
make their home here.

UP DOI SUTHEP
(H1004)

*(Depending on
season, time and
location, foreigners
may have to pay 200
baht entrance fee for
access to the natural
sites in the National
Park, but access to the
temple, palace and
hill-tribe villages is
free. The Park HQ,
which is at KM152+.
Tel: 053 248405 can
provide accommoda-
tion but little else —
see sidebar page 83.
For information
visitors should go to
the visitor centre
opposite the Khru Ba
Srivichai monument
at KM3+.
Red baht buses regularly ply
the road starting from the
entrance to the zoo (KM3+).
They will not leave with less
than 6 passengers. One way
fares range from 30 baht to the
temple to 80 Bht to Ban Maeo
Doi Pui.)* THE HIGHWAY passes
close to several cascades
where the Huai Kaew
tumbles off the mountain —
Huai Kaew Falls (Km3+),
Wang Bua Ban Falls (Km5+)
& Pha Ngoep Falls (Km5+)
all lie close to the road. The
nicest, however, are the
Monthatarn Falls *(KM6+
right turn 1.5kms — the park
fee is collected on this unsealed
access road).* The road crosses
the Phalat stream(KM8+) and
passes two viewpoints before
reaching Wat Phrathat Doi
Suthep (KM14+).

Forest Types on Doi Suthep

The lower dry ridges (400-950 m.) are deciduous dipterocarp, with trees dropping their leaves to survive periods of low moisture. Here the forest is severely disturbed by fire, with trees standing further apart and with grasses prevalent. The dry grasses and fallen organic matter that would otherwise provide nutrients to the soil are regularly destroyed by fire; seedlings from species not resistant to fires are destroyed, further adding to the cycle of disturbance.

Sunrise over Wat Phrathat Doi Suthe[p]

In the gullies between ridges, a higher water table allows evergreen species to survive producing mixed deciduous/evergreen forest. There is much more moisture and a much higher diversity of species here. The thick canopy prevents the grasses from taking hold. During the dry season, the cool, moist gullies become refuges as animals and insects migrate from the dry ridges.

The 'strangling' fig tree starts as an epiphyte in the canopy. The plant sends roots to the ground and puts energy into taking over the canopy of the support tree. Often the support tree slowly dies (but not from strangling), and the fig grows thick roots for support. The fruits of fig trees are very beneficial to animals, which spread the seeds from the fruit.

Evergreen forest survives at elevations (above 1000 m.) where rainfall is higher. The rich soil supplies moisture and nutrients to the trees, which in turn feed the biomass below with leaf fall. The permanent canopy lowers temperatures, and the water retention capability of the rich black soil reduces evaporation. Watersheds high up release precious fresh water that forms the streams running off the mountains. Destruction of this evergreen forest causes the land below to dry up. On the highest part of the mountain (above 1500 m.) there are pine trees as well stands of magnolia, oak and chestnut. For identification of tree species on the mountain, refer to *A Field Guide to Forest Trees of Northern Thailand* (May 2000. English Ed. 750 Bht.)

Monthatarn Falls

Wat Phrathat Doi Suthep
วัดพระธาตุดอยสุเทพ

(KM14.5 see p.58) A LARGE CAR-PARK with a multitude of souvenir shops is thankfully hidden from view by the promontory on which the temple stands. Healthy visitors should go up to the temple by climbing the *Naga* stairway rather than by taking the cable car. A path from the base of the stairway climbs in the opposite direction up the hill to the National Park HQ.

Tham Russi (Hermit's Cave)
ถ้ำฤษี

(KM16+ east side) THIS IS A GOOD area for birdwatching. A path leads down a steep, slippery path to the "cave", an overhang over a wide ledge, and then continues down through evergreen to join the road at the herb garden (KM15+).

Phuping Palace
พระตำหนักภูพิงค์ราชนิเวศน์

(KM.19 Closed December 10 to mid-April/May. Check with the TAT if planning a visit near these dates as the palace may b[e]

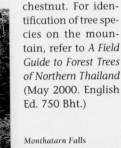

National Parks & Park Fees

The National Parks of Thailand are being improved with better visitor centres and more marked nature trails. Once the nature trails have been established, however, their maintenance becomes uncertain. Most trail brochures (available at the visitor centres or park offices) are in Thai only, but you may find them useful for their rudimentary maps and for communicating with park wardens, who may speak but few words of English.

Most National Parks have official bungalow accommodation which vary in price according to size. Rooms and meals must be booked in advance — walk-in is not advisable unless you plan to rent a tent and have your own food. For reservations call the National Park Division of the Royal Forestry Department, Bangkok (*Tel: 02 579 5269/4849/0529*) The Parks office in the RFD Chiang Mai (*Tel: (0)53 818348*) can process reservations, but they need longer than a day.

The Parks officially charge foreigners 200 baht (*children 100*), while Thais pay 20 baht (*Cars 50 baht, motorcycles 30 Bht for everyone. Resident foreigners who politely ask in Thai may be charged at Thai rates on production of proof of residence, such as a Thai driving license*), but some newer parks have not begun charging this fee yet. A national park ticket is valid for any site within the park for one day. While tourists on limited budgets may need to consider carefully whether a one-off visit to a small site in a park merits the expense, foreign visitors may feel better to know that they are, in theory, contributing to nature conservation.

Phuping Palace

impressed by the rosebeds, particularly as the palace is closed to the public during peak flowering when members of the royal family may be in residence. During the rainy season there are almost no flowers at all.

Ban Doi Pui

บ้านแม้วดอยปุย

(*Ban Maew Doi Pui — 3.5 kms. from Phuping. 4WD*) FROM THE PALACE a narrow road continues up the mountain and forks after one kilometre. The left (south) turn goes down to Ban Doi Pui, a Hmong village in a picturesque location.

A "high street" through the village consists solely of souvenir shops and leads to a terraced flower garden,

osed. *For the rest of the year e flower gardens are open to e public on Friday, Saturday ad Sunday only from 8:30– l:30 AM and 1-4 PM. Entry is ce, but polite dress required. arongs and loose fitting ousers to cover lower legs may e rented for 10 Bt.* THE THAIS ave great respect for their lajesties, and many like to sit the palace, which is used y members of the royal mily as a winter retreat.

The palace itself is an egant, modern Thai-style uilding of moderate size. isitors must stick to paved walkways and may go as far as the front entrance that overlooks a terraced ornamental garden. Entry to both the terraced garden and the palace is prohibited.

Visitors used to European gardens will not be very

The success of FORRU's (see p.96) cooperation with Hmong villagers from Ban Mae Sa Mai in reforestation within Doi Suthep-Pui National Park is significant. While upland peoples contributed to deforestation in the past, many now wish to be actively involved in conserving and restoring the forests on which they depend.

Walks on Doi Suthep

Until 1935 everyone had to walk up to make merit at Wat Phrathat Doi Suthep, but these days people walk up the road in the moonlight to participate in early morning merit making on Visakha Pucha Day only. Four temples, each denoting a level of understanding on the path to enlightenment used to exist on the main path up the mountain, but apart from Wat Sri Soda, these have long since disappeared.

However, you can walk to the Phrathat from the foot of the mountain avoiding the road. The walk begins on a nature trail that starts from the small lane which passes Wat Fai Hin and the southern entrance to the zoo from near Suthep Road. The path goes up to Wat Phalat, a pleasant spot where some Buddha images look over a stream. From the temple the direct route to the right of the stream up to the road is a scramble, or you may take the longer temple access road to reach H1004. The path continues upward about 40m down the road from where the road crosses the stream (*Huai Phalat* KM8+). The path emerges at the very sharp bend just downhill from the temple (Km14+). The entire walk is reasonably maintained and can be done in two hours.

A second walk can be made from the car park of Monthatarn Falls to the National Park HQ (or vice versa). The path crosses to the northern side of the Huai Kaew stream just below the higher level of falls and climbs steeply. After a short section where the climb is more gentle, the path crosses to the south side just when further climbing would seem impracticable. From there it continues upwards till it joins a dirt road. Turn left on this

Images Wat Phralat

road and follow it to the park HQ (approx 800m), or take the trail that forks left a short distance from where you joined the dirt road. This trail rejoins the dirt road about 150m north of the park office, passing a fine specimen of ficus altiss*ima* Bl. Moraceae en route.

Other walks can be found by taking almost any of the paths leading off the road, or from San Ku near the summit of Doi Suthep. The summit of Doi Pui is, unfortunately, off limits. Extensive walks can be found on the back of the mountain, starting from Ban Maew Doi Pui. Head for the flower garden in the village, and, instead of entering, continue walking on the path that goes around and above it. These trails better suit a day-long exploration, so take water and food. A rough idea of where these trails can take you may be found on Map 17 p114. Serious walkers will want a copy of the 1:50,000 army map sheet # 4746 I which is good enough for orientation through study of the contours, but the detail is not enough to show footpaths or even some of the dirt roads in the park.

where the opium poppy as well as other flowering plants are grown for display, as well as to a hill tribe museum. Though other villages in the hills can only aspire to the income generated by this tourist trap, many of the men in the village still work in fields on the mountain slopes beyond the village, and the village is not without interest.

The Summit of Doi Suthep - Pui

THE RIGHT TURN at the road fork after Phuping Palace leads to the summits of Doi Suthep and Doi Pui (there is a fine view west after 1.4 kms.). After the road drops from the first summit of Doi Suthep, a track to the right leads to San Khu, the site of a chedi and a place where

offereings are made to the spirits on the mountain. Tak the track downhill from the chedi for good walking and bird watching.

The sealed road goes to Doi Pui, but in recent years the summit has been closed to visitors. A dirt road (4WI continues down to the Hmong village of Chang Khian (5 *kms.*), a less-visitec village than Ban Doi Pui.

Chiang Mai's Spirit Mountain.

Doi Suthep mountain is the abode of the Chiang Mai's guardian spirits — Pu Sae, Ya Sae and their male child, Sudeva Rishi — who are in turn attended by six minor spirits.

According to legend, the three were aboriginal cannibals who planned to eat the Buddha as he was travelling through the area. Upon becoming aware of their plan, the Buddha stamped his foot into a rock, creating a footprint and frightening the wits out of the cannibals. After a sermon, the cannibals promised to forego human flesh during the Buddha's lifetime, while Sudeva Rishi forswore meat permanently.

Sudeva Rishi became a monk and he (or another rishi who lived some 1500 years

Paying respects at San Ku (Chiang Mai 700 year centenary)

later) is credited with founding Haripunjaya. He later disrobed to became a hermit, a *russi*, and retreated to a cave on the mountain to which he gave his name.

Phu Sae and Ya Sae kept to their promise of forswearing human flesh, but pleaded to be allowed to eat buffalo meat and taste human blood once a year, a request which the Buddha said was not his right to grant. After their deaths, Phu Sae's and Ya Sae's spirits roamed the mountain, and fearful villagers began propitiating them.

In former times the ruling *chao* as well as commoners made annual offerings of buffalo and other food before the start of the rice growing season. In a rite once common to the region, this ancient Lawa practice yet continues near Wat Phrathat Doi Kham, a temple where statues illustrate the myths of the mountain.

The ceremony begins with a pre-dawn slaughter of a young male buffalo and the preparation of offerings of raw meat and blood for the spirits. During the ritual itself, the guardian spirits take over a medium and swig whiskey and chew on the bloody offerings. Later, they remember their promises to the Buddha, who is represented on a large banner swinging from the bough of a tree above the site. Accordingly they leave the medium and, presumably, the supplicants in peace for another year.

Though the propitiation right appears to receive no official support, and certainly none from the Tourism Authority, senior local representatives sometimes attend the ceremony, along with large crowds of local onlookers and numerous photographers.

Apart from being a continuance of tradition, the ritual can be seen as a re-enactment of the victory of Buddhism, of the higher culture of the Mon, over an indigenous head-hunting people (the Lawa) who were characterised as cannibalistic giants.

Suffice to say an influential core of Chiang Mai's citizens regard Doi Suthep-Pui as a sacred mountain, whose spirits they periodically propitiate with offerings of food and liquor, and whose domain they feel has been disturbed enough. Fierce opposition continues to meet any resurrection of plans to build a cable railway up the mountain.

E.J.Haas

Propitiating cannibalistic spirits

2. East to Doi Saket & San Khamphaeng

(Maps 7 & 8 pp.88-89. Half to one Day). THE FERTILE VALLEY FLOOR to the east of the River Ping is bounded by the range of mountains between Chiang Mai and Lampang provinces. With a location close to Chiang Mai in the centre of a fertile rice growing area, the people of Bo Sang and San Kamphaeng became skilled in folk crafts, and the area was to become the centre for production of celadon and other wares in Lan Na. With the instability that came with the Burmese occupation, production all but disappeared. It was not until the 20th century that celadon production was to revive and the tourism boom fuel the development of the area into the main centre for handicraft production.

Once away from population centres, land use remains

Images hide Buddha

typical of a fertile rice basin, with villages and temples marked by groves between the paddy. Located on the periphery of the fertile valley floor, nearby places of interest to visit include Wat Doi Saket, the San Kampheng Hot Springs and Mae On Caves.

Beyond Mae On, sealed

lanes lead up narrow valleys to villages once dependent on *miang* tea cultivation. Two national parks have been established in this mountainous area, an area which until recently has remained somewhat remote and undeveloped despite its proximity to Chiang Mai.

Wat Doi Saket

วัดดอยสะเก็ด

(KM.15) THE TEMPLE sits atop a low hill reached by a *naga* stairway (a road to the right of the stairway leads up to the back of the temple). At the top a small grotto with mythical statues lies to the left. The unique decorations of the *viharn* include unusual stucco motifs. The temple grounds contain a monastic school and a giant seated Buddha image.

The Murals of Wat Doi Saket

Sponsored by a businessman from Nakhon Pathom, Chaiwat Waranon took over three years to paint murals in the main cruciform viharn in the early 90s.

The artist was a student of the iconoclastic teacher Buddadhasa Bhikkhu, who eschewed much of the formal Indic aspects of Buddhism. Thus the murals are in the style of magic realism as they try to impart the meaning of Buddhist *dhamma*.

The sequence of pictures runs clockwise from (picture) 1, which is the left one of three pictures on the south wall. It shows a stylised Thai scripture cabinet with books that appear to be flying out of it in all directions. Titles in Thai are written beneath many of the murals. The same artist also did the gold on black murals around the main image. One of these depicts the symbolic birth of the Buddha.

1. Scriptures Hide Dhamma.
Learning may lead to higher rank but cannot lead to the real truth represented by the monks seated in the "heaven" above the scripture cabinet.

2. Images Hide Buddha.
People worship images but the real Buddha is like a shining purity only found in the heart of people.

3. Robes Hide Monks.
The robes and eight accoutrements of a monk may conceal people who practice black arts in order to deceive others and receive tribute.

4. Truth Beyond Desire.
Thoughts are like a sea of animals constantly churned by the rage of emotion. The ignorant act according to inclination, but those who know truth perceive the illusory and habitual nature of thought. Free from desire, they understand the path to enlightenment lies within.

5. Your Worst Enemy.
People cling to a false sense of self and seek happiness through actions based on lust, anger and delusion. These result only in pain and suffering. Thus we are like writhing animals biting ourselves in our own ignorance.

6. Worldly Bondage.
The destiny of worldly bondage is the funeral pyre

7. Defeating Mara (illusion).
Mae Thorani, Goddess of Earth, pours the cool waters of detachment onto the demons of desire, anger and ignorance — a representation of the Buddha overcoming the final bonds of desire and attachment binding him to family and past as he meditated before enlightenment.

8. Breaking Worldly Bonds.
Happiness is temporary, and causes infatuation which ensnares you in endless chains of cause and effect. You must break the chains for the true path to freedom.

The defeat of Mara, a theme often found on murals above the main entrance of viharns in Thai temples.

9. Loving Kindness Supports the World.
Distinguishing neither race nor language, a pure heart is free and can smile on anyone.

10. Enlightening the Heart.
Wisdom comes from vigilance over mind and body — from watching the constant arising and falling of body, sensation, perception, predisposition and consciousness — and realising that nothing can be truly identified as self.

11. Prior Actions Determine Nature.
Whether our actions are base or wise determines our natures. One who has wisdom is like a flowering species that shelters and protects, but those with desire, anger and delusion in their hearts are like differing growths above faces half hidden with prejudices.

12. Wisdom Beyond Passion.
One who has concentrated wisdom remains untouched by the fires of worldly passion, and looks at everything with a truthful eye, strengthening wisdom even further.

13. Merit Brings Its Own Reward.
People who donate to temples with wisdom in their hearts will receive the knowledge, jewels, protection and keys of the *dhamma*.

Picture 14. Hooked On False Views
The fish are mortals, the bait is what we perceive with our senses, and the fisherman is the cycle of birth and death. Taking the bait we are hooked and put into the three baskets of existence — desire, form and spirit — which constantly leak back again into the sea of samsara.

15. The Temple Shines with Truth (or Free from Theory).
Beyond all definitions and free from the cycle of existence, the figure sits unwavering above a temple roof in the light of shining truth.

16. Balance Beyond Concentration.
The concentrated mind is like a set of scales balancing hate (stones) and love on a sharp point poised on a fragile lotus leaf

17. The Wise Mind Perceives Truth.
One with a wise heart and concentrated mind likens existence to a constantly changing stream of soap bubbles that reflect, but in essence are empty. Weary of attachment, he sees what should and should not be through simple wisdom rather than moral force.

Beyond Doi Saket

BEYOND DOI SAKET, a small district town at the foot of a low hill surmounted by the temple, the main route to Chiang Rai (H118) climbs the upper Mae Kuang valley to a pass at KM.53. From there it descends towards Mae Khachan, passing Khun Chae National Park HQ at KM.55 and the souvenir stalls at the Mae Khachan Hot Springs at KM65. A dirt road to the south-west

Ittipon Elajukanon

The Bo Sang Umbrella festival (held on third week-end of January) features a parade and beauty pageant.

from KM63-64 leads to a upland valley (9kms) with Lahu, Yao and Karer villages. It is one of several tracks off the highway that leads to remote valleys and villages

THE 'HANDICRAFT HIGHWAY' (H1006)

THE ROAD TO BO SANG is lined with emporiums presenting the commercial face of a handicraft tradition that was once exclusively small-scale. Though set up to receive shoppers by the coach

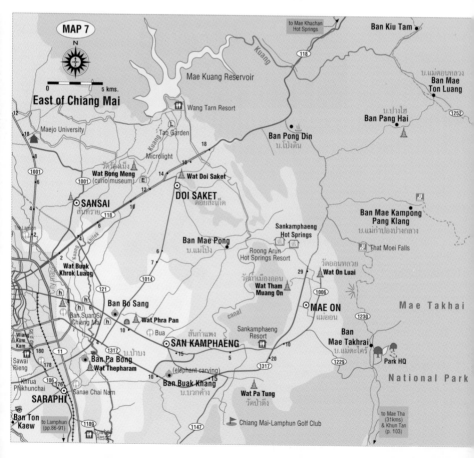

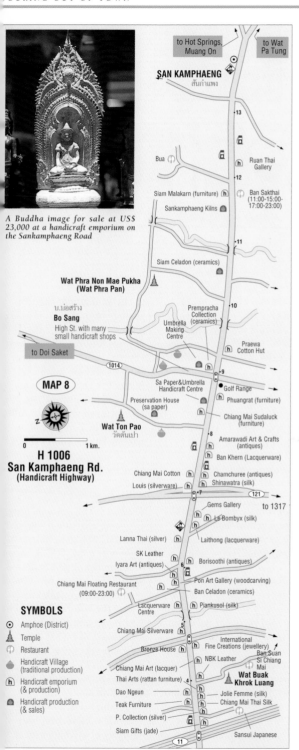

A Buddha image for sale at US$ 23,000 at a handicraft emporium on the Sankamphaeng Road

MAP 8

H 1006 San Kamphaeng Rd. (Handicraft Highway)

0   1 km.

to Hot Springs, Muang On

to Wat Pa Tung

SAN KAMPHAENG
สันกำแพง

13

Bua

Ruan Thai Gallery

12

Siam Malakarn (furniture)

Ban Sakthai (11:00-15:00-17:00-23:00)

Sankamphaeng Kilns

11

Siam Celadon (ceramics)

Wat Phra Non Mae Pukha (Wat Phra Pan)

บ.บ่อสร้าง
Bo Sang
High St. with many small handicraft shops

Prempracha Collection (ceramics)

Umbrella Making Centre

10

to Doi Saket

1014

Praewa Cotton Hut

Sa Paper & Umbrella Handicraft Centre

9

Golf Range

Preservation House (sa paper)

Phuangrat (furniture)

Wat Ton Pao
วัดต้นเปา

Chiang Mai Sudaluck (furniture)

8

Amarawadi Art & Crafts (antiques)

Chiang Mai Cotton

Ban Khern (Lacquerware)

Louis (silverware)

Charnchuree (antiques)

Shinawatra (silk)

121

Gems Gallery

to 1317

Le Bombyx (silk)

Lanna Thai (silver)

Laithong (lacquerware)

SK Leather

6

Iyara Art (antiques)

Borisoothi (antiques)

Chiang Mai Floating Restaurant (09:00-23:00)

Pon Art Gallery (woodcarving)

Ban Celadon (ceramics)

Lacquerware Centre

Piankusol (silk)

5

Chiang Mai Silverware

International Fine Creations (jewellery)

Bronze House

Ban Suan Si Chiang Mai

NBK Leather

Chiang Mai Art (lacquer)

Wat Buak Khrok Luang

Thai Arts (rattan furniture)

4

Dao Ngeun

Jolie Femme (silk)

Teak Furniture

Chiang Mai Thai Silk

P. Collection (silver)

Siam Gifts (jade)

Sansui Japanese

11

SYMBOLS

⊙ Amphoe (District)
🛕 Temple
🍴 Restaurant
🏘 Handicraft Village (traditional production)
ℍ Handicraft emporium (& production)
◉ Handicraft production (& sales)

load, the emporiums welcome individuals and can provide English speaking guides who will show you around demonstrations of the manufacturing process before ushering you onto the sales floor.

Prices are generally good, though items like cabinets made out of rosewood with mother of pearl inlay may cost thousands of dollars. The Jewellery emporiums in particular stretch interpretation of local traditions. Once past the demonstrations of cutting and polishing, you walk into darkened grottoes where pretty salesgirls attend glittering displays of baubles. Shark-like fish swimming in tanks behind

Pon Art Gallery, Sankamphaeng Rd.

the troves of treasure add to the predatory atmosphere. Credit cards are welcomed.

While the emporiums conveniently demonstrate particular processes, to see what remains of small-scale handicraft production, you must venture into the side-lanes and villages in the area.

Wat Buak Khrok Luang

วัดบวกครกหลวง

(KM4-south turn —300m)
THIS TEMPLE has a wooden
Lanna style viharn built in
1857, in which famous 19th
century Lanna style murals
depict the previous lives of
the Buddha.

Ban Ton Pao and Bo Sang

บ้านต้นเปาและบ่อสร้าง

BAN TON PAO *(KM8 —north
turn opposite school. 500-
700m)* produces sa paper,
which is made from a plant
related to the mulberry.
'Preservation House' *(Ban Ton
Pao)* and 'The Sa Paper &
Umbrella Handicraft Centre'
(H1006 KM8+) demonstrate
the process.

Bo Sang's souvenir shops
sell a wide range of handicrafts, though it is most
famous for its umbrellas.
Different parts of the
production process can be
seen beneath some of the
villagers' houses, especially
on the lane east at the north
end of the high street. The
whole process can be seen at
the 'The Umbrella Making

Northern women in the dress of the mid-19th century
(mural: Wat Buak Khrok Luang)

Centre' *(next to Prempracha
Collection).*

East of Bo Sang a north
turn *(KM10 — 1km)* goes to
Wat Phra Pan (Wat Mae
Pukha. Typical murals cover
the walls of a *viharn* built
around a large reclining
Buddha image.

SAN KAMPHAENG, MUANG ON CAVE & THE HOT SPRINGS

THOUGH A FEW handicraft
shops are found in San
Kamphaeng (13kms), the
town is more a prosperous
market centre than a handicraft centre *(to avoid cong-
estion along H1006, take
H1317 for a faster route to Mae
On direct from Chiang Mai).*

The entrance to Muang On
Caves *(H1317 KM28 west
turn — 1km to car-park)*, en
route to the hot springs, lies
about 100m up a steep *naga*
stairway. Make sure the lights
are on before descending
down the stairway deep into
the caverns.

Cliffs on the west side of
the same mountain have been

bolted for climbers *(see
p.182).*

The Sankamphaeng Hot
Springs *(KM29 west turn—10
Bht.)* and the Rung Arun Hot
Springs Resort *(20 Bht.)* have
geysers, mineral baths and
gardens and are popular
places for Thai families at
weekends. Continue past the
hot springs for a return route
through the complex of
narrow lanes east of H1014.

Wat Pa Tung

วัดป่าตึง

*(12 kms from Sankamphaeng.
Go straight on a lane due east
where H1147 turns sharply
right near a low hill).* LOCATED
IN the midst of paddy dotted
with sugar palms, this temple
contains a large teak *kuti*,
where the body of Luang Pho
La Chaiya Janto has been
embalmed in a glass case
(photo p. 92) since he died
aged 96 in 1993.

The temple holds a festival
to commemorate the
Venerable's death *(16th
March)* and a second festival
(8th day of waxing moon of

*Everything in a paper umbrella is
hand-produced*

7th lunar month - around mid-June), when there is a rocket-festival and long-drum contest. A third festival (20-22 September) features a competition for Northern Thai dancing.

EAST OF MAE ON

NARROW SEALED ROADS penetrate along narrow valleys to remote villages high in the mountains to Mae Kampong and Thep Sadet. From Ban Mae Don Luang a 17km nature trail passes over the summit of Doi Langka Luang (2031m) in Khun Chae National Park. This will require advance preparation with a Thai guide to co-ordinate a local guide and camping equipment.

Mae Takrai National Park
อุทยานแห่งชาติแม่ตะไคร้

OCCUPYING MOUNTAINOUS LAND 354,7 km^2) between 400 and 1,997m in elevation in Chiang Mai and Lamphun Province, the park offers two nature trails (brochures available in Thai only) which start from near the Park HQ. The first is 3kms long and goes round a lake created by a dam, while the second (10kms. total return 4hrs) goes to the Mae Tung Falls. The small Tat Moei Falls are easily reached from H1230 (unsealed all-weather) on a 2km circular trail. South of Mae Takrai, H1230 follows a pretty rural route to Mae Tha District (39kms), passing the access road (26kms) to Khun Tan National Park (34kms) en route.

Stucco on wood at Wat On Luai, Mae On

WHERE TO EAT & STAY (EAST OF CHIANG MAI)

(For accommodation listings see p.191) The **Wang Tarn Resort** (*H118 KM.17 west turn by irrigation canal 6kms.*) has pleasant gardens and a pool where the children can play while you enjoy a lazy lunch. Enter the grounds of the adjacent irrigation department to see the dam, go fishing, or take a short drive around the southern rim of the lake.

Further east along H118, the **Mai Pa Rim Than** restaurant (*KM.36*) and **Windmill Country** (*KM.38*) offer 24 hr room service. **Trekker's Lodge** (*KM63-4 right turn 9 kms*) is a base from which to explore nearby hill tribe villages, and **Wieng Doi Cottage** (*KM65*) opposite Mae Khachan hot springs has a pleasant restaurant as well as rooms with mineral baths.

Restaurants off H1006 near Bo Sang include the **Ban Suan Si Chiang Mai** (*KM.4 south turn 400m*), an attractive collection of Lanna style buildings in a grove of rain trees (also has a cooking school), and the **Bua Restaurant** (*KM.11 north turn 400m*), which is in a modern complex with a pool that is part of a housing estate. East of Sankamphaeng, the **Sankamphaeng Resort** is quiet and relaxing (young children can paddle boats on the lake). The government-run **Sankamphaeng**

Hot Springs (*H1317 KM.29 left turn 2kms*) and then privately-owned **Rung Arun Hot Springs Resort** (*H1317 KM.29 left turn 3.5kms*) have gardens with hot springs, mineral pools and accommodation, but the bungalows at the latter look nicer.

Erawan PUC Tours (*see p.199*) runs overnight tours to Mae Kampong to study the local lifestyle based on *miang* (tea) cultivation, and the **Uthayan Thep Sadet Resort** in Ban Pang Hai provides a base from which to explore the mountains beyond Mae On.

Stalagmite chedi in Tham Muang On

3. SOUTH TO WIANG KUM KAM & HANG DONG

*(Map 6 p.80 & Map 9 . Half
— one day. Best on a mountain
bicycle or small motorcycle)*
THE TOUR BEGINS with the old
ruins of Wiang Kum
Kam on a pleasant
rural route that
follows the River
Ping to Pa Dua. After
crossing the river to
the west, you can
visit the woodcarv-
ing centre at Ban
Thawai and pass two
classic examples of
19th woodcarving in
rural Lanna temples
on the return route.

Unless you wish to
visit woodcarving/
antique shops along the road,
avoid the busy main route of
H108 on any local journey
from Chiang Mai.

WIANG KUM KAM

เวียงกุมกาม

WIANG KUM KAM was a
settlement long before it
became King Mangrai's
capital around 1287-90.

Frequent flooding caused
Mangrai to move, but the
place remained important
throughout the Lanna period.

Wat That Khao

The site was later buried
under mud when the river
changed course during the
Burmese period. The area
was restored as a historical
park during the 1980's, and
more renovations and recon-
structions have recently been
undertaken.

The new highway to the
south of the old *wiang* has
only recently been
completed, and the sur-
rounding area maintains a
pleasant rural feel for the

time-being.

Continue on Koh Klang
Road past Wat Chedi Liem,
to reach the McKean
Institute. From
there follow the
riverside road along
the east bank, the
more pleasant bank
for a rural ride.

Wat Kan Thom

วัดกานโถม

WAT KAN THOM is at
the heart of Wiang
Kum Kam. The
temple contains the
remains of a former
temple as well as a
new enlarged spirit house
that is revered as the home of
the spirit of King Mangri.
The temple has a Lanna-style
chedi and a finely decorated
new viharn built in 1987.

*The former home of
King Mangrai's spirit at
Wat Kan Thom*

David Henley

Rice Barns
*The barns are raised on poles and have removable ladders in order to reduce threat
from damp and from animals to the family's seed stock and rice supply. The size of
barns are measured according to the number of poles required to support them, 6 to
8 being considered the average. A larger rice barn was a sign of relative wealth in
landownership and, in northern matrilocal society, provided an incentive for local
men to marry into the family. Rice barns are still fairly common in traditional villages in the countryside beyond Wiang Kum Kam, but they are also being bought up
and rebuilt by private land-owners.*

Vat Chedi Liem

คเจดีย์เหลี่ยม

Koh Klang Rd.) THE MAIN
EATURE of interest is the
Iaripunchai-style chedi built
round 1286. It is a square
tepped chedi with Buddha
mages in niches at each
evel. The chedi is a replica of
he Mahapol Chedi at Wat
Chamadevi in Lamphun.

OUTH TO BAN THAWAI

McKean Institute

งพยาบาลแมคเคน

STABLISHED IN 1908 by Dr

Wat Chedi Liem

James McKean to treat
leprosy, the institute serves
as a local hospital as well as
a rehabilitation centre set
in beautiful, quiet grounds
next to the river. Colonial
style architecture includes
a church with flying
buttresses as well as small
houses for patients. These
can be seen by following a
narrow sealed loop road
clockwise from the main
gate (the dirt road
continues on a loop back
to the main gate).

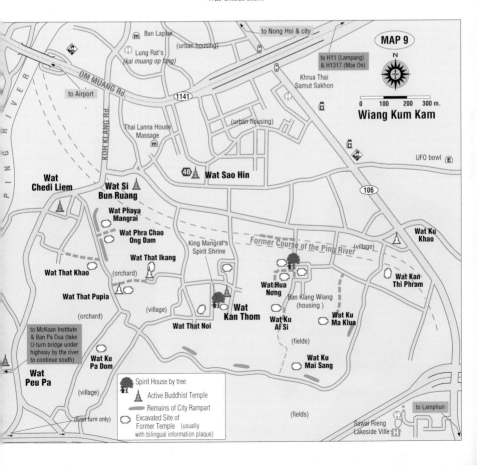

Ban Pa Dua
บ้านป่าเดื่อ

A SMALL MARKET has developed at a crossroads by a bridge across the Ping. Villages and longan orchards, especially along the banks of the canal to the south-east, form picturesque countryside to the south and east of Pa Dua.

Waiting for customers

Ban Thawai
บ้านถวาย

(7 kms direct from Pa Dua, or 3kms from east turn at traffic lights on H108 near Km.15 in Hang Dong District town) BAN THAWAI is the centre of Thailand's woodcarving industry, but many carvings are sent here or completed from roughs carved in the area around Tha Thung Luang *(H1033 KM18)* of Mae Tha District in Lamphun Province. Kilns also operate around Hang Dong and shops

selling woodcarvings and ceramics are frequent along the road between Ban Thawai and Hang Dong. Many of the large emporiums in the area are remarkable wooden buildings in themselves.

Ban Thawai's main street is packed with shops selling both large and small items. Drinks and food are available and this is a good place to shop for small wooden gifts if larger pieces seem a bit much.

The lane continues south from the village till it reaches the River Ping (3.5kms). Approximately 800m from the Pa Dua-Hang Dong road, a narrow lane forking east leads to Wat Thawai, where local skills are on display in the temple buildings.

AROUND HANG DONG
หางดง

H108 DOMINATES this District Town. If travelling west, cross and go through the market and turn right. This will take you past Wat Hang Dong *(see sidebar opposite)* on a route to the quieter canal road.

Visitors with a special interest in wood-carving may want to go south to Ban Roi An Phan Yang *(H108 KM20. 4.5 kms south of Hang Dong. 08:30-16:30 closed Wed. Foreigners 200 Bht. to enter the woodcarving museum)*. There is a shop and a three-floor museum in which Khun Charuay Na Sunthorn displays some delicate carvings.

Ob Khan National Park
อุทยานแห่งชาติออบขาน

(Canal Rd. KM.66 west turn — 12 kms. unsealed after 6 kms. 4WD. Accommodation & camping are available) THE RIVER KHAN flows through a small gorge and into a large natural pool which can be popular at weekends. Follow the path (take water and a picnic if you have children) past the gorge and along the rocky river bed to a better, less visited pool below Ob Hai about 450 metres upstream.

Ban Tawai artesan

Ob Hai gor.

Wat Inthrawat
(Wat Ton Khwen)

ดัตต้นเกว๋น

H1269 KM.37 south turn 100 m. after canal bridge — 200 m.) BUILT AROUND 1858, the temple served as a resting place for the Phra Boromathat Chom Thong relic when it was brought

Stucco and woodcarving Wat Inthrawat- Wat Ton Khwen)

from Chom Thong to Chiang Mai. This temple is a good example of Lanna wooden architecture of the last century. Note the decoration in the viharn and the detail in the cross-shaped hall in the temple courtyard.

Ban Muang Kung

บ้านเหมืองกุง

KM.10 If coming from Chiang Mai do a U-turn at junction of 1269 with H108. West turn at police box — 200 m.) MANY HOUSEHOLDS in this village specialise in making traditional earthenware jugs for serving water. Villagers turn pots on simple hand-driven wheels with an ease that tells of years of practice *(photo page 167).*

Old Temple Buildings

In Buddhism, desire and attachment are seen as leading to suffering. Combined with villagers' wishes to make merit as an integral part of the well-being of a close-knit rural community, this becomes a powerful tool for change in temple architecture. In the past abbots and the local community have been only too happy to replace old temple buildings with bright new ones that may seem more appropriate as symbols of a successful community in which everyone is fulfilling their proper roles.

Slow renovations at Wat Sai Mun, Hang Dong

While the Fine Arts Department has preserved the old buildings of both Wat Ton Khwen and Wat Tung Luang in Hang Dong District, the fate of the crumbling viharn of Wat Hang Dong remains in question. Renovation of old buildings is costly, and funds have been scarce since the crash of 1997.

New temple buildings built in the last decade or so seem very common around Chiang Mai. Whether they will appear as attractive in 100 years as the 19th century wooden buildings appear today is a question for future generations to answer.

Partly carved bargeboards at Wat Thung Luang, Hang Dong

WHERE TO EAT & STAY
(SARAPHI-HANG DONG)

Three main restaurants are located in area covered by this tour *(see p.161 for listings).* The **Sawai Riang Restaurant** (and Resort) offers delicious northern Thai dishes in an exotic setting conveniently close to Wiang Kum Kam(H106 KM179-180 west turn). **Khrua Pikulchai** (H106 KM179) is also reasonable.

Both the **Ban Wang Tan Restaurant** (H108 east turn just before KM9), which overlooks park land, and **the Rainforest** (H108 KM10 west turn), which is set in modern *sala* overlooking a pond are popular large restaurants off H108. The **Panglade Coffee Corner** serves refreshments in Ban Tawai and both Pa Dua and Hang Dong have markets with stalls serving food to order.

The embalmed body of Luang Phu La lies in a resplendent teak kuti at Wat Pa Tung. Embalming of monks is an uncommon practice undertaken as a demonstration of the purity of the deceased. Normally, even the most revered monks are cremated in keeping with the Buddhist value of non-attachment.

The largest standing Buddha in Northern Thailand is at Wat Si Don Chai in Lamphun Province (near H11 KM75). 59 sok high (a sok is the length between the elbow and the tip of the fingers), the image was built with 8 million baht of donations

Forest Conservation & Regeneration

Thailand's newer national parks are part of a broad conservation program which set a

Environmental deterioration is widely recognised as a cost of Thailand's rapid develpment (Mural at Wat Pang Hai, Tambon Thepsadet, Doi Saket)

target of 40% forest cover for the nation. This was to reverse destruction that saw forest cover fall from 53% of total land area in 1960 to 28% in 1989.

The 1985 plan called for 25% of the total land area that remained under forest to be conserved in protected areas such as national parks, while the rest was to be reserved for future timber production through commercial replanting. Unofficial estimates, meanwhile, put forest cover at far less than 20% and the current annual rate of destruction is estimated at about 1000km^2, or one per cent of remaining forested land in Thailand. The ban on logging in 1989 only slowed the clearing caused by illegal logging, devel-

opment projects and the extension of agricultural land.

In the 1990s, the public and private sectors became involved in tree planting to celebrate the golden jubilee of King Rama IX's reign, but results were mixed, with success coming from fire-control preserving natural growth as much as from planting. The Forest Restoration Research Unit (FORRU), a small and underfunded NGO associated with Chiang Mai University, set out to study local species and establish a methodology for successful replanting. Cooperating with Hmong villagers and using local 'framework' species, they have developed a methodology that achieves full canopy cover within a few years. For more information see "Forests for the Future" by FORRU (Tel: (0) 5394 3346 or (0) 5394 3358, e-mail <scopplrn @chiangmai.ac.th>).

Moss falls at Ko Noi, Mae Ping National Park

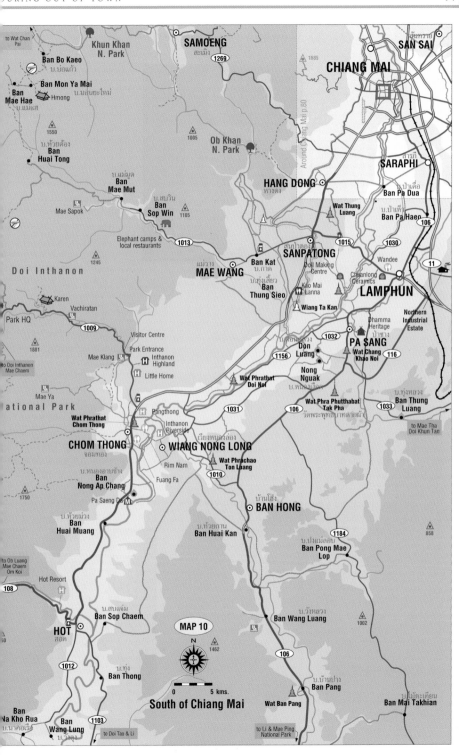

South of Chiang Mai

MAP 10

4. South to Lamphun (H106)

(Maps 10-12. Half to one Day. Return 52 Kms. Lamphun station [see p.198 for schedules] is 2 kms. from the old town. Regular buses begin at Chang Phuak (No 1.) bus station and may be caught at the start of the old Chiang Mai-Lamphun Road near the Nawarat Bridge.) LAMPHUN remains a small provincial town on H106. The quieter pace of the city makes it an attractive destination for those interested in historical culture. The old city is in the shape of an oval surrounded by lotus-filled moats and by the River Kuang on the east side.

HISTORY OF LAMPHUN

Lamphun (formerly Haripunchai) is amongst the oldest cities in Thailand and predates Chiang Mai by several centuries. Northern Thai chronicles suggest the city of Haripunchai was founded by some Buddhist monks in 661 AD, but the actual date may have been as late as the mid-ninth century.

The chronicles tell how the monks wished to establish a city and invited Queen Chamadevi from Lopburi to be the first ruler (a statue of the queen stands in a small park near the south-west corner of the old city moats). The city survived Lawa attacks and eventually assimilated the Lawa and other ethnic groups.

The oval shape of the city demonstrates its older origins as a northern outpost of the

A disciple of the Buddha (12th-13th century Haripunchai style. Chiang Mai National Museum)

Mon Dvaravati civilisation, which developed to the west of the Khmer Empire along trade routes from the Gulf of Martaban to the Chao Phraya River basin in the 7th to 11th centuries. The centre of this civilisation lay in the western part of Central Thailand, but the location of its capital has never been established.

Queen Chamadevi's dynasty lasted till the mid-11th century, when the city may have been temporarily evacuated due to a cholera epidemic. The rich city with its high culture was a tempting prize for King Mangrai, who captured it in 1281, but he was to make it is capital for only four years before moving north, an act which eclipsed further development of Lamphun.

LAMPHUN CITY SIGHTS

Wat Chamadevi

วัดจามเทวี

(Wat Kukut. 1 km. west on R1015 to Sanpatong. Trishaw – 20 Bt.) Two CHEDI that are the most impressive remains of the Dvaravati civilisation in Thailand stand in the grounds of this temple.

The larger of the two ched is a square stepped pyrami made of laterite. Known as th Mahapol Chedi (or the Suwa Chang Kot Chedi), the orig

Dipterocarpus Alatus

903 tall *yang* trees line H106 to Saraphi and end abruptly at the provincial boundary. Chao Phraya Surasi Kitisak, the governor of Chiang Mai is credited with having them planted in 1899. Each tree is numbered, the 779th being a large and healthy specimen. The height of the trees is emphasised by pruning of lateral branches for safety reasons. The trees are protected, and anyone who damages them is liable to a 10,000 Bt. fine.

al chedi dates back at least to the 10th century. It has since been enlarged and renovated. The four sides at each level contain three standing Buddha

Standing Buddha in a niche of the Mahapol Chedi

Hong

The *hong* or *hamsa* is a mythical gander linking the oceans with the sun and the heavens. It serves as a mount for Varuna and Brahma. It represents the breath, the foundation of our existence, and serves as the gatekeeper to heaven. Common in temples with links to the Mon people, the *hong* is believed to take the souls of the builders of the temple to heaven.

The hong at Wat Chamadevi

images in niches. The frames around the niches are highly decorated with stucco. The chedi at Wat Chedi Liem in Wiang Kum Kam is a copy of this design.

A second smaller, octago-

nal chedi of similar age is known as the Ratana Chedi. It has eight standing Buddha images in the first section above its base. The adjacent modern viharn contains a mural that depicts King Viranga of the Lawa throwing a javelin towards the city.

Wat Phrathat Haripunchai

วัดพระธาตุหริภุญชัย

(*Inthayongyot Rd. East side*)
THIS TEMPLE is one of the most famous temples in Northern Thailand. Large lions guard the main entrance gate that faces the River Khuang to the east. A reclining Buddha image fills a small building located nearby.

The temple grounds form a square with a 46 metre high chedi at its centre. The chedi is said to have been built on the site of Queen Chamadevi's palace. Construction on the chedi probably began in the late ninth century, but it was enlarged at the

The Three Javelins

Queen Chamadevi became famous for her tricks in defending herself and the city against Viranga, a powerful local king of the Lawa who wanted to marry her.

In his ardour King Viranga even attacked the city, but he was defeated by the queen's magic elephant which squashed his commander in a narrow gate now known as 'Elephant Crush Gate' (this gate is located at the northern entrance of H106 to the old city).

According to legend, Viranga's final attempt to win Queen Chamadevi's hand was to bring his demise. She promised marriage if Viranga could throw one of three spears into the middle of Haripunchai from a 'nearby' mountain (thought to be a rather distant Doi Suthep).

To achieve such a feat, Viranga would have had to call on magical powers. The queen, meanwhile, had offered Viranga the gift of a hat upon which she had smeared some of her menstrual blood, foiling Viranga's access to magical powers. His javelins were to fall short, and so, stricken with grief, he died as if his broken heart had been impaled by one of his own javelins.

Viranga casting a javelin (mural at Wat Chamadevi)

beginning of the 12th century, reaching its final shape in the reign of King Tilokarat in the 15th century.

The parasols at the corners and on the pinnacle of the chedi were placed by Kawila. The nine-tiered parasol at the top is said to be made of over 68 kilograms of gold. On the dome below the outlines of repoussé Buddha images can still faintly be made out. The chedi is in the Sri Lankan style, which reflects the origins of Theravada Buddhism in the region. On the full moon day of the sixth lunar month, an annual homage and bathing ceremony of the *phrathat chedi* is held.

The main viharn, a large structure containing the *Phra Chao Thongtip* Buddha and several smaller images, was rebuilt in 1925. South of the viharn there is a small 19th century scripture repository. Moving west along the south wall of the sanctuary one finds a small *sala* with four footprints of the Buddha within each other.

The Chedi of Wat Phrathe Haripunche

In the south-west corner a small museum (*hrs: 09:00-16:30*) has several fine Buddha images, some of which were reportedly dug up in from within the confines of the temple. The collection includes fine examples of 15-16th century Lanna images. Next to the museum

...side the Than Chai Viharn

...n the viharn, which ...ontains a standing Buddha ...mage as well as some ...emarkable murals that were ...ainted in the 1950's. The ...est and north walls depict ...uddhist hells and the east ...nd south walls scenes from ...e coming of the next ...Maitreya) Buddha.

In the north-west corner, ...e small Suwanan Chedi was ...uilt in 1467 as a replica of ...e original at Wat ...hamadevi. Finally, the ...ompound contains a red ...han-looking structure ...olding a bell and a large ...ong cast in 1864.

Wat Phra Yeun
วัดพระยืน

(1 km. east across narrow ...ridge over the River Kuang in ...ront of Wat Phrathat ...aripunchai.) LOCATED in a ...rove, the temple has a chedi ...ith a large square base and ...ur tall standing Buddha ...nages in arched niches. The ...ld site is said to go back to ...e 11th century when a large ...tanding Buddha image was

built in the grove.

The temple was expanded when Phra Sumana Thera stayed for two years around 1370. His visit is recorded on one of the oldest stela in the valley, which still stands under a small shelter near the entrance to the temple. An English explanation of the writing is provided at the site.

Old residents have recorded that the original structure at the site of the present chedi was a *mondop* with a pinnacled wooden roof (the *mondop* in the *ubosot* of Wat Phra Singh is thought to be a loose copy of this vanished structure). The structure had four standing Buddha images twice the height of the present ones. The chedi was rebuilt in a Burmese-style at the beginning of this century.

Haripunchai National Museum
พิพิธภัณฑ์แห่งชาติหริภุญชัย

(Inthayongyot Rd. opp. Wat Phrathat Haripunchai. Weds-Suns 08:30–16:00. 30 Bt.) THE MUSEUM contains a good display of stelae (basement) and some fine examples of Haripunchai religious art.

Ku Chang
กู่ช้าง

(1.5 kms. — follow the narrow lane north-east along the banks of the Kuang for a kilometre; a lane to the north-west called Thanon Kuchang leads to the site.) THIS PLACE will be of less interest to foreigners than to Thais, who leave carved wooden

The Lohasimbali Hell

This hell is the 15th auxiliary hell for those who commit adultery. The kapok trees are one *yojana* tall (approx 13 kilometres) and have flaming thorns of red hot iron sixteen finger lengths long. Lovers who have committed adultery are reborn into this hell.

The guardians of hell at the bottom of the tree pierce the lover low on the tree with lances, urging him or her to

Modern cynics say they no longer fear the thorns because they have been worn down.

hurry up the tree to join the other at the top. Though in mortal pain, the lover is driven by fear of the guardians to the top, only to discover that the other is at the bottom.

elephants in front of the first of two chedis at the site, and who believe that Queen Chamadevi's legendary elephant is buried there.

Weaving Co-operatives

LAMPHUN THAI SILK on the lane to Ku Chang, and the *Klum Satri Tho Pha Muang Yu* (the woman's weaving cooperative of Muang Yu) are two cooperatives located near Lamphun. The Yong women of Wiang Yong across the river from Lamphun are renowned for their weaving skills, which includeds a style known as *yok dok*. A Thai speaker would be helpful if planning to visit these cooperatives. More cotton weaving villages are located near Pasang.

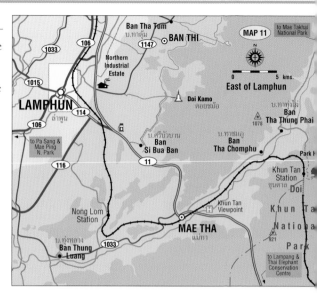

WHERE TO EAT & STAY IN LAMPHUN

The Suphamit offers good value air-con rooms in Lamphun, and there are several good places to eat. The **Dao Khanong** Restaurant on H106 is well-known for its northern Thai food, but aficionados might want to try the **Wan Di** Restaurant (*H1015 KM3 north side— no English menu!*). **Rabieng Nam** is the most respectable looking of restaurants overlooking the river. For noodles and market food try **Kwang-Tung** noodles just north of the National Museum, or the extensive street market, which stays open to late, next to the Chamadevi Monument.

Accommodation may be available by advance arrangement at the Dhamma Park and Heritage Garden in Pasang, while **Khun Tan Viewpoint Resort** (see p.191) offers bungalows not far from Khun Tan.

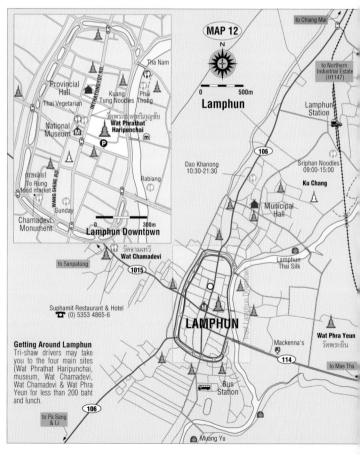

Getting Around Lamphun
Tri-shaw drivers may take you to the four main sites (Wat Phrathat Haripunchai, museum, Wat Chamadevi, Wat Chamadevi & Wat Phra Yeun for less than 200 baht and lunch.

OI KHUN TAN

ขุนตาล

Map 13. By train: Morning
pt. from Chiang Mai 06:25
07:35. Return dep. Khun Tan
:18 only — don't miss it! A
m footpath leads up from the
ation straight to the visitor
ntre and Park HQ. Foreign-
s 200 Bht. Accommodation
see p.83. Food is best at
oodle stalls by the station, but
ring the season kiosks sell
acks at weekends near the
mps to crowds of students.
ke a day pack with food, a
ange of clothes and a warm
cket for the return journey if
ing in the cold season.
  By road: H11 KM47-200m
st turn at Ban Tha Pladuk.
kms to side road and another
ms —2kms unsealed—to the
rk HQ. Apart from park
commodation, the Khun Tan
ew Doi Resort is the only
her place to stay in the area.)
STABLISHED in 1975, the park
as a former hill station
hose history may be studied
the visitor centre. Hiking

A small shrine near the entrance to Khun
Tan tunnel commemorates those who died
building it. The primary bore to the tunnel was completed in 1918. Its completion
ended the relative isolation of Lan Na,
hastening the economic integration with
Bangkok.

the clearly marked 8.3 kms
trail — a climb of 793m—to
the summit and returning to
the station for the only
evening train back to Chiang
Mai can easily be done if
reasonably fit. The early start,
the picturesque train ride and
the hike through some
pleasant mixed evergreen
forest will make this a
memorable day out.

SOUTH FROM LAMPHUN ON H106

THE ROAD south from
Lamphun to Thoen passes
Pasang, an area well-known
for its cottonweaving, and
continues through a wide and
flat part of the valley. The
highlight of a longer journey
south of Pasang is the Mae
Ping National Park(Map 16
p.113. 108kms to park
entrance from Lamphun.
Accommodation on rafts).

Pasang

ป่าซาง

THE DHAMMA
PARK & HERITAGE GARDEN
(H106 KM145 left turn and
follow signs —2kms. Open Sat
& Sun 10:00-16:00, weekdays
by appointment only. Tel: (0)
5352 1609. Donation) will
delight art and dhamma fans,
who will discover the works
of Venetia Walkey and Inson
Wongson in this tranquil
private sculpture park.

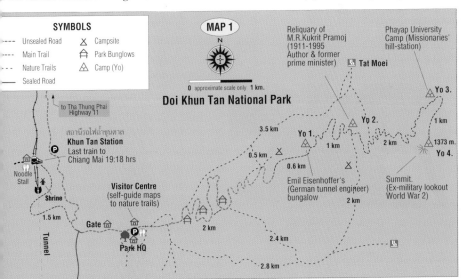

SYMBOLS

----	Unsealed Road	✕	Campsite
----	Main Trail	⌂	Park Bunglows
- - -	Nature Trails	△	Camp (Yo)
——	Sealed Road		

MAP 1
N

0 approximate scale only 1 km.

Doi Khun Tan National Park

Reliquary of
M.R.Kurit Pramoj
(1911-1995
Author & former
prime minister) ⚑ **Tat Moei**

Phayap University
Camp (Missionaries'
hill-station)

to Tha Thung Phai
Highway 11

สถานีรถไฟน้ำขุนตาล
Khun Tan Station
Last train to
Chiang Mai 19:18 hrs

Noodle
Stall

Shrine

1.5 km

Tunnel

Visitor Centre
(self-guide maps
to nature trails)

Gate ⌂

Park HQ

3.5 km

Yo 1.

0.5 km ✕

0.6 km

Yo 2.

1 km

2 km

Emil Eisenhoffer's
(German tunnel engineer)
bungalow   2 km

2 km

2.4 km

2.8 km

Yo 3.

1 km

1373 m.
Yo 4.

Summit.
(Ex-military lookout
World War 2)

The Asian Elephant in Thailand

The Asian elephant, especially the sacred white elephant, has a special place in Thai lore and unofficially is considered a national symbol of the country. Above all comes the white elephant called Erawan (Airvata), who was the mount of the Vedic chief of gods, Indra, the god who controlled thunder and lightning (and so rain). The symbolic importance of the white elephant has carried into Buddhist mythology, such as in the Vessantara Jataka (see p.68), and images of Erawan can be seen on many temple buildings as a result.

To this day possession of auspicious white elephants has been considered an attribute of a universal ruler, and so they have long been prized as tribute. A baby white elephant found in the Borneo Company's logging herd in Chiang Mai was presented in an elaborate ceremony to King Prajadhipok (r. 1925-1935), when he visited the city in 1926.

Auspicious white elephants (they are not albino elephants) are ranked in three classes according to characteristics that even a trained eye can take long to determine. Along with the fact that taking care of auspicious elephants in the prescribed manner was expensive, that such elephants appear indistinguishable from ordinary elephants may account for the use of 'white elephant' in English idiom to mean an 'expensive burden of doubtful value'.

Ironically many of Thailand's estimated two and half thousand ageing elephants, most of which are privately owned, have become 'white elephants' for their owners. Once valued as beasts of battle and burden, elephants have become redundant. Since the logging ban in 1989, only an estimated quarter to one-third can find work in the tourist market. With perhaps ten births amongst the entire population per year, the Asian elephant in Thailand is endangered.

Elephants may often be seen around cities, their hapless mahouts trying to quickly raise money for their families (or the animal's owner) before leading their animals back to sources of essential rough fodder. In former times an elephant usually had two mahouts, perhaps a father and son, who would look after the animal for its expected 50-60 years of life. Being a mahout, however, is no longer a desirable calling, and the expertise of masters is increasingly scarce. Mistreatment of elephants has resulted in numerous deaths amongst mahouts, for the elephant is a potentially dangerous animal which has never been selectively bred and domesticated.

The elephant camps are helping by generally treating the animals well and providing work for them. They usually run programmes in the morning, when mahouts (many of whom are Karen) get the animals to show their skills and then take tourists on basic rides.

The Thai Elephant Conservation Centre *(30kms south from Lamphun on H11 at Km 28-29 in Hang Chat district, Lampang Province. Tel: 054 228034, 054 231150. Daily bathing 09:45; shows at 10:00 & 11:00, weekends and holidays additional show 13:30 adults 50 Bht. Short rides 10 min. 150 Bht. 08:30-15:30)* is the only government run camp. It contains the Mahout and Elephant Training School, where foreigners may learn to handle elephants, as well as an elephant Hospital which became famous for the treatment of Motala, an elephant injured by a land-mine. The Centre is home to the Lampang Elephant Art Academy and the Thai Elephant Orchestra.

The Elephant Nature Park *(Mae Taman. Contact through Gem Travel only. Tel: (0) 5327 2855. <www.thaifocus.com> 1-3 day programmes 1500-3500 Bht.)* provides opportunities for hands on experience that includes homestays with mahouts.

Most people prefer to mount elephants.
(Elephant training: Thai Elephant Conservation Centre)

Cotton weaving villages are
cated to the south-west of
asang. Ban Don Luang
(บ้านดอนหลวง) (KM140 west turn
00m before junction with
116. 1km to shops) and Ban
ong Nguak (บ้านหนองเบือก)
KM138-300 West turn on lane
ter bridge & proceed 2.5 kms
shops near T junction.) have
ops selling hand-woven
ttons.

emples South of Lamphun

AT PASANG NGAM in the
iddle of Pasang, Wat Chang
hao Noi Tai and Nua
KM142) and Wat
nkamphaeng (1km down
ne to Nong Nguak) all have
atures of interest.

Best known is Wat
araphuttabat Tak Pha (วัด
ะพุทธบาทตากผ้า KM136 east
rn —2 kms) where,
cording to legend, the
uddha hung his robes
dry. The temple
came famous under
hru Ba Phroma
kko, who died aged
7 in 1984, and
hose wax effigy
ay be seen in his
ti. The temple has a
vered Buddha
otprint and a
rominent hilltop chedi
69 steps to top)
onouring his father
d two brothers,
ho also became
nior monks in the
ahanikai sect.
Wat Ban Pang(H106
M89.), Khru Ba Srivichai's
rthplace and home temple,
ontains a museum and
odern, ornate buildings. It
worth visiting if en route to
e Mae Ping National Park.

*High relief at Wat
Chang Khao Noi Tai*

Singha

Singha are the lion-like beasts
that act as guardians to temple
entrances, and may be shown
in different postures on each
side of a gate. *Singha* are particularly popular in the north and indicate a Burmese influence.

In some temples the figure of
a woman may be seen in the
mouth. In the time of the Buddha this woman was collecting
the fruit of a banyan (Indian
fig) tree that had particularly
sweet fruits. A jealous *singha*
wh guarded the tree for him-
self was about to devour the woman when she complained
that anyone had the rights to the fruit. The matter was taken
to the Buddha who judged that the woman was right and commanded the *singha* to release her.

Singha at Wat Chang Khao Noi Tai

Mae Ping National Park
อุทยานแห่งชาติแม่ปิง

*(H106 KM47 west turn on
H1087. 20kms to Park
HQ Tel: (0)5351 9031
or (0)2579 5734, and
a further 20kms to raft
landing at Kaeng Ko,
where you can stay on
rafts overnight —
check availability and
prices in advance. See
p. 191)* THE BHUMIPHOL
dam created a
picturesque lake over 300 kms in length, but
blocked the river route to
Chiang Mai. Cruises on the
lake can be enjoyed aboard
the Edelweiss Princess
(p.199) as well as on the rafts
or long-tails from Kaeng Ko.
Rafts are also available at Tha
Nam Doi Tao *(H1103 west
turn at KM33)*. The Ko Luang
Falls in the park can be easily
reached by car, but visiting
other places (for details
contact the park's visitor
centre), involves 4WD
and/or trekking.

*Cruising home
(Mae Ping
National Park)*

5. Southwest to Doi Inthanon

(MAP 10 P.97 & MAP 14 P.109) THE JOURNEY south to Chom Thom (60kms) and Hot (80kms) takes an old route through a heavily populated part of the Ping Valley. H1009 from Chom Thong to Doi Inthanon, the highest mountain in Thailand, becomes increasingly dramatic as it climbs to the summit(47 kms from Chom Thong — start early to make the return journey in one day).

H108 south of Chom Thong to Hot passes weaving villages, and then takes a pretty route to Ob Luang National Park. This is part of a circular route (overnight recommended) via the picturesque Mae Chaem valley west of Inthanon, or of a longer journey to Om Koi District.

AROUND SANPATONG
สันป่าตอง

THE SATURDAY morning cattle market (KM.25 west side) is the best-known feature of this small market town. At the front of the market,

tarpaulins cover stalls selling clothing and household goods, while the middle part is a huge second-hand motorcycle market. The cattle market itself is at the back. There you can see animals change hands for 6-8,000 baht and listen to forlorn calves mew for their mothers. The adjacent Wat Pa Charoentham has numerous gaudy modern statues including a huge reclining Buddha.

Continue through Sanpatong to the first set of traffic lights at KM23 and follow signs for the **Chiang Mai Doll Making Centre** (6kms. Hrs: 08:00-17:00. Tel; (0) 5383 7229) to see an impressive collection of dolls and get a souvenir for a little one. Keep following this road to reach the River Ping and riverside lanes suitable for two-wheel transport.

Mae Wang Valley
แม่วางวาเล่ย์

(H108 KM22-23. West turn on H1013) PAST THE DISTRICT offices, the road enters a narrow valley and runs alongside the river. Numerous food stalls and sala line the side of the road overlooking the river between KM21&24. Elephant tour operators offers hour-long elephant rides (Mae Wang Elephant Camp Tel:(0)53 201315-6 early mornings or evenings only, or try 01-883 9265. 300 Bht./elephant) to

either a Karen or a Hmong village in the surrounding hills, as well as short bamboo rafting trips down the river.

H1013 continues up the valley to Ban Wang Pha Pun at KM28, and then becomes a cobbled lane and a sealed road through uplands to Ban Huai Tong. At KM6 (from the end of H1013 at KM28) a concrete lane to the left goes to the Mae Sapok Falls(2kms), and at KM16 a sealed road south leads to Ban Khun Wang. This route (5kms sealed, 10kms unsealed — possibly difficult in the rainy season — before joining H1284 near Khun Wang) eventually joins H1009 to the summit of Doi Inthanon near KM30.

From Ban Huai Tong (KM19 —Karen), a combination of cobbled, sealed and dirt roads go on a somewhat complex route (22 kms from Ban Huai Tong) via the Hmong/Northern Thai villages of Mae Hae, Ban Mor Ya Mai and Ban Bo Kaeo, to the Samoeng-Wat Chan road (3kms) near KM26.

Wiang Ta Kan
เวียงท่ากาน

(KM30 Turn south at lights in Tung Sieo — 2kms) THIS ANCIENT SETTLEMENT is similar to Wiang Kum Kan, though it is smaller. Bounded by a moat in the shape of a half rectangle, much of the site is covered by a village in the

Sanpatong cowboy

iddle of which a large open
ld contains some old
edis, reconstructed temple
mains and a visitor centre.
wide area of well-irrigated
nd surrounding the site has
elded relics from the
aripunchai era (12-13th
), and chronicles suggest
e area has been a rice
anary since at least Lan
a's golden age.

Several other ancient sites
e located in the Sanpatong-
ot area. Chiang Mai Green
ternative Tour (p.199) may
able to provide the expert
idance necessary to make
siting the sites more than a
easant trip into the country.

The Naga and the Garuda

Nagas are considered to be strong guardians on temple balustrades, yet on temple roofs they appear to be victims in the clutch of a *garuda* (much as snakes in the clutch of an eagle in flight). The sworn enemy of the *naga*, the *garuda* is symbolised by the *cho fa* at the apex of the roof.

The *garuda*, an eagle-like bird with a human-like head and torso, serves as a mount of Vishnu (the *garuda* is the

WAT PHRATHAT SI CHOM THONG

วัดพระธาตุศรีจอมทอง

(H108 KM.59) Chronicles suggest the origins of Wat Phrathat Si Chom Thong, one of the most important temples in the valley, go back as early as 749 AD, when the highly revered Phra Boromathat Chom Thong relic was found. A viharn has been on the site since at least 1466.

The current viharn was built in 1817 and is extensively decorated with wood carvings. The building

Chedi of Wat Phrathat Chom Thong

symbol of the Thai government). A legend states that a *naga* was once caught by a *garuda* at the time of the Buddha. The *naga* grasped onto a bo tree under which the Buddha was seated and asked for his help. Whereupon the Buddha taught both creatures the value of the *dhamma* — sym-bolised in the temple by the *cho fa* and *naga* on the barge- boards.

Cho Fa and Naga bargeboads (Wat Phrathat Sri Chom Thong)

According to legend, the Phra Boromathat Chom Thong relic (a piece of bone in the glass above) was found in a broken stucco Buddha image illuminated by a supernatural light in 1499

contains a *mondop* — a chedi-like reliquary which houses the Buddha relic — decorated with golden stucco. The revered Buddha images and finely carved elephant tusks around the *mondop* give the *viharn* the feeling of a museum.

On the main Buddhist holidays, the relic, which is reputed to be from the cranium of the Buddha, is brought out of the *mondop* for display. At the back of the *mondop*, past cages containing valuable Buddha images, a small room contains a ' Buddha bed' donated by King Muang Kaew, (r.1495-1526) who probably sponsored development of the temple. The temple is also an active meditation centre.

CHOM THONG & SOUTH

CHOM THONG'S MARKET is close to Wat Phrathat Si Chom Thong, and is a good place to stock up with grilled meats and fruit for a picnic on Doi Inthanon. Some 15 kilometres south H108 passes an area well-known for weaving.The

Weaver at Ban Rai Pai Ngam

Nong Ap Chang women's weaving group (*KM68 east side just after the concrete elephant*) and Ban Rai Pai Ngam — Pa Saeng Da Textile Museum (KM68 east side 400m. Hrs 08:30-17:00.) offer weaving displays, a textile museum and a shop.

Side roads off the main highway to Hot lead to some pretty areas. At the small district town of Hot, H108 turns west on a scenic route following the River Mae Chaem to Ob Luang (*see p.112*), while H1103 goes south to Doi Tao and a back route to the Mae Ping National Park (*see p.105*).

WHERE TO EAT & STAY
(Sanpatong - Chom Thong)

(*Listings p.191*) The **Kao Mai Lanna Resort** (*H108 KM29*) offers stylish rooms in converted tobacco drying houses; it has a large shop specialising in handwoven cottons. **Inthanon Riverside** is reasonable, and **Inthanon Highland Resort** has small houses in a spacious orchard. The nearby **Little Home Guest House** (*H1009 KM6*) offers inexpensive but serviceable huts. For a meal try either the **Rim Nam** (*H108 KM60 east turn on a lane just south of police station – 1km*) or the **Fuang Fa** restaurant (*H108 KM61east side of the road*).

DOI INTHANON NATIONAL PARK
อุทยานแห่งชาติดอยอินทนนท์

(*H108 KM57 west turn onto H1009 — 47kms to summit. Checkpoint KM8. Park Fees. Keep tickets for access on the same day through any of the park checkpoints. The Visitor Centre at KM9 has brochures and video shows at 09:00, 10:30, 13:00 and 14:30. Food is available at stalls by the main waterfalls, by the Park HQ (tel: (0) 5335 5728 general business) at KM31 till 20:00 hrs and at a canteen at the Royal Chedis at KM40 hrs. 08:00-17:00.*

Accommodation is available at resorts around KM7, at the park HQ (Tel: (0) 5331 1608 or see p.83), and in Mae Chaem. At the basic Karen Ecolodge near KM26, guides offer day and night programmes. Tel: 01-881 7346, 01 258 6071) AT 2,565 METRES, the granite mass of Doi Inthanon is over 200m higher than anything else in Thailand and is climbed by H1009, which was built to

Karen terraces during the rainy season on the lower slopes on the east side of Inthanon

reach a radar station at the summit. The 482km² of the park contains true upper montane forest and provides a habitat for species of primate, deer and small cats.

Hmong villages are located on the high ground around the edge of the core forest covering the mountain, and in the surrounding upland valleys, the Karen practice their skilled terraced farming techniques.

Mae Ya Fa

Mae Ya Falls
น้ำตกแม่ยะ

(*H1009 KM.1 south turn — 1 kms.*) TO VISIT these falls you must buy or show a park entry ticket at the gate located just after the road begins to climb. The falls, which drop 100 metres in a stepped cascade, are best seen in the early morning. It is possible to get to H1009 up Doi Inthanon by taking a concrete road north from the Mae Ya approach road just before it begins to climb up t the park gate. The road becomes a dirt track that skirts the hills.

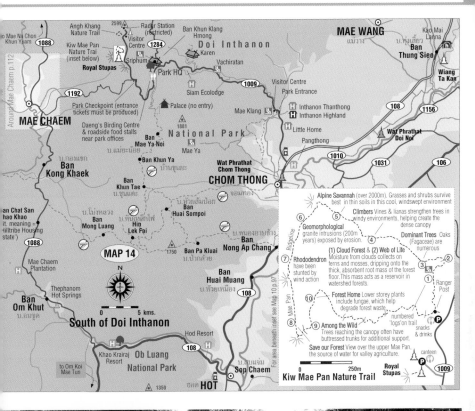

Angh Khang Nature Trail

2599

Radar Station (restricted)

Ban Khun Klang Hmong

MAE WANG

Kao Mai Lanna

บ.ทุ่งเสี่ยว

Visitor Centre

Ban Thung Sieo

Kiw Mae Pan Nature Trail (inset below)

1284

Doi Inthanon

มาแวง

Wiang Ta Kan

Sriphum

Karen

Royal Stupas

Park HQ

Vachiratan

1088

io Mae Na Chon Khun Yuam

1192

1009

Visitor Centre
Park Entrance

108

1156

Siam Ecolodge

Palace (no entry)

Inthanon Thanthong
Inthanon Highland

MAE CHAEM

Park Checkpoint (entrance tickets must be produced)

Mae Klang

Daeng's Birding Centre & roadside food stalls near park offices

1881

National Park

Little Home

Wat Phrathat Doi Noi

Ban Mae Ya Noi

บ.แม่ยะน้อย

Mae Ya

Pangthong

1010

1031

106

Ban Khun Ya

บ้านขุนยะ

Wat Phrathat Chom Thong

Ban Kong Khaek

Ban Khun Tae
บ.ขุนตะ

CHOM THONG

จอมทอง

1088

an Chat San hao Khao it. meaning = iilltribe Housing state')

บ.โม่งหลวง

Ban Mong Luang

บ.พนอกน่าไฟ

Hin Lek Fai

บ.ห้วยสัมป๋อก

Ban Huai Sompoi

1750

Ban Pa Kluai

บ.ป่ากล้วย

บ.พนองอมข้าง

Ban Nong Ap Chang

MAP 14

N

Mae Chaem Plantation

Ban Huai Muang

บ.ห้วยเหมือง

108

Thephanom Hot Springs

Ban Om Khut

บ.อมขูด

0   5 kms.

South of Doi Inthanon

Hod Resort

Khao Krairaj Resort

108

H

Ob Luang National Park

บ.สบแจ่ม

Sop Chaem

to Om Koi Mae Tun

1350

HOT

ขอด

For area beneath inset see Map 10 p.91

Kiw Mae Pan Nature Trail

Alpine Savannah (over 2000m). Grasses and shrubs survive best in thin soils in this cool, windswept environment

⑤ **Climbers** Vines & lianas strengthen trees in windy environments, helping create the dense canopy

⑥ **Geomorphological** granite intrusions (200m years) exposed by erosion.

④ **Dominant Trees** Oaks (Fagaceae) are numerous

(1) Cloud Forest & **(2) Web of Life** Moisture from clouds collects on ferns and mosses, dripping onto the thick, absorbent root mass of the forest floor. This mass acts as a reservoir in watershed forests.

Ridgeline

⑦ **Rhododendron** have been stunted by wind action

③

②

①

Ranger Post

⑩ **Forest Home** Lower storey plants include fungae, which help degrade forest waste

⑧   ⑨ **Among the Wild** Trees reaching the canopy often have buttressed trunks for additional support.

Mae Pan

numbered 'logs'on trail

snacks & drinks

P

Save our Forest View over the upper Mae Pan, the source of water for valley agriculture.

0   250m

canteen

P

Royal Stupas

1009

Cloud forest on the Aangka Nature Trail

Up Doi Inthanon (H1009)

THE FIRST attraction on the road to the summit are the Mae Klang Falls *(KM7 left turn 1km)*, which are very popular at weekends. Cross over the bridge to enter the tidy gardens of the Kamphaeng San Buddhist college or walk up past the falls to the visitor centre.

To reach the Brichinda Cave *(Km 8. Right turn 750m on rough dirt road to where walking 750m is obligatory)*, a partly collapsed cavern on the north side of a low ridge, you must leap the torrent at the bottom of the gully.

A new access lane to the Vachiratarn Falls *(KM19. left turn 750m)* means that visitors no longer have to walk from the old car park near KM20 down past a chute to where the water tumbles over the main drop.

Unsealed lanes *(KM23 & 25)* climb north into narrow, terraced valleys tended by the Karen, who live in villages on the slopes above the cultivable land *(no motorable through route to H1284)*.

H1284 *(KM30 — north turn sealed 15 kms. Turn right at research station for a through route to Sanpatong via Mae Wang Valley. 4WD)* first

Tiled mural on the Queen's Chedi

passes a Hmong village, where a road to the left lead to the Siriphum Falls, before skirting the southern flank c Inthanon to terminate at the Mae Chon Luang Agricultural Research Station. On H1009 just past KM31, A concrete road south goes to private royal lodge *(7 kms— no entry)*, and to a dirt road which passes Hmong and Karen villages on a high route over the hills.

Food stalls (open till 20:0 hrs) operate in front of the National Park HQ *(KM30-31. Tel: 053 311-608. Get permission here first before continuing if you want to wal on the Kiw Mae Pan Trail at KM42).* Mr Daeng's Birding Centre *(100m up from Park HQ on west side of road. Call Mr. Daeng to book his limited accommodation or get a summary of conditions on the mountain. Tel 01 884 8108)* consists of a basic restauran where you can get advice on where and when to see the more than 380 species foun on the mountain.

H1192 to Mae Chaem goe left just after a checkpoint a KM38, where the final very steep climb to the summit begins. On the way up the

Walking on Doi Inthanon

The easiest walk is the short Aangka Nature Trail at the summit, but far better is the Kiw Mae Pan *(KM42. 3+kms. min 2hrs. Closed May through November. N.B. You must first get permission to enter the trail from the park HQ at KM31! Trail closes 16:30hrs).* The trail leads through evergreen forest before emerging onto a grassy range above the west facing ridge. Numbered logs on the trail link with text on a large park brochure (not available in English). A very brief synopsis and a small reproduction of the map in this brochure are found on the inset of map 14.

The area around the Mae Pan Falls (H1192 KM6) is also pleasant for walking

A 'Thousand Year Rose' (Rhododendron delavayii Fran. Ericaceae) on west facing scarp of Inthanon.

road (very steep!) passes two chedis built in honour of Their Majesties (*left turn KM40*). The southern Napamethaneedon Chedi commemorates the 60th birthday of H.M. King Bhumiphol Adulyadej (5 Dec.1987) and the Napapolphumsiri Chedi that of H.M Queen Sirikit (12 Aug.1992). The modern chedis contain stylistic Buddha images and are decorated with interesting tiled murals. The best views (no views higher up except from the Kiw Mae Pan Trail) and the best restaurant on the mountain are found here.

The Summit of Doi Inthanon

OFTEN SHROUDED in mists, the trees on the flat summit of the mountain are coated with moss; this can be seen on the Angka Nature Trail(*KM47*), a short boardwalk through cloud forest surrounding a small bog. A side path leads to a shrine at the site of a helicopter crash.

A visitor centre opposite has a good display (English and Thai) on local ecology, and nearby a small chedi marks the spot where the ashes of Chao Inthanon, who died in 1897, were buried.

ACROSS TO MAE CHAEM (H1192)

H1192 goes 22kms to Mae Chaem, from where you may

take H1088. *The return to Chiang Mai via Ob Luang and Hot is 156kms.*) THE NARROW highway descends steeply through many switch-backs to Mae Chaem. Do not let the impressive views distract you from the road and the frequent oncoming pick-ups!

Turn right near KM6 (*unsealed track 4WD descends 2.7kms, then take track that climbs*) to reach the Mae Pan

Mae Pan Falls & Inthanon's west scarp

Falls beyond Huai Sai Luang and the forest station. A series of spectacular drops link natural pools ideal for swimming in the afternoon.

In the Mae Chaem valley country lanes go through picturesque rural scenery to the small market town of Mae Chaem. The uplands to the west (*follow signs for Pang Hin Fon*) offer a maze of possibilities for exploring dirt roads in the mountains.

H1099 follows the valley of the Mae Chaem from near Ob Luang north to Mae Na

19th century northern women took great care of their long hair, unlike the women of the central region, who kept their hair short (mural at Wat Pa Daet).

Chon, before becoming a rugged all-weather dirt road. The latter links to a newly sealed road (*6kms north of Mae Na Chon*) on a very scenic route to Khun Yuam in Mae Hong Son Province.

Mae Chaem
แม่แจ่ม

THE RELATIVE isolation created by the massif of Doi Inthanon has helped preserve a more traditional way of life in the Mae Chaem area, though it is the nearby rural communities rather than the small town which gives the area its special atmosphere. The villages of Ban Thong Fai and Ban Tha Pha are famous for *tin chok*, which is a type of weave used for the decorative strip at the hem of a woman's tube skirt.

Rural Temples near Mae Chaem

THE ISOLATION has also helped preserve some of the small temples in the valley. The addition of a new classic Lanna-style *ubosot* surrounded by a lotus pond has added to the ambience of Wat

Pa Daet (*H1088 - west turn at sharp left hand bend 1km south of junction with H1192*), a charming rural temple in a tree-lined compound set amidst rice-fields. The renovated *viharn*, which was originally built in 1877, contains some relatively well-preserved murals. Wat Yang Luang nearby is also pleasing.

Cross the river to reach Wat Putta En, which was built in 1868 and has a rare example of an *ubosot* set on posts above a lotus pond. Further along the same lane (*7 kms*), Wat Kong Kan contains a large, old seated Buddha image.

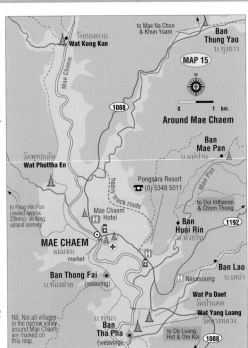

Around Mae Chaem

"Travel agents call it (Ob Luang) the 'Grand Canyon' but my readers will not be taken in ..." (Hudson's Guide to Chiang Mai and the North 3rd Ed. 1967)

TO HOT (FROM MAE CHAEM - H1088)

(*68 kms.*) H1088 PROVIDES a pleasant drive across valleys between uplands before dropping down to join H108. A local restaurant overlooks the river at Ban Om Khut (*KM10*), which lies close to the Thephanom Hot Springs(*KM9. Keys to the huts for mineral baths are available from the building left of the entrance gate*). After H1088 has joined H108 at KM21, the latter follows the river in a scenic stretch that passes Ob Luang on the way to Hot and Chiang Mai.

The best way to see the Mae Chaem River is by raft. Both Mae Sot Conservation Tour (*see p.199*) and the Forest Industry Organisation at the Mae Chaem Plantation (*KM15*) run such tours.

Ob Luang National Park

อุทยานแห่งชาติออบหลวง

(*H108 KM17. Park Fees*) THE MAE CHAEM river thunders through a very narrow gorge spanned by a footbridge. A second footbridge at the Khao Krairaj resort 500m upstream make a circular walk possible on a good nature trail.

A walk uphill from the downstream bridge passes an ancient burial site ("Land of Prehistoric Human"), the remains of which are in the National Museum in Chiang Mai. One may question the authenticity of ancient rock drawings higher up as they appear today, but a fine view over the valley can be enjoyed from the rock outcrop above at Doi Pa Chang.

OM KOI & MAE TUN

(*H108 south turn at KM39. Om Koi 50kms and Ban Mae Tun 138kms from H108*) CHIANG MAI province extends south to the district of Om Koi, in the upper valley of the Nam Mae Tun. This river flows south into the reservoir created by the Bhumiphol dam, which blocked river/land routes south when it was completed in the early 1960's. Since then the only way into this area has been by H1099.

1099 to Mae Tun

HE DRIVE south begins on the
rested Bo Luang Plateau,
hich has been cleared in
arts by the Lawa and Karen
grow cash crops. The road
asses through wooded
plands on the route to Om
oi, a place that is little more
an a village with a market
d district offices.

Further south, sparse
Karen, Lawa or Thai)
abitations near pockets of
rraced farmland can be
en from H1099 as it climbs
ver the summit of Doi
usoe *(1320m - KM43 from
m Koi. Thais like to trek
om the nearby sanctuary
ation and stay overnight on
oi Mon Chong to appreciate
e sunrise — a permit must
st be obtained from the
oyal Forestry Department's
fices in Chiang Mai).*

While the summit of Doi
usoe has been cleared for
ltivation by the Lahu, the
rrounding forests are part
the Om Koi Wildlife Sanc-
ary *(KM65 on H1099)*, an
tensive area of forested
nd that appears to have
rvived the logging
oncessions first granted
wer in the Mae Tun Valley
the 1890's.

The villages and paddy-
elds of Tambon Mae Tun are
ominated to the east by a
all of mountains over
300m in height. A local
ide would help you reach
e tumbling waters of the
stant Huai Tat Falls, which
e clearly visible in the
iddle of this range.

WHERE TO EAT & STAY
(Inthanon, Mae Chaem & Hot)

(Listings p.191) Those with a taste for
basic facilities in the middle of rice
paddy will enjoy **Siam Ecolodge's**
(H1009 KM26) thatch huts; otherwise
you must depend on bungalows and
camping at the National Park HQ at
KM31 *(see p.83)* for accommodation
within the National Park itself,. Apart
from the self-service restaurant *(Hrs.
08:00-17:00)* near the Royal Chedis on
the mountain, food is provided at
stalls near the Park HQ, at **Mr Daeng's**
Birding Centre *(just uphill from the
Park HQ on south side of road)*, or at
stalls by the waterfalls.

On the west side of Inthanon, the
Navasoung Resort (H1092 KM20)
and the **Pongsara Resort** (H1088)
offer the most comfort near Mae

Chaem, otherwise there is only the
basic Mae Chaem Hotel in town. To
the south, the Forest Industry
Organisation's **Mae Chaem Plantation**
(H1088 KM15) has a few wooden
cabins en route to Ob Luang. You can
enjoy the excellent location and nice
rooms of the **Khao Krairaj Resort**
(H108 KM17), as long as you don't
expect a service to match. Service is
probably better at the **Hod Resort**
(H108 KM4 from Hot), which also
enjoys a riverside location.

The **Om Koi Resort** has pleasant
cabins in a grove, but there are only
local style restaurants on this route.
Staying in Mae Tun depends on
traditional hospitality, which may be
found by going to a temple such as
Wat Chom Chaeng, one of several old
temples in the tambon, and asking
where you can stay.

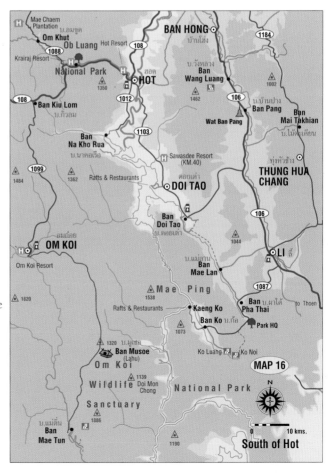

6. North & West to the Mae Sa Valley & Samoeng

(Maps 17 & 18 p.117. Half to one day. Samoeng is reached either by going south on H108 to KM10 and turning west onto H1269, which ascends into the valley of the Tha Chang, or by going north on H107 to Mae Rim and turning west onto H1096 at KM17. Round trip to Mae Sa 66 kms; the loop via Samoeng 103 kms. Yellow pick-ups to Samoeng via the Mae Sa Valley wait near the Bangkok Bank on Chang Phuak Rd.) EXTENSIVE uplands divided by narrow north-south valleys lie to the west of the River Ping. The two picturesque upland valleys of the Mae Sa and the Tha Chang, which bound the massif of Doi Suthep-Pui to the north and south respectively, give access to the west and are favourite locations for resorts and other attractions. They may be driven as a loop.

Many companies run tours to the Mae Sa Valley, the prime rural attraction near Chiang Mai, and Samoeng can be easily reached by public transport. West of Samoeng there are fewer facilities for tourists on the route to Wat Chan.

H107 TO MAE RIM

(Take H107 to KM17 and tur west onto H1096 for the Mae Sa Valley & Samoeng)
The road to Mae Rim passes entrances to golf courses an sports clubs (*see p.182*) as

Lazy lunching at Huai Tungth

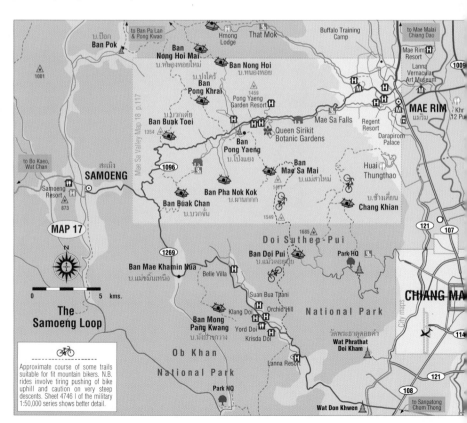

ell as a side road to Chiang
Mai's beach at Huai Thung
hao (H107 KM9 west turn —
ms. 10 Bt.). The latter is
ainly an excuse to enjoy
rilled meats and fish — try
e catfish baked in foil (ปลา
) — together with sticky
ce and liquor at *salas* set
ound a small reservoir.
indsurfing is possible (*first
ght after left turn at T
nction beyond ticket gate*),
ut there's seldom much puff.
The interest in Mae Rim
es in the Darapirom Palace
nd small-scale up-market
ops near the Regent Resort
nd Spa (*H1096 KM1 left turn
— 400m*). The surrounding
ea is full of attractions.

TTRACTIONS NEAR
MAE RIM

Museums

HE BEST of the three small
useums located close to
Mae Rim is the **Darapirom
alace** (*H107 KM16 west turn
tween footbridge and police
ation — enter the grounds of
e Dara Rasmi Border Patrol
olice Camp and drive straight
r 200m. Hrs: 09:00-17:00.
dults 50 Bt. Children 20 Bt.*),
quasi-government museum
anaged by Chulalongkorn
niversity in Bangkok. The
nal home of Chao Dara

Chao Dara Rasmi

Princess Dara Rasmi was born
in 1873, the 11th daughter of
Chao Inthawichayanon, the
seventh *chao luang* of Chiang
Mai. In 1886 the Royal Commissioner arranged for her to
join the royal service of King
Chulalongkorn (Rama V) as
Princess Consort in the
InnerCourt at the age of
twelve. She gave birth to a
daughter by King Rama V in
1889, and was raised in
status, but the little girl died,
officially from tuberculosis,
when she was three year old.

*Princess Dara Rasmi was herself a keen
photographer. Some of her work can be
seen in the library of Yupparat School.*

In fact the Princess was also
kept in Bangkok in part as a
hostage, a common practice between royal houses of the region. While living in Bangkok she practised the arts, playing
her greatest role as a promoter of northern culture in a court
which had hitherto looked down upon the north. When King
Rama V died aged 57 in 1910, fears of secession by the north
prevented her return home for a further four years.

Upon her return to Chiang Mai, she continued to promote

Lanna arts and culture and sought
to improve the lives of poor farmers.
She arranged for the reliquaries of
Chiang Mai royalty to be kept at Wat
Suan Dok, and she ensured that the
proper etiquette was observed during
King Rama VII's visit to Chiang Mai
in 1926. In her final, happier years
she endowed temples and the
McCormick Hospital, and she gave
land for two of Chiang Mai's schools.
She died in 1933.

Courtesy of Darapirom Palace

The Darapirom Palace

Rasmi, the eighth and last
daughter of Chao Inthanon,
the museum features an
extensive display of photo-
graphs, furniture and
clothing. From this collection you can get an impres-
sion of the lifestyle of
Northern Thai royalty at the
turn of the century in the
colonial period.

The other two museums are
small private displays that
specialise in artefacts from
different social levels.

The Chateau Kum Une Art Museum
(*H1096 KM4. Adults 100 Bt. Children
50 Bt. Hrs: 09:00-17:00 closed Tues.
Tel: (0) 5329 8068*). Antique and art
connoisseurs will appreciate the
rarefied atmosphere created by the
art-loving Central Thai family who

Wat Phra Non Rocket Festival

the most artistic rocket. The rockets are launched in the afternoon from a site in scrub land just to the north of the 700 Year Sports Complex. Local temples are represented by teams who compete for best launch and flight and who often become quite intoxicated. Contestants are very friendly and will offer you drinks. The polite response is to accept at least a sip.

Unlike festivals which allow use of metal pipe, the rules only permit natural materials such as bamboo reinforced with hemp rope in rocket construction. The results are therefore quite unpredictable.

Participants are advised to light the touch paper and stand well back, for rockets sometimes explode.

(H107 KM.4 east turn opposite provincial hall – 600 m. Call TAT to confirm the date) Rocket festivals are common in the sixth and seventh lunar months throughout the north and north-east of Thailand. They are held to herald the rain. Wat Phra Non hosts a festival on the day of the new moon of the 7th lunar month (June).

Contestants take rockets to the temple in the early morning to compete for prizes for

created this museum. There are displays of Victorian and Chinese furniture and art, and paintings by the family, the younger of whom have

Farmers now use 'khwai lek' — iron buffaloes.

studied at famous art colleges in the United Kingdom.

The Lanna Vernacular Art Museum & Chiang Mai Terracotta Gallery *(H1260 KM2. Hrs: 00:00-17:00. Adults 100 Bt. Children 50 Bt. Tel: (0) 5329 8897)* Called in Thai "Mae pun din-Pho tum suan", which means "mother sculpts with clay, father does the orchard/garden", this museum displays Lanna folk artefacts in a large converted rice barn. The informed members of the family who own this museum also organise lessons in terracotta sculpture at a workshop beneath the house and attached kiln. They also

plan to run educational tours into nearby farm communities and have a few Lanna style rooms, offering the possibility of an educational vacation.

Snakes and Elephants

The **Mae Sa Snake Farm** *(30 min. shows at 11:30, 14:15, &15:30. Tel: (0) 5386 0719)* and the **Mae Rim Snake Farm** *(KM5 Hrs 09:30-16:30 -3 min show on demand includes "water fighting" 200 Bt. adults, children 100 B* put on "snake shows". The Thai Buffalo Training Camp — **Ban Khwa Thai** *(H107 left turn after KM18 —800m. 1 hour shows at 08:00, 09:00 10:00, 15:00, 16:00 Adults 200 Children 100. Tel: (0) 5330 1628. <www.bannkwaithai.com>)* demonstrates the buffaloes'

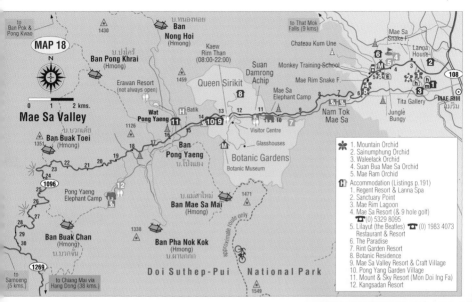

MAP 18

N

Mae Sa Valley

0 1 2 kms.

The Mae Sa Valley
แม่สาวาเล่ย์

THE MAE SA RIVER tumbles out of an upland valley in a series of cascades through picturesque forest. These may be seen at the Mae Sa Falls (*H1096 KM6 south turn— 500m Adults 200 Bt. for a day pass to all falls within the National Park*), or at Suan Damrong Achip (*KM11*), a pleasant spot for a meal or snack overlooking the torrent.

The scenic nature of the valley has attracted resorts, which provide tranquil

...aditional role in local farming actices, a role that has been so ndermined by modern tractors that e water buffalo population is pidly declining and may become dangered.

Of the two elephant camps, the **Mae Elephant Camp** (*KM10. Shows at :00 & 09:40 80 Bt.. Rides from 07:00- :00. Rides per head from 80 Bt for a ort waddle to 1000 Bt for 60 min. (0) 20 6247-8*) is the more convenient d is packed out with coach and van ur groups in the morning, but the **ng Yaeng Elephant Camp** (*KM18 uth turn —1.5 kms. Shows 09:15, :15. 100 Bt. Elephant rides 1—6 hrs 1000 Bt./hour. Tel: (0) 5321 5943*) is a more spectacular location.

Hmong life, Ban Nong Hoi Mai

settings for gardens and restaurants, as well as a craft village (Mae Sa Valley Resort). These places charge a nominal fee for visitors to enter and enjoy the gardens.

In the upper part of the valley, recreational land use gives way to flower cultivation beneath numerous shelters made of plastic sheeting. Some of the cultivation is done by the industrious Hmong, and several lanes from H1096 climb up to their villages in the surrounding heights.

Mae Sa cascades at Suan Damrong Achip

Orchids

Most orchids in Thailand are epiphytes (non para-
sitic plants that grow on other plants), and they were
once common in the perfect conditions offered by
the mountains of Northern Thailand.

The demand from orchid growers for wild stock,
however, has meant that their occurrence in the wild
is now severely threatened, and in many cases have
disappeared altogether. Collection from the jungle
is banned and the Convention on International
Trade in Endangered Species (CITES) bans trade in
wild-collected plants.

The export of plants propagated in nurseries is
legal however, and specimens may be purchased
from the orchid farms. To export them a
phytosanitary certificate and CITES certificate must
be obtained from the Chiang Mai International
Airport Plant Quarantine Office (next to the Immigration Office. Tel: 277182).

Orchid nurseries are found at the farms west of Mae Rim,
where visitors may contemplate rows of blooming colourful
hybrids as well as butterflies bred in special enclosures. They
have restaurants or snack bars as well as shops selling orchid

*Cymbidium — a cultivated orch
exhbited at a sho*

Hans Benziger

*The lady slipper orchid
(Paphiopedilum callosum),
one of more than 250 spe-
cies of orchids which once
populated the Doi Suthep-
Pui National Park. Be-
cause of its horticultural
value it has been over-col-
lected and is now extinct
on the mountain.*

jewellery and plants in a form that may be exported (check
for CITES procedure).

The most comprehensive collection of plants including orchids, however, may be seen at the **Queen Sirikit Botanic
Garden** in the Mae Sa Valley. The market with the largest
choice of plants for sale is to be found at the **Kamthien Market** in Chiang Mai (169.B9)

The **Sainumphung Orchid & Butterfly Farm** (*H1096 KM1 south turn —
400m Hrs 07:00-17:00 Tel: (0) 5329 7892*), **Mountain Orchid** (*H1096 KM1 south
turn — 400m Hrs 08:00-17:00 Tel: (0) 5329 7343*), **Suan Bua Mae Sa Orchid**
(*H1096 KM4 Hrs 08:00-17:00 Tel: (0) 5329 8564*) and the **Mae Ram Orchid &
Butterfly Farm** (*H1096 KM5 Hrs 07:00-16:00 Tel: (0) 5329 8801*) charge the
same nominal entrance fee (10 Bt.), but to the author's knowledge only the
Sainumphung Orchid and Butterfly Farm cages Thai breeds of cats and dogs.

The Queen Sirikit Botani
Garden

สวนพฤกษศาสตร์สิริกิตดิ์

(*H1096 KM12. Hrs. 08:00-
17:00 Adults 20 Bt. Children
10 Bt. Cars only 20 Bt.
Motorcycles are not allowed
within the gardens. Visitor
centre near entrance gate.
Tel: (0) 5329 8171 <http://
qbg.hypermart.net>*) OCCUPY-
ING 2,600 acres between 600
and 1200m in elevation on
both sides of the Mae Sa
Valley, the botanic garden
was created in 1992 to collec

Farming butterflies

nd conserve rare species of plants. Extensive facilities ave been developed, hough unfortunately this as been at the cost of ormer forest on the site.

These facilities now nclude a glasshouse omplex, a natural science useum and three nature rails on semi-paved /alkways through the iving collections. Trail 1 200m) goes to the Thai Orchid nursery, Trail 2 600m) through the rboretum and Trail 3 800m) through the imbers collection. As yet hese trails do not extend to ie higher levels where the lasshouses and museum are ocated. If you do not have a ar you may have to walk the oncrete lanes to reach them. Iopefully this will change.

AMOENG & BEYOND

ะเมิง

Map 19 p.121) LITTLE MORE ian a village with a market nd district offices, Samoeng s the start of H1269, a leasant rural route down the ha Chang Valley that joins ie Hang Dong Road (H108 M10) south of Chiang Mai. little broader than the Mae a Valley, the Tha Chang alley has also become a ocation for a number of esorts. A return trip via this alley to complete the Samoeng Loop" is a gentle nd pleasant way to see some pland scenery.

While the Mae Sa and Tha hang valleys have been ommercialised, the country eyond Samoeng remains aditional and remote,

Man-made rainforest in the Sirikit Botanic Gardens

perhaps because many of the roads remain unsealed.

Samoeng is the start of a back route to Wat Chan (*92 kms - sealed for 31kms to Ban Mae Yang Ha. The all-weather unsealed road may have heavily rutted and muddy sections during and just after the rainy season. Allow a full day*) and Pai. Like H1095, the main highway to Pai, the route travels through spectacular country, passing Hmong and Karen villages as well as taking a route through upland pine forests near Wat Chan.

The small valleys north of Samoeng have become more accessible due to small hand-painted bilingual signs put up at some intersections. Routes into the hills can be made by turning north either from H1096 at KM4 to pass the That Mok Falls (*9kms. Park fees for Doi Suthep Pui National Park*), or from past KM15 to Ban Nong Hoi (Blue Hmong), or on the small concrete lane at KM16+400m

to Ban Pok, Pong Kwao hot springs (*25kms — a private company has built covered baths. Camping possible. Cold drinks and instant noodles available*) and a through (dirt) route via Ban Mae Loei to Pa Phae on H1095 near KM30(*one rough muddy patch in rainy season — see map p.121*)

WHERE TO EAT & STAY (MAE SA & SAMOENG)

The **Tea for Two Restaurant** (Samoeng Resort) at the end of the loop marks the last outpost of the regular tourist trail. En route the **Pong Yaeng Garden Resort**, the **Kansadan Resort** and the **Yord Doi Resort** all have restaurants with pleasant vistas, but good food in less formal circumstances can also be found at the small restaurants.

Every resort is nice, but for an intimate stay the author's choice remains with the **Pong Yaeng Garden Village** for the sheer beauty of its location, and the **Regent Resort and Spa** for luxury that will please the most sensitive taste. **Mount and Sky**, **Ban Klang Doi Resort** and **The Lanna Resort** all have pleasing locations and make good use of local architectural style. The flower gardens of **Krisda Doi** become very popular in season.

The **Mae Sa Valley Resort** not only has a nice location but also offers day programmes to learn handicrafts, and it is rumoured that visitors can actually pay for the privilege of mucking in on their model farm. The extensive facilities of the **Suan Bua Hotel & Resort** (the resort has a full-service spa) and the **Belle Villa** would seem suitable for company junkets.(*listings p.191-192*)

Nymphaea 'gypsy'

7. North-West to Pai

(Maps 19 &20. H1095 starts from H107 at KM35 in Mae Malai. Chiang Mai-Pai 131kms) THE ROUTE TO PAI begins at the market town of Mae Malai and climbs through increasingly spectacular scenery to a high ridge line (KM60-75), passing Huai Nam Dang National Park, before descending into the valley of the River Pai, a tributary of the Salween. Pai lies is a picturesque part of the valley wide enough to grow rice.

The Hao Valley

(23kms. Left turn from H108 at KM18+300 signed Ban Khwai Thai/Thai Buffalo Training Camp. Joins H1095 near KM10). A SLOWER rural road following the small River Hao and cuts a corner if travelling from H108 to H1095. At least three temples close to this route — Wat Walu Karam, Wat San Pa Yang and Wat Tha Kham — have murals of interest.

Following the signs above, turn west from the Hao Valley route at Wat Prakat Tham (a little north of KM15) for a route to Muang Ga (9kms—unsealed), a Lua village purporting to be either King Viranga's birthplace or a sanctuary when he was fighting Haripunchai. The route climbs a further 9kms through forest to the Phraphutthabat Si Roi — a Buddha foot-print containing the footprints of the three previous Buddha's, symbolising the previous presence of the dhamma.

Villager in the Hao Valley

ACROSS TO PAI (H1095)

(Mae Malai-Pai 95kms) NUMEROUS BENDS on the route west from Mae Malai to Pai make travel slow, but the highway is one of most scenic in the country.

Places to visit off this road include Mok Fa Falls *(KM23 south turn 1.5 kms. 200 Bt Adults/100 Bt. children includes day-ticket to all sites in Doi Suthep-Pui NP)*, a fall that drops into a deep pool a the end of a ravine.

Huai Nam Dang National Park

อุทยานแห่งชาติห้วยน้ำดัง

(Pong Duet Hot Springs and Huai Nam Dang Lookout. Park fees — see p.83 —gives access to all sites in the park on the same day). LOCATED IN a pretty wooded valley, the Pong Duet Hot Springs *(H1095 KM.42 north-east turn — 6kms.)* are not yet over-commercialised. Rock dams form shallow open-air pools cool enough for a hot soak downstream from steamy, bubbling geysers.

The Japanese may have first developed this site when they were building the road to Mae Hong Son during World War II, for its atmosphere is close to that of a small *onsen*. Camping is possible and a walking trail leads north into the hills.

Huai Nam Dang Lookout *(KM65 — 6 kms)* is located on a summit with a beautiful prospect over the upper Mae Taeng Valley towards Doi Luang Chiang Dao. The lookout is famous for its dawn view in the cold season. Dirt roads north of this point continue far through high country, passing Lisu and Haw Chinese villages.

Pai

ปาย

RECORDS show that in the 1870's the hitherto empty or depopulated settlement of Pa was used as a base by a mino Shan sawbwa (chief), who was a source of irritation in Anglo-Siamese relations. Until recent years Pai remained an insignificant town with a Shan and Muslim Haw Chinese population.

Today the town serves numbers of hedonistic travellers (in the peak season more than 40 guest houses are open) drawn to the town by its village atmosphere and cheap, easy living in scenic surroundings. The once relaxed attitude towards drugs that gave the town a reputation amongst back-packers has become a thing

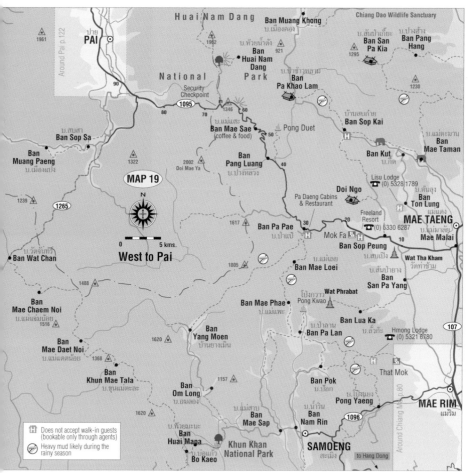

MAP 19

West to Pai

Around Pai p.122

PAI

Huai Nam Dang

Ban Muang Khong

Chiang Dao Wildlife Sanctuary

National   Park

Ban Huai Nam Dang

Ban San Pa Kia

Ban Pang Hang

Security Checkpoint

1095

Ban Pa Khao Lam

Ban Sop Sa

Ban Mae Sae (coffee & food)

Pong Duet

Ban Sop Kai

Ban Muang Paeng

Ban Pang Luang

Ban Kut

Ban Mae Taman

Doi Mae Ya

Doi Ngo

Lisu Lodge (0) 5328 1789

Ban Ton Lung

Pa Daeng Cabins & Restaurant

Freeland Resort (0) 5330 6287

MAE TAENG

Ban Pa Pae

Mok Fa

Mae Malai

Ban Wat Chan

Ban Sop Peung

Wat Tha Kham

Ban Mae Loei

Ban San Pa Yang

Ban Mae Chaem Noi

Ban Mae Phae

Wat Phrabat
Pong Kwao

Ban Lua Ka

Hmong Lodge (0) 5321 6780

Ban Yang Moen

Ban Pa Lan

Ban Mae Daet Noi

That Mok

Ban Khun Mae Tala

Ban Om Long

Ban Pok

Pong Yaeng

MAE RIM

Ban Mae Sap

Ban Nam Rin

1096

SAMOENG

Ban Huai Mapa

Khun Khan National Park

Bo Kaeo

to Hang Dong

Around Chiang Mai p.80

Does not accept walk-in guests (bookable only through agents)

Heavy mud likely during the rainy season

the past since the government's rigorous use of death sentences on drug traffickers.

round Pai

map 20) THE QUIET VALLEY good for walking and xploring by mountain icycle. Dirt roads into e mountains are perfect r motorcycles. Several mpanies run treks into e hills, and highly

Dawn view at Huai Nam Dang

Shan temple near Pai

recommended is the Thai Adventure Rafting's

(*Rungsiyanon Rd. Tel: (0)5369 9111) over-night rafting trip through inaccessible reaches of the Pai River to Mae Hong Son.*

Places to visit include the Mo Paeng Falls (*H1095 KM101 south-west turn — 4 kms. Motorcycles only for last kilometre*), the Mae Yen Falls (*2-3 hours walk from Ban Mae Yen — start early!*) and Tha Pai Hot Springs to the south (*6 kms from Pai town*).

Rafting near Pa

WHERE TO EAT & STAY (PAI)

Pai is the place for home-made bread, herbal massages and reggae. Local restaurants serve food near the new market, and the **Nong Bua Restaurant** has long been reliable. A late night bite at the **Pai Corner Bar** can be enjoyable, but the best recommendation to make for Pai's new-age fare is to follow your instincts.

Inexpensive guest houses are sprouting like mushrooms in former paddy on the east side of the river, as well as in the nearby village of Mae Yen. **Sipsongpanna**, the **Sun Hut**, **PP Orchid** and **River Corner Guest House** are amongst the better guest houses. **Hut Ing Pai** and the **Muang Pai Resort** are the best at the higher end of the market, but **Spa Exotic Home** or **Tha Pai Spa Camping** might appeal to air hot-tubs enthusiasts (non-residents may enjoy these for 50 Baht). (*up-market listings p.192*)

MAP 20

Around Pai

Selected Downtown Guest Houses & Agencies
1 Baan Nam Pai E-m: baannampai@hotmail.com
2 Golden Hut ☎ (0) 5369 9949
3 PP Orchid ☎ (0) 5369 9159
4 River Corner ☎ (0) 5369 9149
① Back Trax (trekking) ☎ (0) 5369 9739
② Elephant Camp Office
③ Northern Green Tours (mountain biking) ☎ (0) 5369 9385
④ Pai Enduro Team (motorcycle trekking) ☎ (0) 5369 9395
⑤ Permchai's Trekking ☎ (0) 5369 8048
⑥ Thai Adventure Rafting ☎ (0) 5369 9111

Pai Town
0   500m

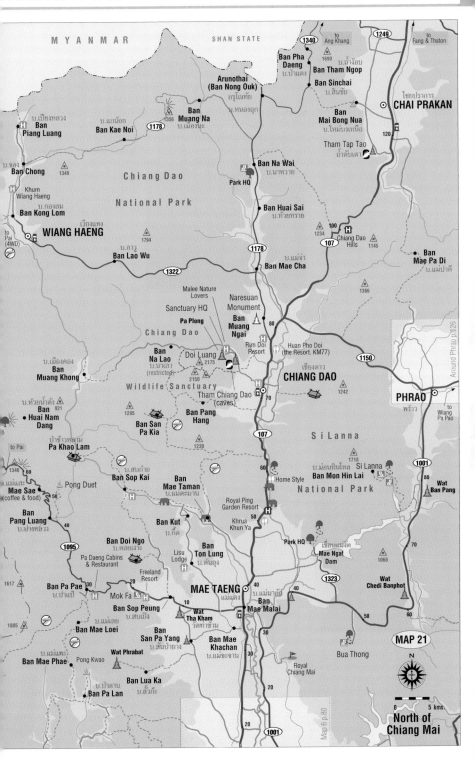

MAP 21

North of
Chiang Mai

0   5 kms

8. North to Chiang Dao, Phrao, Fang & Thaton

(Map 21 p.123 & 22 p.126. Full day. Chiang Dao caves round trip 154 kms.) NORTH OF MAE MALAI, H107 follows the Ping upstream through a gorge before the valley opens out into a rice basin dominated by the spectacular peaks of Doi Luang Chiang Dao (2240m), Thailand's third highest mountain.

Sri Lanna National Park protects the highlands between the River Ping and Mae Ngat, which flows through Phrao. From Chiang Mai, H1001 takes a rural route to the quiet market town of Phrao, which is set amidst an area of traditional wet-rice cultivation. H1150 is an quick link to from Phrao to Chiang Dao *(50 kms)*, thus by staying overnight in the area, it is possible to do an easy but simple loop.

The older of the two Hmong Saelao brothers of Ban Mae Doi Ngo, a village high up on the watershed between the Hao and Mae Taeng rivers, entered the 1999 Guiness book of records as one of the several people claiming to have the longest hair (over 16Ft 10 inches long grown over a period longer than 65 years). Yi Saelao (83 in this picture taken in 2000) survives his brother, who died in 2001.

Preparing paddy (Mae Taeng)

AROUND MAE TAENG

AN UNSEALED ROAD follows the narrow, scenic stretch of the Mae Taeng Valley between Sop Kai and Mae Taman. It can be reached from Sop Peung *(23kms)*, Ban Kut *(H1095 north turn by KM3+700m —18kms)* and Mae Taman *(from H107)*. The road to Sop Kai from Sop Peung *(H1095 KM12+400 north turn unsealed)* climbs to a pass *(10kms)*. Take either of the roads left at this pass to reach Hmong villages higher up on the ridges. The main road later becomes unsealed — turn right at junction on a long down grade *(18kms)* and then sharp right again off the concrete lane at the bottom of the steep incline in Ban Kai Noi *(18Kms+700m)*. The unsealed road will take you to Ban Sop Kai *(4kms)*, a Northern Thai village which can serve as a trekking base.

Upstream from Sop Kai a rough dirt track passes Akha

and Lahu villages on a route to the Karen village of Pa Khao Lam *(17kms. Trail bike or 4WD only!)*.

Downstream the road goes to a bridge at Ban Kut and onwards to Ban Mae Taman, *(H107 KM.43 east turn — 10 kms.)*, where three elephant camps stage shows and offer rides on elephants to hill tribe villages. Day programmes include lunch, rides on ox-carts, and a final bamboo rafting trip down the Mae Taeng.*(Programmes allow time for transfer from Chiang Mai, and finish around 15:00 hrs. Prices below do not include transfer).*

Mae Taman Rafting and Elephant Camp *(under the same ownership as the Mae Sa Elephant Camp. Tel (0) 5329 7060. Show 09:30hrs. 1500 Bt. full programme)*, the largest of the camps, has set up their own hill-tribe villages inhabited by salaried Lahu Shi Ba Lan and Palaung villagers.

Mae Taeng Elephant Park *(Tel: (0)*

320 6047. Show 10:00 hrs. Full
rogram 1250 Bt.) and the smallest
amp, **Jungle Raft** (Tel: (0) 5320 4301.
how 09:00 hrs. Full program 900 Bt.)
rganise elephant rides to a Lisu
illage.

Mae Taeng Tour (through agents
nly) operates a smaller camp in a
retty location 8kms up the Mae Taeng
alley.

The Elephant Nature Park (Mae
aman. Contact through Gem Travel only.
el: (0) 5327 2855.<www.thaifocus.com>
-3 day programmes 1500-3500 Bht.)
nvites visitors to a hands-on
xperience taking care of elephants and
aying at the site with mahouts. Shows
re not put on for visitors.

Thai Adventure Co (Contact
ravel. Tel: (0) 5327 7178) runs
rofessional rubber rafting trips down
he gorge and is best for a rafting day-
ip from Chiang Mai. 500 Bht/head.

Downstream near the
onfluence with the Ping,
Vat Tung Luang (H107 KM42
est turn through ornamental
ate—2.5kms) honours Khru
a Thammachai, who died in
988 aged 73, and whose
ax effigy and preserved
ody are kept in the main
harn. Donor's names and
mounts given are clearly
nown on the ornate
ecorations on the temple
uildings.

ri Lanna National Park

อุทยานแห่งชาติศรีลานนา

H107 KM41 east turn —12
ms. 200 Bt. adults/100 Bt.
hildren. Overnight stays on
fts on the Mae Ngat
eservoir. The Park HQ is
cated near the north end of
ae Ngat Dam. Nature trail
rochures available in Thai)
REATED IN 1989, Sri Lanna
ational Park covers 1,406
m² to include most of the
ighlands surrounding the

upper valley of the Mae
Ngat River around Phrao.

The park is best known
for the rafts some 8kms up
the reservoir from the Mae
Ngat Dam (listing p.193),
but it also includes the
popular local picnic spot
near the small Bua Thong
Falls and Seven Colours
Spring (H1001 to Phrao
KM.48 south turn —3kms).
Visitors may be able to
enjoy other less well-
known natural features in
this park in virtual
solitude.

The park has three nature
trails, though their state of
upkeep is uncertain. The
Huai Mae Wa Trail (3kms —
get information from park HQ)
is located near the Park HQ
by the Mae Ngat Dam, and
the Mon Hin Lai Trail (1km.
West turn from H1001 to
Phrao KM80. Continue
straight where sealed road
turns sharply left. The track
turns right by a reservoir
before going steeply uphill
through evergreen forest. The
Nature Trail — if you can
make it out— begins by a sign
near KM13 by your odometer.
Continue up to road to the
village from where a view over

*Chedi Banphot & flowering teak trees
(H1001 KM64)*

the valley and the top of the
falls may be enjoyed at the end
of the orchard and pasture in
front of the village.) visits the
waterfall of the same name.
The most accessible trail is
the Huai Kum Trail (3 kms —
cross suspension bridge near
KM60 on H107).

Other strictly local
attractions include the Huai
Pa Phlu falls, a seven level
series of cascades which may
only be reached on foot (to
the north of Phrao), and the
Pha Daeng Caves (H1150
KM10+700m approx. north
turn on unsealed road—
12kms).

Upland orchards (Mae Taeng).

NORTH TO PHRAO (H1001)

(Maps 21 and 22. H1001—93kms. from Chiang Mai or 30 kms on H1055 from its junction with H107 at

Thalaeo in rice-field (Phrao)

KM83 north of Chiang Dao.) Places to visit on H1001 to Phrao include those in the Sri Lanna National Park (*see above*), as well as Wat Mae Pang (H1001 KM76). Founded by Luang Phu Suchindo (who died in 1985 aged 98), the temple has modern architecture which breaks with tradition. The abbot became famous after pilots during the Vietnam war reported seeing a monk flying in the clouds.

Phrao

พร้าว

EARTHEN WALLS enclosing an oval shaped settlement around Wat Phra Chao Lan Thong are a sign of early inhabita-

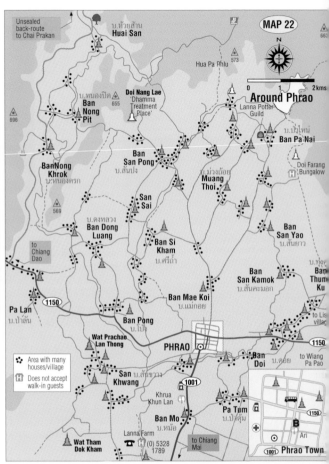

(Right) Bullock cart in Phrao in mid 90's — a sight now rarely seen in Northern Thailand. (Below) A Phrao mother and her 14 year-old daughter.

tion in this valley. In the troubled 18th century, the remoteness of this *wiang* made it a refuge; indeed its remoteness and absence of major attractions has preserved its ambience. As a

Mae Chi Saengtham Suttawan (Wat Tham Dok Kham, Phrao)

esult the quiet rural
ountryside is pleasant,
hough not spectacular.

While the town in the old
quare *wiang* has developed
s a small market centre, the
urrounding area is a
astiche of villages and
emples amongst paddy
elds. The narrow concrete
anes linking the villages
ake for leisurely explora-
on by bicycle. The irrigation
ystem linking the paddy fields
a good example of *fai
uang*, the northern Thai
ethod of water sharing that
onds people in the commu-
ity. Some villages also share
emples, which may be seen
etween villages in groves
urrounded by paddy.

Temples of interest include
e small cave temple of Wat
ham Dok Kham, Wat Phra
hao Lan Thong (the viharn
ontains a large Lanna
uddha image cast in 1527,
ut it is usually kept locked),
d the 'dhamma treatment
ace' at Doi Nang Lae of Phra
ikhon Thammawathee, a
ealthy cult figure who
ecame embroiled in a sex
andal and had to disrobe.

View north towards Chiang Dao

NORTH TO CHIANG DAO (H107)

เชียงดาว

H107 FOLLOWS THE RIVER PING
as it flows through a gorge
south of Chiang Dao. Two
elephant camps are located
along the route as well as the
Huai Kum Nature Trail.

Mae Ping Elephant Village (H107
KM53. Tel: (0) 5396 0532 Show 08:30
& 10:00 60 Bt. Rides 07:30-11:30. 60
mins. includes visit to Lisu village 600
Bt/head) is the newest camp on the
Ping.

**Tang Dao Elephant Training
Centre**, which originally began as a
logging camp, was amongst the first
camp to serve tourists in Chiang Mai
(Tel: (0) 5329 8553. H107 KM56
Shows 09:00 & 10:00. Bt 60. Rides
08:00-11:00. 60 mins. 500 Bt/head.
Rides 90 mins. includes visit to Lisu
Village 600 Bt. /head). The camp has a
very pretty location on the River
Ping.

Dominated by the massif of
Doi Luang, the picturesque
part of the Ping Valley near
Chiang Dao was a place to
which people were banished
if they were branded as
witches in the 19th century.
The small market town
serves Akha, Hmong, Lisu
and Palaung villagers living
in the uplands nearby.

Chiang Dao Caves and Muang Khong

ถ้ำเชียงดาว

FROM NEAR THE MARKET
(KM72 west turn 5 kms &
7kms) a sealed lane leads to
Chiang Dao Caves. Guides
with lanterns will take you

Mae Thorani — the goddess of the earth — wrings the cool waters of detachment out of her hair, dousing the fires of temptation sent by Mara as she bears witness to the Buddha's worthiness as he meditated under the bo tree (Wat Tham Chiang Dao. Also see p.87).

deep into the caves, which
are extensive and generally
easy, but in one or two places
you must crouch.

The road past the caves

A limestone outpost of the upper Tennasserim range, the Chiang Dao massif offers a unique habitat for different species of flowering plants. It remains a prime site for bird-watching, especially near the ranger station at the western end, where rare species are known to make their habitat. Unfortunately hunting has virtually eliminated many other forms of wildlife despite the mountain's classification as a wildlife sanctuary since 1978. The situation is aggravated by the local villagers' somewhat equivocal attitudes towards extinction of species in the area.

The U-shaped massif itself is formed by a line of peaks, the highest of which is Doi Luang (2240m). These peaks enclose a high valley which opens to the west (photo facing page). Using soils that produced the best opium of the north, years of cultivation by the Hmong and Lisu has reduced most of this once forested valley to grassy swards that are regularly burned off in the dry season. As a result, in the seven year interval between the author's last two visits, the valley has got noticeably drier. Though opium cultivation has virtually ceased, the fire-prone valley appears to have little chance of recovery.

To climb the mountain you must get permission from the sanctuary headquarters near Wat Pa Bong, and it would be wise to get advice if not a guide through Malee Nature Lovers Resort. A fit hiker can reach the summit in 5-6 hours by any route, but you have to have transport to reach the paths that approach from the west. Very fit hikers could make the summit and back in a day by climbing the front route (the author took 5 hours to ascend by this route once), but you must carry your own water for the mountain is bone dry. You must also bring out everything you take in (a lesson sadly lost on many visitors). Campfires are theoretically banned on the summit due to the scarcity of firewood and distubance to the biomass.

If climbing into this beautiful place, please respect it.

(Main Picture) A view from the trail that follows the valley up to the summit of Doi Luang Chiang from the west. The summit of Doi Luang is particularly interesting for the flowers found there. (Photo left) A crevice plant on the summit of Doi Luang (Sendum Sarmentosum Bunge.Crassulasceae)

rminates at Wat Pa Plong
.5 kms. *Chiang Dao Wildlife*
nctuary HQ is located to the
ght just before the temple),
 active meditation centre.

rmer in Chiang Dao Valley

A concrete lane continues
 a quite spectacular route
 Muang Khong, a small
lated *muang on the River*
ae Taeng (Lane starts at a
rth turn approx 850m before
at Pa Pong— sealed 28kms.
uang Khong 35kms. Onward
eep and rough tracks suitable
ly for trail/ mountain bikes go
 Huai Nam Dang 26kms and
iang Haeng 25kms. Taking a
ide is recommended).

WHERE TO EAT AND STAY (MAE TAENG, CHIANG DAO & PHRAO)

The **Freeland Resort** (H1095
KM17) is comfortable and
conveniently located for
mountain bikers, and guest
houses are found in Sop Kai.
If open, the **Khrua Khun Ya
Restaurant** (H107 KM50) is
in pleasant surroundings and
the **Royal Ping Garden
Resort** (H107 KM52) is a
large resort aiming at the
upper end of the market.

Chiang Dao town has a
wooden hotel with a
restaurant serving local food,
and street stalls at night offer
warm fare to cold riders. The
Chiang Dao Inn Hotel hotel
provides mid-market comfort,
and the **Khrua Chiang Dao** opposite is
the best restaurant in town. Those
wanting something different, however,
might try **Malee's Nature Lovers
Resort**, which is in a fine location near
the mountain.

To the north the inexpensive **Rim
Doi Resort** (H1178 KM1) has a lively
coffee-shop at night that makes the
pretty mid-market **Chiang Dao Hills
Resort** (H107 KM100) look staid by
comparison.

Rafts on the lake formed by the
Mae Ngat Dam are operated by
**Rimtarn Floating Bed/Breakfast &
Restaurant** and other local operators.
To reach the boat landing you must
make your way through irrigation
department property to the northern

Legends surround Chiang Dao Mountain.
Its name translates as 'city of stars', and
the mountain is one of the main centres of
the spirit world in Northern Thailand. The
most famous legend concerning a spirit is
that of Chao Luang Kham Daeng, a 'Chao'
of Phayao.

It was after a successful campaing
defending his kingdom aginst Chinese
invaders that he was out hunting. Near
Chiang Dao he came across a golden deer,
which was a spirit who could manifest as a
beautiful woman. This spirit lured Kham
Daeng into Chiang Dao cave and he was
never to return (a statue of Chao Laung
Kham Daeng is located in a 'sala' not far
from the cave entrance).

The area is noted for its spiritual
vibration, and several Buddhist centres for
meditation and spiritual retreat utilise the
caves of the area (Photo: Images near the
ntrance to Tham Chiang Dao).

end of the L shaped-dam.

In Phrao things are pretty local,
but good food can be enjoyed at
Khrua Lan Khun 2 (H107 KM91west
side) and the local **Ari Phochana** (by
the market in town). The **Ban Doi
Farang** resort is the only place to stay
worthy of mention apart from a
pleasant local guest house whose
owner is sensitive about who stays
there (contact only through Duang
Dee Guest House in Chiang Mai).

Fires burn all over the mountains every hot season (Late
Feb-May), periodically blanketing the entire north in
haze. Set by locals, who burn off ground for cultivation
or for increased yields of forest products such as
mushrooms, the fires degrade forests by destroying
saplings. Effective measures to replant (see p.96) and
truly protect forests in the north are urgently required
to ensure future water security for much of the Kingdom,
(Photo: Fire on the mountain: Doi Luang Chiang Dao).

Sam Phi Nong from Doi Luang Chiang Dao

NORTH TO THATON (H107)

Wiang Haeng & Arunothai
เวียงแหง, อรุโณทัย

H1178 AND H1322 form a scenic high country loop (156 kms via Piang Luang from H107 KM78 to H1178 KM31. Fuel at Wiang Haeng) Via Wiang Haeng, a place with little more than district offices. More interesting is Piang Luang, a small town with a mixed ethnic population.

H1178 (79 kms to Ang Khang from H107KM78) passes the Si Sangwan Falls, a series of small cascades by the HQ of the recently created Chiang Dao National Park. From Arunothai (Nong Ouk) H1340 takes a pretty route to Ang Khang, passing General Li Mi's former Kuomintang 3rd army stronghold at Tham Ngop en route. (Expect checkpoints on all border routes!)

Doi Ang Khang
ดอยอ่างขาง

(H017 KM128 west turn onto H1249 —26kms, or via Arunothai) THE ROAD TO ANG KHANG climbs steeply to a high valley (1000m +) which enjoys cool temperatures year round. A Royal Project was set up in 1969 to experiment in temperate cash crop cult-ivation, and the place became popular as a hill station. Nature trails lead to views over the spectacular country-side, and the local Lahu (Khob Dong) and Palaung (No Lae) villagers have been encouraged to continue wearing traditional dress.

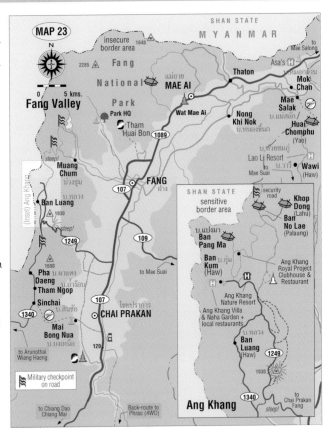

Fang & Thaton
ฝาง, ท่าตอน

AT THE SOUTHERN END of the valley, a side road leads to the Tap Tao Caves (H107 KM118 west turn —3kms). A path into the northern cave leads several hundred metres to a cavern in which primitve Buddha images are formed from stalagmites. To reach them, you must crawl through a chute, brave humidity and put

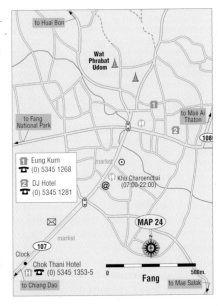

Bordering on Instability

The territory in Chiang Mai Province contiguous with Myanmar's Shan State is populated by Northern Thai, Shan, Akha and Lahu peoples. Most noticeable, however, are the Chinese, who predominate in places such as Piang Luang and Muang Na.

Chinese migrations to Chiang Mai began in the early 20th century with 'overseas' Chinese migrating north from the central plains and mainly Muslim Haw ('overland') Chinese moving south from Yunnan as local traders.

The communist victory in China in 1949 contributed to migrations of rural Yunnanese, but many Yunnanese Chinese including remnants of the Kuomintang armies fled to Burma from China.

Aided by the CIA, who supplied both the Kuomintang and the Thai military in the gathering fight against communism, the Kuomintang increased opium production by more than tenfold in the Shan States of Burma (local opium production had developed as a result of British policy in the first place), creating what became known as the 'Golden Triangle'.

In 1961 the Burmese and Chinese cooperated militarily and drove the Kuomintang out from Burma. Remnants of the 3rd and 5th armies established bases at Tham Ngop (Chiang Mai Province) and Mae Salong (Chiang Rai Province), where in line with American and Thai policy, they continued to protect Thailand against communism while funding themselves from the opium trade. Haw traders bought opium from the hill tribe farmers and collected it for the Kuomintang who dominated the trade in the hills through their military control of the caravan routes. The opium was refined and sold on as heroin through Chinese syndicates with the knowledge if not complicty of the CIA *(see: "The Politics of Heroin in Southeast Asia" by Alfred McCoy.)*

The Yunnanese who had first gone to Burma after 1949 were also to come to Thailand when discrimination against foreign business interests began in Burma after the military coup in 1962. Many were to settle in Chiang Mai

Province and, through their contacts in Burma, help develop a lucrative cross-border trade.

When the threat of communism dimished in the 1980's, American and Thai support for the Kuomintang evaporated and they were obliged to concentrate on farming and legitimate business. Today, the Chinese in the area produce tea, lychees, oranges and other cash crops, but they also continue to participate in cross-border trade.

Across the border, meanwhile, local Sino-Shan warlords took over from the Kuomintang,

In his travels in the Shan States in the 1890's, Sir George Scott noted that the Panthays (Haw) had better rifles than those of many British troops. It was the ability to provide well-armed transport suited to the terrain that allowed the Haw Chinese to dominate overland trade to the north. (Photo: a pack-mule with a saddle typical of Haw trading caravans)

and their fortunes were to rise and fall as circumstances changed. Currently the border area of Shan State is under the control of the former Burmese Communist Party, now referred to as the *wa daeng* (Red Wa) who, with the connivance if not support of certain Chinese and Burmese authorities, have been financing their operations in the time-honoured tradition, not just producing opiates, but amphetamine as well.

The flood of amphetamine into the Thai market and general deterioration of relations lead to hostilities and the temporary closure of all border crossings into Burma for several weeks in 2001. In Thailand penalties for drug traffiking were stiffened, and fire-fights between smugglers and Thai border forces became more frequent as patrols were stepped up.

After high level visits between Thai and Burmese authorities, the relationship was stabilised, the border was reopened and things seemingly returned to the *status quo ante* for a time. However, instability continues and the area beyond the border remains a centre of drug production. Thai authorities continue efforts to stem the flow of drugs into the country and checks on vehicles on highways linking border areas are frequent.

---

up with harmless beasties such as wood-lice and cave pythons.

From the caves, a network of lanes continues north through Chinese and northern Thai villages. Extensive lychee groves are found amongst the

orchards nestling on the side valley west of Fang.

Fang itself has a history dating back to at least 1268, when King Margrai made it is capital, and the town has some interesting back streets.

Most visitors prefer to stay at Thaton, a stop-off point fo tourists travelling north or down the Mae Kok River to Chiang Rai. Wat Thaton overlooking the town is worth exploring for its

nusual structures and the
ews over the valley.

H1089 continues north of
haton passing the wealthy
su village of Lao Ta (KM38
est turn 1km) and the
alika hot springs (KM40)
route to Mae Salong in
hiang Rai Province. A side
rn (KM34 straight ahead at
arp north turn of highway)
ads to the Shan village of
n Mok Cham and then
ross a bridge to Mae Salak,
om where a dirt route
imbs up to the tea growing
ea around Wawi.

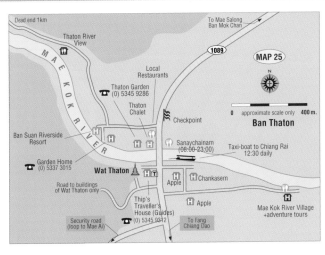

ae Fang National Park
ทยานแห่งชาติแม่ฝาง

OVERING 524 km², the park
corporates Doi Phahom
ok (2285m), Thailand's
cond highest mountain.
he park HQ (H107 Fang
ypass KM2.5 west turn and
rk right after 100m —8kms.
l: (0) 5345 1441 ext 302.
ark fees p.83) is by some hot
prings, the ambience of
hich have been compro-
ised by a small geothermal
ower station.

The park can organise
uided treks to the summit of
oi Pahom Pok. A dirt road
ads close to the summit

passing a Lahu village and a
side turn to Huai Bon Cave
(H107 KM6 left turn 6kms.
*You will need a torch for the
cave and are supposed to get
permission to go up the
mountain on a road that leads
past the turn off to the cave.)*

A security road (omitted
from maps) that follows the
Burmese border is in plain
view from the summit . A
narrow sealed lane 52kms
long, it passes only
occasional border guard
camps on a spectacular but
insecure route. If you are not
stopped before entering, you
go in at your own risk.

WHERE TO EAT AND
STAY (FANG & THATON)

(Listings p.192) Between Wiang
Haeng and Piang Luang, the **Kum
Wiang Haeng** has a couple of
bungalows that may be rented, and in
Piang Luang, a functional guest
house offers rooms in single-floor
row. Otherwise there is all regular
accommodation until Ang Khang,
where two small resort offer average
quality huts at relatively high prices.
The much more luxurious **Angkhang
Nature Resort** is the place to stay if
spending a night on the mountain.

There is nothing luxurious in
Fang, but good food may be enjoyed
at the **Khu Charoenchai Restaurant**
and the **UK (Eung Kum) Hotel** has
the best local ambience for an
overnight stay.

In Thaton the (Comfort) **Thaton
River View Hotel** has a good
restaurant and the most comfortable
bungalows along the banks of the
river in Thaton. Both **Ban Suan River
Side** and the **Garden Home** also
enjoy pleasant riverside ambience.
The **Mae Kok River Village** offers a
wide range of comfortable family
bungalows which are ideal if
planning to enjoy the range of soft
adventure activities the resort offers,
see <www.trackofthetiger.com>

'**Asa's House**' (Tel: (0) 1961 0268),
a Lisu run guest house in Lao Ta
village, organises local treks, and
there is a local hotel in Wawi on the
upland route to Mae Suai.

View south from Ang Khang

THE MOUNTAIN PEOPLES

THE MOUNTAINS were once the preserve of aboriginals and were avoided by the lowland farmers. With the arrival of logging interests and the so-called 'hill tribes', people penetrated into the high hills in a process that has resulted in dirt roads now reaching most of the remote places in the Kingdom. Many villages are not populated by 'hill tribes', however, for many upland villages are occupied by Shan and *khon muang* escaping the pressures of lowland development.

The Hill Tribes

SIX MAJOR AND SEVERAL MINOR HILL TRIBES are found in Northern Thailand. Each tribe is divided into clans or sub-groups, which have distinct customs, rituals and clothing.

The Lahu, Akha and Lisu have languages with common linguistic roots (Yi/Lolo of the Tibeto-Burman family of languages) and migrated into Thailand from Yunnan via Burma. The Hmong and Mien (or Yao) speak languages from the Sino-Tibetan family and came from south central China via Laos. These five tribes are all found in larger numbers beyond the borders of Thailand. The majority of the largest 'hill tribe' found in Thailand — the Karen —

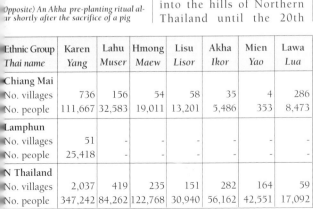

A Hmong farmer with home-made basket in fields above Ban Mae Sa Mai

(Opposite) An Akha pre-planting ritual altar shortly after the sacrifice of a pig

similarly live beyond Thailand's borders in Myanmar, but their origin is a mystery.

With the exception of the Karen, the hill tribes did not start migrating in numbers into the hills of Northern Thailand until the 20th century. The largest migrations only came after the political upheavals triggered by the communist and socialist revolutions of China (1949), Burma (1962) and Laos (1974).

Until the late 1950's the hill tribes were left to practice subsistence agriculture relatively undisturbed in the remote uplands. Then their increasing numbers, their poverty and the threat of insurgency encouraged the government to exert greater control. The National Committee for the Hill Tribes was formed in 1959 to "integrate the hill people into Thai society, while allowing them to preserve their culture",

Ethnic Group Thai name	Karen Yang	Lahu Muser	Hmong Maew	Lisu Lisor	Akha Ikor	Mien Yao	Lawa Lua
Chiang Mai							
No. villages	736	156	54	58	35	4	286
No. people	111,667	32,583	19,011	13,201	5,486	353	8,473
Lamphun							
No. villages	51	-	-	-	-	-	-
No. people	25,418	-	-	-	-	-	-
N Thailand							
No. villages	2,037	419	235	151	282	164	59
No. people	347,242	84,262	122,768	30,940	56,162	42,551	17,092

Hill Tribe Population 1998 (Tribal Research Institute, Chiang Mai University)

Lawa/Karen grandmother and children.)

Subsistence Agriculture in the Hills

By tradition the hill tribes believed in a world of spirits. Using a shifting (swidden) system of cultivation by moving the village when the land became exhausted after a few years, the hill tribes produced enough to survive, to propitiate the spirits and to feast for prestige.

Depending on mountain rice, corn (maize), opium, vegetables, pigs and chicken and whatever they could hunt, they produced most of what they needed themselves. They worked hard enough to have a surplus to barter for things they could not produce, such as sulphur for gun-powder, metal for tools, and needles .

Women made clothing, while men produced tools. Each village also had special artisans such as blacksmiths and silversmiths, who enjoyed special respect. To get supplies people would travel to lowland markets, or trade with itinerant Haw merchants.

Akha-Lahu blacksmith near Thaton

and the government began an extensive primary school programme in upland areas. However, the slash and burn techniques of shifting cultivation used by the hill tribes to grow food crops and opium poppies increasingly conflicted with national efforts to preserve watersheds against deforestation and to curb drug production.

To address these problems, H.M.King Bhumiphol initiated royal projects and both government and international aid development began promoting cash crops such as coffee, red kidney beans, potatoes and cabbages. These programmes were very successful in bringing hill tribe villages into the cash economy and in reducing opium production.

The success led to the loss of the subsistence agriculture as a way of life, however. The tribes had to abandon shifting cultivation in favour of rotational cropping and permanent field systems. In addition they have often had to relocate from preferred habitats in high areas near primary watersheds.

Increased contact with the

Karen village west of Chiang Da

(Left) Akha and Lisu children learning Thai at a Hilltribe Welfare Division Day-Care Centre. Large villages on main dirt roads usually have a primay school, but children in smaller, more remote villages may still have to board at distant schools to get an education

lowland culture and with missionaries has also led to partial abandonment of customs based on beliefs in the spirit world and annual farming cyles.

Despite obstacles such as difficulty getting identification papers, different groups have adapted with different degrees of success. The Karen, who traditionally inhabit the lower areas, have been integrating for centuries and many are now like northern Thais. The Hmong, Lisu and Yao, who usually occupy the highest areas on mountains (but who may have been lowland peoples in the very distant past) have shown skill in making money while keeping their traditions. The Akha and Lahu have also had some success, but as with all hill peoples, this has varied according to community.

Karen men keeping warm in the early morning

KAREN

THE KAREN began to move into Thailand around the 17th century and are found in large numbers in the western part of Northern Thailand, particularly to the west and south of Doi Inthanon. The main groups in Thailand are White Karen composed of the Skaw and the Pwo sub groups.

The Karen live in villages of around 25 raised houses, with villages tending to cluster in areas usually below 800m in elevation. Each household consists of the parents and unmarried children. Married daughters and their families may also live in the same house. The highest authority is the village priest who runs the village along with the elders.

The Karen have rituals to live harmoniously with the 'Lord of the Land and Water', as well as with nature spirits in the rocks, trees, water and mountains that surround them. They also have guardian spirits and believe in the soul.

Their desire for harmony with nature may account for their practicing ecologically sound systems of swidden agriculture, using long-term rotation over large areas of land. They do not cut all the large trees down when they clear a plot. They are also the only group to have built terraces to grow wet-rice in Thailand.

Karen cloth is hand-woven on back-strap looms and is predominantly red with white, blue or brown vertical stripes. Stitching is clear and decorative. The men may wear

Job's seeds in Karen needlework

simple forms of this material in a sleeveless tunic, while the women wear more elaborate styles on their sarongs. The women's blouses are made of dark homespun cotton with

Karen family

traditional kitchen (Karen)

Lahu Shehleh girl at New Year Festival

horizontal embroidered patterns decorated with seeds woven onto the lower half. Unmarried girls of the Skaw group wear plain white shifts. Those of the Pwo are more decorated. The Karen are famous for their use of beads for ornamentation.

THE LAHU

THE LAHU are divided into two groups; the Black Lahu form over 75 percent of the Lahu and consists of three subgroups — the Lahu Na, the Red Lahu and Shehleh Lahu. A second group is

known as the Yellow Lahu. The Thai call the Lahu *muser* because of their skills at hunting in the forest. The Lahu are concentrated close to the Burmese border west and north of Chiang Dao and Pai.

Houses are generally built on stilts, with villages consisting of 15-30 households. Households consist of families with unmarried children and maybe a married daughter and family. The Lahu believe in the soul, a house spirit, nature spirits and a supreme being who is administered to by a priest.

Silver rupees (Red Lahu belt)

Traditional clothing of the Lahu is black with bold embroidered patterns and bands of cloth for decoration. The trims of sleeves, pockets and lapels are often decorated, with each subgroup using different colours.

Lahu man prepares roofing

HMONG

THERE ARE two subgroups of Hmong in Thailand; the Blue Hmong and White Hmong. Blue Hmong villages are located on high mountain areas north from Doi Inthanon to the Burmese border. They are the closest group to Chiang Mai, with villages in the Doi Suthep-Pu National Park area.

Hmong houses are built on the ground in clusters, with several clusters forming a village. The oldest male controls the extended family household

(Right. The Blue Hmong women wear skirts (girl on the right) and the White Hmong wear pantaloons (New Year).

(Left) Working with a hand stained by dye, a Blue Hmong woman takes wax for batik from a pot on the fire (Ban Buak Chan)

hat will include married sons nd their families. The Hmong re divided into clans, which lay an important part in rituals nd relationships.

The Hmong believe in a umber of household pirits as well as souls. ituals are per- ormed by household eads, but each illage will also ave a shaman to xorcise evil spirits nd restore health to he sick.

The pleated skirts of lue Hmong women are 1ade of hemp died vith blue and white atik patterns. The omen's jackets re made of black loth decorated

A Hmong dancing and playing qeej. At funerals, Hmong shaman play qeej all night to guide the souls of the deceased.

vith elaborate embroidery for vhich the Hmong women are enowned. Men's clothes are lso made of loose-fitting lack material, with embroi- ery on the jackets. The Imong use silver both for dornment and as a show of vealth.

LISU

HE LISU originated from unnan and are divided into ix original patrilineal clans, ut not all are found in Thailand. Lisu villages can be ound near Chiang Dao, Pai nd Phrao.

Villages vary in size, and ouses may be raised on stilts r built on the ground. xtended families with 1arried sons may live in the ame house. The Lisu are ompetitive and thus are utgoing, social and hard- vorking.

Lisu villages have a shrine for a guardian spirit set above the village. There are spirits for the ancestors and several other entities such as water, trees, the sun and the moon. Priests will officiate at ceremo- nies involving the village guardian, while shamans dispel spirits causing sickness. Lisu costumes of the 'flowery' sub-group found mainly in Thailand are very distinct. T h e women wear a knee length tunic of light blue or green cloth, often with red sleeves. The upper sleeves of the women's tunic and a yoke of black cloth are heavily decorated with many bands of bright cloth. The women also wear plain belts from which hang multi-coloured tassels. Young men's trousers are made of the same blue or green cloth, while their jackets are often of plain black material.

AKHA

THE AKHA originally came from Yunnan, moving into Burma in the mid-19th century. They did not come

Lahu who migrated from the troubles in Shan State (just be- yond the ridge-line in photo) live next to the Lisu of Lao Ta (middle of photo), who give them work.

Lisu villagers reading portents from a pig's liver at a funeral after a 'bad death'

to Thailand until early in the 20th century, but the large migrations due to persecu- tion and instability in Burma have only been quite recent. Akha villages can be found near the Burmese border in the northern part of Chiang Mai province, but mainly in Chiang Rai province.

Villages vary in size and have elaborate gates with carved wooden fertility figures nearby, demarcating the realm between humans and good spirits and that of the jungle spirits. Ancestral spirits are paramount and are

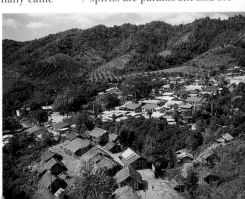

Ulo Akha House

worshipped at an altar in the house.

The Akha have a special 'way' which covers all aspects of their daily and ritual life. The "Akha Way" helps the tribe to maintain continuity and is administered by the village priest, who has more power than the elders and village head.

Lomi Akha Woman in the border area

Akha clothing is made of a homespun cotton cloth died to near black with indigo. For women this cloth is embellished with embroidery and strips of coloured cloth decorated with coins, seeds, or what-ever might catch the fancy. Women's outfits consist

of hip length jackets worn over a halter, a short skirt, a sash, and leggings.

The most distinct item for women is the headdress, which gets more elaborate as the wearer matures. Men tend to wear loose jackets that may have an embroidered strip down the front and back.

MIEN

THE MIEN are commonly referred to as the Yao in Thailand. They originated from China, but much of Thailand's small population settled in the eastern part of Northern Thailand after migrating from Laos during the Vietnam conflict. Mien villages in Chiang Mai province are found off Highway 118 near Pong Nam Ron and north east of Thaton, but the majority are found in to the east in Chiang Rai and Nan provinces.

Villages are small with up to 25 houses built on the ground. The Mien are divided into 12 clans, with more than one clan living in a village. Households can be very large, consisting of extended families that include married sons and their families.

The Mien have rituals that must be performed correctly for a hierarchy of ancestral spirits. This system appears to have been influenced by Taoist

beliefs that originated in Chir in the 13-14th century. Pries will attend to the Taoist ritu als, while shamans will cu the sick afflicted by lesse natural spirits.

A carved figure outside an Akha village gate keeping away bad spirits

Mien women are unmistakeable for they wear a long black tunic with a bright red ruff around their neckline. Black trousers beneath the tunic are heavily embroidered. In addition they wear a black turban cloth embroidered at the ends. Men wear loose black jackets which tend to be only lightly decorated and loose fitting black trousers.

Yao bridesmaid

ao men enjoying a morning smoke. ulturally the Yao are very close to the hinese

HE LUA AND PALAUNG

HE LUA have been in Chiang Iai the longest of all hill eoples. They are thought to ave originated from the awa who were pushed into

awa woman at a festival in Mae Chaem

le hills by the Mon from aripunchai and the Tai.

The Lua accept alien ways irly easily and over the years iany have integrated and be-ome like the Northern Thai. Iowever a group of Lua have iaintained a distinct identity, specially in upland villages. hey are found in the areas round Bo Luang (H108) and uth towards Om Koi.

They practice swidden agriculture as well as wet-rice cultivation and favour villages on the crests of hills. They believe in good and bad spirits and profess a belief in Buddhism. The women may wear costumes that have blue tunics and skirts to below the knees as well as a turban, but the men dress ordinarily.

The Palaung are the newest hill tribe to arrive in Chiang Mai. Like the Lua they may have originally been a lowland peoples. Both Lua and Palaung speak a language related to the Mon-Khmer family of languages. The Palaung have been living in the Shan State of Burma for several centuries but have only started moving into Thailand since 1984 to escape from the fighting in their homeland. They number more than 2000 and live in six villages in the Doi Ang Khang and Chiang Dao areas.

The Palaung are noted for their skill in raising crops. They are strict Buddhists who also believe in nature and animal spirits. Their villages must have a Buddhist temple or shrine as well as a shrine for propitiating the spirits. Living in raised houses, families are extended

Palaung gathering corn for pig feed

with married sons usually living with the parents. Villages have headmen, who usually come from the largest families, as well as monks and shaman for curing sickness.

Only Palaung women wear costume. They wear a short bright (often blue) long sleeved jacket with decorated trim and a red tube skirt with narrow horizontal white stripes. The women also wear large belts made of rattan coils which protect them and let them go to heaven when they die. Both women and men like to have silver and gold in their teeth.

Most hill peoples build temporary field shelters in which they may live during critical parts of the crop cycle (Hmong)

Papaver Somniferum

Opium originated in the Mediterranean region and was first brought to the east by Arab traders around the seventh century AD. It came to Thailand when hill tribes migrated

The poppy head is mature when the petals fall off.

south from Yunnan, where opium growing had been encouraged to stop British control of the trade in the 19th century.

Though opium consumption in Siam from the late 19th century was controlled by a royal monopoly and was a useful source of income, it was never approved of. In 1959 poppy cultivation and all other narcotics were made illegal, but by 1967 Thailand was still producing 145 tons due to the corrupting influence of the Vietnam War.

Intensified Western efforts to stop the drug epidemic resulted in a cash crop substitution

program that was so successful that by 199 annual opium production in Thailand was o ficially estimated at 3.7 tonnes.

The success has not been without cos Opium addicts have turned to heroin and HI has followed the sharing of needles. Toxic po lution from heavy use of pesticides to grow cas crops is also widespread. And the success is als mitigated against by the fact that beyor Thailand's borders opium production virtually out of control. Production i Myanmar in 1999, for example, was estimate at 895 tonnes.

Even though amphetamines have fe outstripped heroin and opium as the proble

Slitting and collecting from each head is done twi

drug in Thai society, the Thai government h remained determined to prevent large-sca opium production within its borders. The Thi Army destroys plantations annually, but tot eradication remains illusive, for one army Colonel put it, "hilltrib people can get more for a have sack full of opium than a pick-u truck full of cabages".

The Hmong, Yao, Lahu and Lis are the main cultivators of th poppy. The plant likes altitud above 850 metres near limeston ridges or below cliffs. Fields a cleared early in the hot seaso (March) and burnt, then a fas growing crop like corn is plante The poppy is sown in Septemb and plants thinned out i November. Vegetables are grow

Opium fields in Thailand cover less than 740 hectares.

ollecting raw opium

ɔ add minerals to the soil and ɔ supplement diet, if not to elp conceal opium plants. he vegetables are cleared and ne plants begin to flower in anuary. When the petals drop ff the pods, farmers slit them 1 a way that causes the resin ɔ ooze out and congeal. The ticky congealed opium is craped off a day later.

Hill tribe cultivators tradi-ɪonally have used the drug as medicine for old age. ddiction amongst the young, owever, has been a curse that ventually leads to dire poverty.

he pungent smell of burning opium makes ‑tection of addicts easier.

Getting into the Hills

D IRT ROADS often follow high ridges in a network that goes all over the hills of Northern Thailand. To use them a motorcycle or 4WD vehicle is essential. You should allow plenty of time to cover what may look like short distances and should be prepared to face difficulties.

Firstly, in the rainy season, tracks become very muddy and dangerously slippery, if not impassable. Turning around can be difficult. Hill folk may help if you get stuck, but you should offer payment for their help.

Secondly, signs (if there are any) are usually in Thai and indicate distant villages by their schools. This can be very helpful if you recognise Thai characters and have appropriate maps. But even with these aids, road junctions can still be confusing, so some spoken Thai is very helpful. Consider taking a guide *(rates 500-1000 baht/ day—contact your hotel or a nearby guest house or trekking agency).*

Interesting routes for self-exploration to see Karen villages may be found off H1013 *(see p.106)* and H1009 *(see Map 14. p.109).* Where Karen villages occupy areas low in elevation, Hmong and Lisu villages are found higher up. Easy routes to Hmong villages are found off H1095 in the Mae Sa Valley *(see map 17 p.114 and Map 18 p.117),* and Hmong villages can be gained from the roads into the Mae Taeng Valley *(see p.124).*

A concrete road from H108 *(KM67+500m)* becomes a dirt road that climbs up over the south shoulder of Chiang Dao to the Hmong village of Pa Kia. To the north of Chiang Dao, Lisu and Karen villages lie close to the road to Muang Khong *(see p.127).* Lisu and Karen villages are commonly found off H1095 to Pai *(see map 19 p.121),* and Pai itself is a great base from which to ride or trek to Lisu and Lahu villages.

The Akha tend to occupy more northerly areas and are most common in Chiang Rai province, and, like the Yao, can be found to the north of Thaton *(see Map 23 p.130).*

David Unkovitch's (The Golden Triangle Rider) motorcycle guides and maps are the most useful for those who want to ride indepen-dently into the hills, and Christian Gooden's *Trek It Yourself in Northern Thailand* (Jungle Books, UK 2000) gives comprehensive infor-mation for both motorcycle and trekking tours.

TREKKING

GOING ON A TREK with a guide is the best way to see the hill tribes. Experienced guides lead you on walking trails (the support vehicle often takes your backpack by a dirt-road route) to the destinations for each night. In the villages you will see how the hill folk are living. Though modern facets of their life may seem familiar, many things will be quite different, and good guides will also be able to explain the tribal spirit world and associated rituals.

Visiting Hill Tribe Villages

Hill people are usually happy to have their photos taken when dressed in their best costumes (Lisu new year).

The best time to visit a village is during a festival, especially the tribal New Year festivals, when the women and men are dressed in their finest costumes. The Lahu, Lisu and Yao hold New Year festivals around the time of the Chinese New Year, which falls on the new moon of the second lunar month. The Hmong and the Akha have festivals in late December.

Times for festivals may vary between villages and clans as well as tribes. The Akha, for example, have their 'swing' ceremony (August-September) 108 days after a rice-planting festival. The latter takes place when the village elders feel the time is right (May-June).

Even if you have a guide, knowing something of the customs, beliefs, and taboos before entering a village will make your visit more meaningful. Be very careful not to touch anything that could be sacred, no matter how ordinary the object might look. Do not enter houses without being invited or take photos without first asking permission.

Several books explain the customs of each tribe, such as *Meet the Akha* by Jim Goodman and *Life in a Lisu Village* by John Davies, and much material can be found at the Tribal Research Institute.

Tourists have complained that they no longer see 'authentic' hill tribes, for they expect to see people in quaint costumes practising shifting agriculture as if their world had not changed since the 1950's. With tens of thousands of people going trekking each year, and with more than 30 years of continuous operation, tourism has been but one of many factors affecting the lifestyle of the hill peoples.

The use of ordinary clothing suggests that many hill people have been losing their cultural identity in reaching for material standards advertised on Thai TV, but this is not necessarily the case. It is important to go into the hills without expectations of meeting people willingly maintaining old traditions to please visitors.

Whatever the reality of life in the hills may be, if you have not been on a trek, you should find the experience interesting if not enjoyable. Treks often include elephant riding and bamboo rafting, but illegal activities such as 'opium smoking' are now seriously discouraged.

You do not have to follow the beaten path if you decide to go on a trek. You can organise your own group and then approach one of the companies to plan you own trek. Expect to pay more than 1000 baht per head per day for a reasonable tour if the group is between 6 and 10 people, and you don't want something done on the cheap.

WHAT TO TAKE ON A TREK

WHEN TREKKING, travel light. Keep at least one clean change of clothes dry for wearing in the evening and night. Warm clothing and a sleeping bag are essential in the cold season. A rain poncho (sold to protect motorcyclists from rain and widely available for around 70-90 Bt.) serves both as a raincoat and ground sheet.

A Lahu man in default dress.

Eco-Trekking

In order to counter what is perceived as a 'deterioration of the product base', i.e. that when you walk into a village you see satellite dishes and women thrust souvenirs in front of you, 'Ecotourism' is being promoted as a method of sustaining tourism in the hills. Apart from bringing environmental benefits, it is thought to help foster the preservation of the ethnic identity of the various hill tribes.

Trekking companies, however, may just be using the term as a marketing tool. Though cutprice trekking companies are unlikely to be able to do much more than initiate very low cost measures to green their business, trekkers themselves can help leave an eco-footprint by working actively to make everyone involved more aware of what 'eco-tourism' means.

Eco-photography? Having initially refused permission for a photograph, this Karen woman readily changed into her traditional blouse (this was not requested) and resumed work on her waist loom upon being offered 20 baht for the shot.

1. Minimising impact on the local environment.

Trekking companies have had some success with reducing the size of the ecological 'footprint' left behind. While things will have to go further before the impact is seen as positive, leaving no litter, using biodegradable materials and not damaging plants is a good start.

2. Maximising learning about the people and environment

It is particularly important that there is an educational component before and during the trek. Hill tribes have complained that visitors do not respect their taboos, that trekkers touch sacred objects or females enter sacred areas. A good guide will advise you carefully on how to behave, but you can also study available sources to learn about the hill peoples. Ask trekking companies for information on the peoples to be visited prior to departure, and see what is available in the local shops. If you have something that will tell your hill tribe hosts about life at your home, then be prepared to show it during your trek.

3. Maximising Community Participation

The involvement of the hill people beyond being passive participants in the commoditisation of their culture is often little. At present only a few villagers may benefit from the average of 30-40 baht per tourist per night that goes to the village*, and therefore selling souvenirs as a source of income may be very important to other villagers.

Ask before-hand whether the trekking company employs local guides to work at each village, and evaluate how much company and village cooperate to control trekking activities in the village. Offer suggestions to the company if you have any, and, if you feel a guide or a company is acting inappropriately, report the matter to the TAT**.

The situation is complex, of course, but your actions may help offset a sense of unease that may come from participating in a process that uses hill tribe people and villages as tourist attractions, but which may bring little benefit to them.

* *"Eco-tourism in Chiang Mai: Problems and Prospects — an Examination of the Trekking Industry in Chiang Mai, Northern Thailand" by Sarah Murfitt (MSc Thesis, Royal Holloway College, London University 2001)*

** *For industry guidelines on interaction between tourism and the mountain peoples see <http://www.lanna.com/html/guidelines.html>*

Basic medical supplies to erilise and cover cuts, settle ɔset stomaches, and sterilise ater may be useful. Use ɔsquito repellent and ɔthing to keep mosquitoes vay in the evening and early orning. Malaria is more of a ɍeat near the Burmese border than close to Chiang Mai. Do not rely on either a mosquito net (you may not be able to put it up) or an anti-malaria drug.

Whether you take your valuables is your choice. Good hotels will have a reliable safe-keeping service, and guest houses should be able to provide the same, but there can be no absolute guarantees. The hills are generally secure and local people are not naturally given to dishonesty, but you should always keep valuables hidden from sight.

ENJOYING LIFE IN CHIANG MAI

Modern convenience and mountain ambience provide the basis for a lifestyle that is hard to match in the region. From the tap of a smithy's hammer on a languid day to the beat of drums on a brisk night, the city offers variety and choice for the enjoyment of residents and visitors alike.

FOOD IN CHIANG MAI

Thai cuisine — an indigenous tradition that has been enriched by Arab, Indian, Malay and Chinese influences — has become world famous. Yet for the Thais, the heart of food is the simple, plain rice. Without rice, many Thai will feel that they have not eaten.

Rice and food — *khao* in Thai — are synonymous, and Thais often refer plain rice as 'beautiful rice' or 'nob rice'. A common greeting in Th with the force of "How are you translates as "Have you eaten yet (*k khao laew ru yang*)?" The dishes th provide the nutrients and flavours whic complement the rice are referred to as *k khao*, which means 'with rice'.

Thai Food

KEY INGREDIENTS in Thai cooking come daily from the fresh markets, which become busy in the pre-dawn hours. Thai cooking requires the vigorous use of a variety of herbs, which commonly include garlic, shallots, and fresh coriander. The hot soups and curry pastes require lemon grass, galangal (Siamese ginger), and the leaves of the kaffir lime (you are not expected to eat the chunks of herb when they are served in the famous hot soups — *tom yam*). Other commonly used fresh herbs include mint and three kinds of basil.

The herbs and spices provide the pungent and bitter range of flavours in Thai dishes. Seasonings are used to add salty, sour and sweet flavours; fish sauce and shrimp paste provide the salty tastes, lime and tamarind the sour, and coconut and palm sugar the sweet.

In preparation of dishes, ingredients are chopped into small pieces. This requires longer preparation, but allows for shorter cooking times; it also makes the use of knives at the table unnecessary.

THAI TABLE MANNERS

AT THE TABLE the bulk of a meal consists of rice, which Thais flavour by taking small helpings (two or three mouthfuls) from shared central dishes. They use serving spoons to place sma portions onto their own plates, from which they eat. The politest way to eat is to serve yourself from one central dish, eat what you have taken, and then return to another portion. Amongst intimates, it is a sign of goo manners to serve delicacies such as prawns (using a central serving spoon) to th plate of a fellow diner.

In this way the full flavou of each dish is savoured in a equable atmosphere. In time of past hardships, this natur manner of sharing food also allowed a small amount of spicy flavouring to go a long way with plain rice

The Restaurant Guid

IN CHIANG MAI, restaurants a numerous. You can find good food in plain basic sho houses as much as in elegan garden restaurants. Word of mouth counts in Chiang Ma so if a Thai restaurant is oft completely empty, then ther is usually good reason for it

While it is hard to go

Lunch break from preparing bundles of rice seedlings for transplanting into wet paddy. Typically the food will consist of sticky rice flavoured with a very spicy dip made from fish and fresh herbs — all found in the nearby fields and hedgerows.

rong at Chiang Mai's long-
erving classic restaurants,
ome of the best food in the
ty can be found at the
ewer, smaller restaurants.
he listings cannot cover all
f the many restaurants in the
ty. Included here are a
ariety from the common (but
od) to some of the more
xclusive and expensive.

Thai Restaurants catering
ostly to foreigners usually
ne down the stronger
avours of Thai cuisine and
are suitable for visitors
ith delicate palates. Some of
e more up-market restau-
nts in Chiang Mai are
cated in the major hotels
ee p.154).

Enjoying food is also very
uch part of a night out in
e city, and many 'pubs' have
ands to accompany the
ting and drinking. More
ely places to eat are listed as
ibs in 'Nightlife'.

This guide has no recommen-
ations to make for the
expensive and popular *Mu
ta* (pork pot) restaurants.
rving themselves from
atters of raw meats and
h, customers at these
aces grill raw morsels on
t pots in the centre of their
les. The Thai part is in the
icy sauces served to flavour the
eats. Thus the freshness and
ality of the raw ingredients
d the inventiveness in the
icy sauces are important. Try
y of the places in the
immanhaemin Road area.

Out of town restaurants
ose to the city are men-
ned on page 161 and
ggestions for restaurants on
e touring routes are found
the maps.

Wet Rice Cultivation

There is plenty of work in the villages at the time of planting and harvesting, when teams of people work through the fields. Each person plants up to five rows (the width the arms can conveniently stretch laterally in front of the body without moving the legs).

Rice, *Oryza sativa*, was domesticated in the region more than 4000 years ago. The life cycle of the plant takes 100-210 days depending on the variety. In the North, the cycle begins with plough-ing when there has been sufficient rain (May-June) to allow water to stand in the fields. Seeds are planted in specially prepared nurseries and the seedlings are allowed to grow to a height of about 15-30 centimeters (3-6 weeks).

Then the work of transplanting the young plants into fields flooded to a depth below the tops of the seedlings begins. The water level is maintained throughout the growing season, which helps keep down weeds as well as provide a source of protein from the numerous fish and crabs that live in the water and mud. At the end of the rainy season the fields are drained and the rice matures, whereupon it is harvested and threshed (September-October).

In Northern Thailand, glutinous rice, which has a kind of starch that breaks down easily when cooked, is widely grown. It is

better suited to areas with poor soils, erratic rainfall and shorter growing sea-sons. It tends to keep better after cooking, making it convenient to steam the days consumption in the morning, and to be carried in baskets into the fields; its higher sugar content also makes it better for making mash and distilling alcohol.

Though the minimum wage for Chiang Mai Province is set at 143 baht per day, day labourers and fac-tory workers may not earn that much for their labour.

Though machines are increasingly being used, harvesting in the traditional manner can still be seen in the valley. The rice is first threshed by hand into a large basket (or onto a tarpaulin) and then winnowed with hand fans.

Northern Thai Food

Sticky rice, *khao nieo*, is commonly eaten with northern dishes. It is first soaked for several hours and then steamed in a conical basket of woven bamboo. This reduces the stickiness as well as the sweetness of the rice. It keeps well after cooking and may be kept in baskets for a long time.

The ingredients used to flavour rice were originally those that came from hunting, foraging and fishing. Older Northern Thais may wistfully tell you about the flavour of venison in their youth, but most wild meat has been hunted to extinction. The more adventurous visitor may, perhaps, like to sample the various dishes that use insects and innards that are popular in the north.

The herbs and spices for flavouring are those commonly used in all Thai cooking, but northern Thai dishes have been influenced by the Burmese and Shan. Northern cooking uses more fresh chilli (as opposed to dry chilli) and virtually no coconut in curry sauces as compared with central Thai cuisine.

Dishes served with sticky rice are of several kinds: *nam phrik* — hot dips served in small bowls along with fresh or lightly steamed vegetables and crispy pork skin, *kaeng* — curries (dry or watery); *yam* — vegetables and meat mixed with a variety of herbs, spices and chilli.

Sticky rice is usually eaten by taking a small lump and pressing it with the fingers to form a hard ball. Then the ball is dipped into some spicy flavouring and eaten. In Thai homes it is quite acceptable to take the ball of rice and, holding it with your fingers, delicately dip it into a central dish (watch your host for a lead). Avoid leaving grains of rice in the central dish if eating this way (most Northern Thai restaurants provide hand basins for cleaning hands before and after eating)

PRICES & LISTING SYMBOLS

The cheapest food is sold in markets and at street stalls and noodle shops. *Aharn tam sang* (food to order) costs 20-25 baht per dish.

Because of the way Thai food is served, it is best to go to a restaurant a a small group in order to enjoy sharin a choice of dishes. Though Chiang Ma cannot compete with Bangkok for culinary choice, it certainly can on price. Chiang Mai's restaurants are necessarily tied to the local market, and most Thais are not prepared to pay more for their food. The majority of restaurants charge 50-90 baht for regular dishes, with various fish or meat dishes costing 100-200 baht. Excluding alcoholic drinks, expect to pay on average 150-250 baht per heac for four people at normal restaurants.

In general only restaurants at hotel and those serving foreign food will cos 500 baht per head or more (excluding alcohol drinks). Where restaurants are slightly more expensive than usual for their class, they are marked with ⓑ (NB a Thai restaurant marked in this way will be cheaper than a restaurant serving foreign food similarly marked Even the more expensive restaurants are modestly priced by international standards, however.

Tipping has become customary in better restaurants with serving staff, who will depend on tips for part of their income. Thais will only tip well i service has been special. Large tips are unnecessary, 20-30 baht usually being enough for a 500 baht meal.

⊘ = no English Menu. Take a
        Thai friend!

☞ = air-conditioned

☀ = in a building or under shelter o
        some kind (*sala*).

⚜ = *al fresco*, open air (no shelter)

💳 = accepts at least one major
        credit card (Visa or Master)

Northern Dishes & Restaurants

Most Chiang Mai restaurants serve some northern Thai food. Some northern Thai dishes and restaurants are listed below.

Northern Dishes

cho pakkad : จอผักกาด
fresh cabbage boiled with shrimp paste, fermented fish (pla ra) and tamarind

kaeng hang lae : แกงฮังเล
a Burmese style pork curry in a rich brown sauce made with curry paste, tamarind and soy.

kaeng khae : แกงแค
beans, egg plant, mushrooms, and other vegetables with meat in a watery curry flavoured with shrimp paste, fermented fish, garlic, shallots and lemon grass.

kaeng ho : แกงโฮ๊ะ
Flavouring of *kaeng hang lae* and *kaeng no mai* mixed with vegetables and glass noodles

kaeng no mai : แกงหน่อไม้
a very popular curry made with young bamboo shoots and fresh green chilli, shrimp paste, fermented fish, garlic and shallots.

khaep mu: แคบหมู
deep-fried crispy pork skin

lab : ลาบ
finely chopped meat (raw or cooked) with shallot, chilli, lime, coriander and mint.

naem : แหนม
chopped pork fermented within banana leaf.

nam phrik num : น้ำพริกหนุ่ม
baked green chilli, shallot and garlic pounded into a dip. Be careful as this one can be very hot!

nam phrik ong : น้ำพริกอ่อง
finely chopped pork with tomato and baked red chilli pounded into a spicy dip.

sai ua : ไส้อั่ว
northern style sausage.

yam chin kai : ยำจิ้นไก่
a watery, but spicy chicken curry flavoured with similar ingredients to *lab*.

tam makhua : ตำมะเขือ
a milder dip made with baked egg-plant.

Northern Restaurants

Ban Rai Yam Yen *169.A11*
14 Mu 3, Tambon Faham. Hrs. 11:00–24:00.
Northern food in an atmospheric terrace with live music.
Tel: (0) 5324 4796

Come-In House (Ruan Kham In) *168.B6*
79/3 Sirithon Rd., Chanphuak, Chiang Inn Plaza, Chang Khlan Rd. Hrs. 10:00–22:00.
Good Northern Thai food in the tranquil surrounds of a large, luxurious wooden house. Call the restaurant for free transportation.
Tel: (0) 5321 2516

Huan Penn & **Kaeng Ron Ban Suan** — two excellent restaurants — *see Six Chiang Mai Favourites*

Sri Pen
103 Inthawarorot Rd. Hrs. 10:00–17:00. 184.E7
Northern Thai food is served at tables in open-fronted shop. Good for *som tham* — hot raw papaya salad.
Tel: (0) 5321 5328

(left to right) Lab, Kaeng Hang Lae, Sai Ua, and (lower centre) Nam Phrik Num (Come-In House)

Northern-style noodles

khao soi : ข้าวซอย
Northern Thailand's distinctive 'noodle' dish consists of soft and crispy egg noodles served up in a spicy curry sauce with chicken or beef. Pickled cabbage and fresh shallots as well as condiments are always served with this dish. Many restaurants serve *khao soi*, but some specialise.

Khao Soi Islam Very good *khao soi* (see Halal food).

Khao Soi New Lamduan Faham
352/22 Charoenrat Rd. on east side 300 m. north of the Rama IX bridge. Hrs. 09:00–15:00. 169.B11
This restaurant enjoys a reputation amongst Thais from Bangkok for its *khao soi*. Other places nearby also serve equally good versions of this dish. Tel: (0) 5324 3519

Help! There are 200 items on the menu.

Curries, whether watery or dry, are called *kaeng. Yam* are spicy hot salads, and the fiery soups are known as *tom yam*. Other dishes may be *nung* — steamed, *op* or *yang* — baked or grilled, or *thot* (pronounced like 'tort') — fried.

If you know little about Thai food, here are 15 central Thai dishes to begin your exploration. In general you should order one dish per person and one extra; avoid choosing more than one dish from each of the groups except for the last one (but don't forget that rules are made to be broken if not selectively adhered to, especially in Thailand).

Soups/watery curries

1. **tom yam pla** : ต้มยำปลา
   tom yam soup with fish
2. **tom kha kai** : ต้มข่าไก่
   spicy coconut soup with chicken
3. **kaeng lieng** : แกงเลียง
   spicy soup with vegetables and prawn

Thicker curries

4. **kaeng khieo wan** : แกงเขียวหวาน
   green curry (usually with chicken, or pork)
5. **kaeng kari kai** : แกงกะหรี่ไก่
   yellow chicken curry, 'Indian-style'
6. **phanaeng nua** : พะแนงเนื้อ
   beef with creamy red curry

Fish

7. **pla pae sa** : ปลาแป๊ะซ๊ะ
   fish in sour soup with vegetables
8. **pla nung manao** : ปลานึ่งมะนาว
   steamed fish with lime
9. **pla thot khrop** : ปลาทอดกรอบ
   crispy fried fish

Spicy salad

10. **yam makhua yao** : ยำมะเขือยาว
    spicy salad with egg-plant
11. **yam pla duk fu** : ยำปลาดุกฟู
    spicy salad with crispy shredded fish

General dishes

12. **phak bung fai daeng** : ผักบุ้งไฟแดง
    flame-fried morning glory with chilli
13. **tort man kung** : ทอดมันกุ้ง
    fried prawn cakes

14. **kai phat met mamuang himaphan** : ไก่ผัดเม็ดมะม่วงหิมพานต์
    chicken with cashew nuts
15. **mu thot krathiam phrik thai** : หมูทอดกระเทียมพริกไทย
    pork fried in garlic and pepper

See 'Thai Food to Order' (p.157) for more dishes.

Alcoholic Beverages

Thai menus often have a section called *'kap klaem'*, which refers to dishes suitable as accompaniments to drinking. Many Thais will carry bottles of whiskey into restaurants, especially *black* — the Thai word for a Johnnie Walker distillation, and often there is no corkage charge if you take your own liquor. Local blends of Scotch are more palatable than the local liquors (*Mekhong* and *Saengsom*), which are vaguely related to rum. Local liquors are usually sold in half bottles and served with mixers (try coke and soda and quarters of fresh lime — *manao sik* มะนาว ผ่าซีก) and a bucket of ice.

Wine has become widely available and most established restaurants offer table wine if not a modest choice from a wine list. Chilled beer, however, is the alcoholic beverage most frequently drunk with Thai food, and, as with all locally brewed spirits and beers, the effect is quite noticeable the next morning.

'ya dong' — herb liquor — is made from '35 degree', a local white spirit, which is infused with herbs which have strong and invigorating properties. These may fire up the palate if not the gonads.

Help! My mouth is on fire.

Spicy Thai dishes do not have to be hot! *Yam* — the spicy salads — and curries can be very hot if they contain a lot of *phrik khi nu* — the little green chillies known as 'rat shit chilli'. They are commonly used in the spicy salads and can be hard to see. Just their presence in a dish will make the food hot (Thai chefs tend not to cut them up as this can makes the dish extremely hot), and you are advised to separate them from the food on your plate before you eat. If you don't want your food to be hot at all, tell the restaurant staff not to add chilli.

ไม่ใส่พริก : *Mai sai phrik* — Don't put in chilli.

In fact most restaurants with foreigners counting amongst their customers tone down the use of hot spices in their cooking, but if you do find yourself with a burning palate, the hot element in chilli is a chemical called capsaicin, which is soluble with oil, particularly pork fat, and sweet syrups or sugar. Anything containing oil or sugar (preferably both) mixed with plain rice will wipe and cool the mouth far better than water.

'hot little fellahs!'

ix CHIANG MAI FAVOURITES

asserie Bar & Restaurant (บ้านร่มริมน้ำ) *185/201.D10*
 Charoenrat Rd. Hrs. 17:00–02:00 (Kitchen closes 01:00)
 lk through the Bohemian R&B atmosphere (see p.162) in
 e main building to enjoy Thai food & folk music on the
 ieter riverside terrace beyond. Dishes to try include *lap
 khrop* (ลาบเป็ดกรอบ) — spicy crispy duck salad, *mu kata
 acha* (หมูกระทะผัดจ๋า) — stir-fired marinated pork, *thalae
 imao chan ron* (ทะเลขี้เมาจานร้อน) — spicy fried sea food in
 t dish, *pla kao rat chuchi* (ปลาก๋าราดฉู่ฉี่) — fried rock-fish
 pped with red curry sauce, *nam phrik long rua* (น้ำพริก
 เรือ) — spicy shrimp past with preserved egg.
: (0) 5324 1665

allery Bar & Restaurant (เดอะแกลอรี่) *185/201.D10*
-29 Charoenrat Rd. Hrs. 12:00–24:00.
notable restaurant for Central Thai Food, it is set in an
d wooden mercantile house and a very pleasant leafy ter-
ce overlooking the river. House specialities include *po bia
ng* (ปอเปี๊ยะกุ้ง) — shrimp spring roll, *kuang kae* (คั่วแค) —
uted mixed vegetables with pork, beef or chicken, and *ho
ng kai* (ห่อหนึ่งไก่) — steamed spicy chicken in banana leaves.
: (0) 5324 8601

uan Penn (เฮือนเพ็ญ) *184.E7*
2 Ratchamankha Rd. Hrs. 08:00–15:00, 17:00–21:30.
ie of the best-known northern Thai food restaurants in
iang Mai. At lunchtime, when you can peruse the fare in
splay trays in the main *sala*, the restaurant is often very
owded. Without doubt the pork ribs, *si khrong mu* (ซี่โครง
) and crispy pork skin, *kheep mu* (แคบหมู), are both deli-
ous and necessary complements to their fiery *nam phrik
m* (น้ำพริกหนุ่ม). Many other less spicy northern dishes are
 the lunch menu. In the evening the same fare is served in
 more genteel atmosphere of an adjacent wooden house.
: (0) 5327 7103

Hong Tauw Inn (ห้องแถว) *168.C5*
95/17-18 Nimmanhaemin Rd. Hrs. 11:00–22:00.
Located in a stylishly decorated double shop-house, this restaurant serves good Central Thai food. Try *pla chon hong tauw* (ปลาช่อนห้องแถว) — deep fried water fish with carrot dressing, *naem thod* (แหนมทอด) — deep fried northern sausage served with vegetables, *kaeng khiao waan hed horm koong* (แกงเขียวหวานเห็ดหอมกุ้ง) — green curry with fresh black mushrooms and shrimps, and *yam thua poo* (ยำถั่วพู) — spicy wing bean salad.
Tel: (0) 5321 8333, (0) 5340 0039

Kaeng Ron Ban Suan (แกงร้อนบ้านสวน) *80.C2*
149/3 Mu 2 Soi Chomdoi, Khlong Chonphratan, Chang Phuak. Hrs. 10:00-22:00.
A spacious restaurant beneath trees and in the open-air space under a large wooden house, this is another restaurant known for its *kaeng no* (แกงหน่อ)— bamboo curry, *lap khua mu* (ลาบคั่วหมู)— minced pork northern style, and *kai muang nung* (ไก่เมืองนึ่ง)— steamed chicken northern style. On the principle that you should try anything once, order their fried crickets or bamboo beetles as a sample of northern 'fries'.
Tel: (0) 5321 3762, (0) 5322 1378

Tha Nam (ท่าน้ำ) *202.I 10*
43/3 Mu 2, Chang Khlan Rd. Hrs. 07:00–23:00.
Dining is on a pleasant riverside terrace and upstairs on the second floor of a large wooden building. Fare includes Northern and Central Thai dishes. Try *hors d'oeuvres muang* (ออเดริฟเมือง) — sausage, pork, crispy pork skin and chilli dip; try also *pla chum* (ปลาจุ่ม) — raw fish or beef and vegetables for cooking in soup served in an earthenware pot on coals, *yam mu kham wan* (ยำหมูคำหวาน) — spicy pork salad.
Tel: (0) 5327 5125

THAI RESTAURANTS TO TRY

Aroon Rai 185.E9
45 Kotchasan Rd. nr. Thaphae Gate.
Hrs. 08:00–23:00. Long established restaurant now serves many foreigners with Northern Thai and Thai-Chinese food. Tel: (0) 5327 6947 ☢

Aw Chittichai 169.B10
43/8 Wang Singh Kham Rd.
Hrs. 10:00–13:00, 17:00-22:00
A Chinese style *khao tom* restaurant with a local reputation.

Banana Leaf 168.E3
93/4 Liam Khlong Chonlaprathan Rd (to Wat Umong). Hrs.17;00-24:00
Folk music accompanies good food on a terrrace overlooking the canal. Tel: (0) 5328 0372 ☢ ⚘

Cafe Chic 184.E8
105/5 Prapokklao Rd. Hrs.10:00–20:00
Cool out to Thai food in the middle of the old city.
Tel: (0) 5381 4651 ☐ ☐

The Drunken Flower (Mau Dok Mai) 168.C5
295/1 Soi 1 Nimmanhaemin Rd.18:00-01:00 Pleasant garden and cool house setting. Hot & spicy fare includes Mexican food.
Tel: (0) 5321 2081 ☐ ☢ ⚘

Gàgade 184/200.D8
Coffee House and Restaurant
18 Ratchawithi Rd. Hrs. 09:00–24:00.
Food is served on tiered terraces beneath a high roof. Live music, but not noisy.
Tel: (0) 5322 5453 ☢

Galae Restaurant 168.D1
65 Suthep Rd - go to end of road and enter grounds of irrigation dept. Hrs: 11:00-21:00 Pleasant setting for lunch in copse overlooking small reservoir.
Tel: (0) 5327 8655 ☢ ⚘ ☐

The Gourmet 185.E10
9 Charoenrat Rd. Hrs: 11:00-23:00
Very fresh food served in pleasant, quiet riverside setting.
Tel: (0) 5326 2419-20 ☢ ⚘ ☐

Kafe 185/200.E9
127-9 Mun Muang Rd. Hrs. 09:00-24:00. (F3) Small restaurant in cosy wooden building. Happy hour bar.
Tel: (0) 5321 2717 ☐ ☢

Kai Wan 168.D5
45 Soi 9 Nimmanhaemin Rd. Hrs. 11:00–14:00 & 17:00–23:00.
Dining on raised terrace at this long serving Chiang Mai Restaurant.
Tel: (0) 5322 2147 ☢ ⚘ ☐

Karawek 184.D6
Bungruanggrit Rd. Hrs 18:00-01:00.
Good food & low-key folk music.
Tel: (0) 5321 5912 ⚘

Khrua Sabai 168.H6
Chiang Mai Golf Driving Range at Airport Plaza intersection Hrs. 11:00-23:00. Comfortable middle-class restaurant at golf range.
Tel: (0) 5327 4042 ☐ ☐

Khrua Rattana 185/200.E9
320-322 Thaphae Rd. Hrs 09:00-22:00 Thai-European food in small diner for lonely travellers. Tel: (0)5387 4173 ☐ ⚘

Khantok Dinner

At a *khantok* dinner, a form of entertainment revived in the 1950's, guests sit on mats or thin cushions around low tables (known as a *khantok*) in locations that are often outside. A meal of typical Northern Thai food is accompanied by entertainment of singing and dancing. Settings vary from the house of a former *chao* (Khum Kaew Khan Toke, Vista Hotel), the old house of a rich merchant (*Lanna Khantoke Dinner, Diamond Riverside*), a hotel garden (*Imperial Mae Ping*) and a converted cinema (*Nakorn Lanna 1296, Sridonchai Rd* — the latter describes itself as a dinner show).

The *Khantok* dinner menus normally include *kaeng hang lae* (Burmese pork curry), *nam phrik ong* or *nam phrik num* (spicy dips) with *khaep mu* (crispy pork skin), fried chicken or pork-ribs, steamed vegetables and sticky rice. The spice factor is toned down to foreign tastes, so such dinners offer a simple introduction to northern Thai food in a convivial atmosphere with entertainment. If you have special re-

quests such as vegetarian or *halal*, you must order in advance. Food is normally served around 7 p.m. and shows of traditional dance and preformances last longer than an hour, with most programmes finishing around 9 p.m. or after. Prices vary between 200-300 baht per head, and seats must be booked in advance.

Khum Khantoke 202.C14
Chiang Mai Business Park. Hrs. 18:30–22:00.
Sophisticated show in elegant custom-created setting.
Tel: (0) 5330 4121-2. ☐ ☢ ⚘ ☐

Old Chiang Mai Cultural Centre 169.G7
185/3 Wualai Rd. Hrs. 19:00–21:30. A show in two parts in created wooden village setting.
Tel: (0) 5327 5097, (0) 5320 2993-5 ☐ ☢ ☐

Sipsongpanna Khantoke 168.F3
66/2 Mu 10 Ban Umong Hrs.07:00-09:00.
Set in a large raised Northern Thai wooden house. Drink on in adjacent restaurant after show. Tel: (0) 5381 0690-6 ☢ ☐

A Lanna dancer with rose petals to welcome guests

m Mae La Pla Pao *169.C10*
7 *Charoen Rat Rd. Hrs: 11:00-23:30*
cal atmosphere at this pleasant fish
staurant on the Ping. Folk Music.
l: (0) 5330 6660

mon Tree *168.C6*
/1-2 Huai Kaew Rd. Hrs. 10:30–
:00. Eat good food at back to escape
ary lemon decor.
l: (0) 5321 3812

ango Tree *185/200.E9*
/1-2 Huai Kaew Rd. Hrs. 08:30–
:00. Unexpected class in midst of
r-strip for foreigners.
l: (0) 5320 8292

Nang Nual (Thai) & **Yamato**
(Jap.) *202.I10 27/2-5 Koh Klang Rd.*
Hrs. 08:00–23:00. Large, flashy
seafood place —good if you choose
the right dishes. Tel:(0) 5328 1961-
2

Oriental Style *185/201.D10*
36 Charoenrat Rd. Hrs. 09:00–14:00
& *16:30–20:30.* Thai European food
in stylish back patio of old
mercantile house.
Tel: (0) 5326 2746

Ouan He Ha *184.D7*
9 Arak Rd C.M. 50200. Hrs. 16:30–
22:30. Local no frills fresh-water
fish restaurant.

Noodles

Lanna noodle vendor

Noodles make a simple, inexpensive meal
that can be enjoyed anytime. Thai noodles
are amongst the best in Southeast Asia, and
no visit to Thailand is complete without
trying them at least once. The current price
for a bowl from a street stall is 20 baht. The
price of a bowl of noodles offers a ready mea-
surement of inflation. In 1975 the price was
3-5 baht.

Noodle stalls
How to order. Combine items in the way
you want. i.e.:
bami/nam/kai : บะหมี่/น้ำ/ไก่
   wheat noodles/in soup/ with chicken
sen lek/haeng/nua : เส้นเล็ก/แห้ง/เนื้อ
   medium noodles/served dry (without
   soup)/with beef

Noodle menu
sen yai	เส้นใหญ่	wide rice noodles
sen lek	เส้นเล็ก	medium rice noodles
sen mi	เส้นหมี่	fine rice noodles
bami	บะหมี่	egg noodles
nam	น้ำ	soup (in this context)
haeng	แห้ง	served dry without soup

Meats with noodles
kai	ไก่	chicken
nua	เนื้อ	beef
mu	หมู	pork
lukchin	ลูกชิ้น	(meat/fish) balls
kiao	เกี๊ยว	dumplings

Other dishes made with noodles
phat si iew ผัดซีอิ๊ว noodles fried with soy
   sauce (usually served with pork)
lat na ลาดหน้า noodles served with
   sauce (usually served with pork)
phat Thai ผัดไทย fried noodles Thai-style

Noodle shops
These are usually only open till mid/late
afternoon. Prices are inexpensive (all).

Lim Lao Ngwo ลิ้มเหล่าโหงว *200.E8*
53/ Inthawarorot Rd.

Kuai Tieo Rua Koliang ก๋วยเตี๋ยวเรือโกเหลียง *200.E9*
Mun Muang nr. intersection with Ratchamankha Rd.
Good 'boat noodles' (rich meaty flavoured soup).

Rot Nung รสหนึ่ง *163.X3*
45/6 Charoen Prathet Rd. opp. Diamond Hotel.

Rot Sawoei *Kai tun ya jin* รสเสวย *184.F6*
91 Arak Rd.Hrs 09:00-21:00 Excellent noodles with
chicken stewed in Chinese herbs.

Sa-at สะอาด *200.E8*
*Inthawarorot Rd. — double shop unit just west of Buddha
images and chedi. Try bamifor* บะหมี่

Yong Tour Rot Det ยังทัวร์รสเด็ด *184.E7*
*98/4 Ratcha-
damnoen Rd.*

*'Khao Soi' —
Northern Thai Noodles
(Regent Resort, Chiang Mai)*

Market and Vendor Tips

In the cold season, hot soya milk and a couple of fried batter rolls known as *pa tong ko* can keep the chill out. Add an egg to the soya milk (*sai khai*) for something more fortifying. This, along with instant coffee, is also served in the early morning at main markets in northern towns.

Several stalls sell tasty snacks from in front of the Bangkok Bank on Chang Moi Road, and the *phat thai* served on the north side of Thaphae Road close to the gate is also good.

A vendor prepares 'khanom khrok' in Lanna style food market (Seup San Lanna)

If you have a sweet tooth and want to sample Thai desserts, go to one of the markets, (Sompet market on Mun Muang Road is good) where you find vendors selling desserts in plastic bags for just a few baht. In the evenings vendors sell sweets in two baht portions from carts.

The markets also provide the best opportunity to sample some of Thailand's fruits. Particularly good in season is mango with sticky rice. Try Thap Thim Khrop (*163.Z2*) for Thai desserts.

Phuket Laikram *168.D4*
1/10 Suthep Rd. west of Phayom market.
Hrs. 08:00–14:00 & 16:30–20:30.
Southern Thai food in clean shophouse.
Tel: (0) 5327 8909

Regina *185/201.D10*
69-71 Charoenrat Rd. Hrs.
10:30–01:00. Thai & European fare in quiet riverside garden + shop and guesthouse.
Tel: (0) 5326 2882

The Riverside Garden *202.H10.*
407/2 Charoen Prathet Rd. Hrs. 07:00–23:00. Pleasing setting for quiet dining by river. Jazz on Saturdays.
Tel: (0) 5327 5309

Rot Saep Muang Ubon *163.Z3*
116 Anusarn Market, Charoen Prathet Rd. Hrs. 16:00–02:00. Isan (Northeastern Thai) dishes served in small platters best washed down with beer or liquor.

Wang Pla 2/Pluak Mai *202.I9*
11 Chang Khlan Rd., C.M. 50100. Hrs. 11:00–23:00. Riverside fish restaurant.
Tel: (0) 5327 5961

The Wok *184/200.E8*
44 Ratchamankha Rd., C.M. 50200.
Hrs. 11:00–22:30. A garden setting in which to enjoy Thai food for foreign palates.
Tel: (0) 5320 8287

MARKETS, FOOD CENTRES & STREET FOOD

STALLS IN ANUSARN MARKET (*Chang Khlan Rd. near the Night Bazaar*) and Sompet Market (*Chaiyaphum Rd. a little north of Thaphae Gate*) serve Thai food to order and have English menus. Anusarn Market (*163.Y2*), the larger of the two features an open air terrace with many stalls serving food at prices only slightly above regular market prices elsewhere. More restaurants are located nearby in the market. 'Wang Kung Rena' 24 Hrs. Tel: (0) 5327 4588) serves good fish and fresh prawn priced by the kilo, and food is cooked at prodigious speeds at 'Ouan Heha' (*Hrs 17:00-24:00 Tel* (0) 5381 8441).

Inexpensive food centres using coupon systems are found at the Airport Plaza (fourth floor), Kat Suan Kaew (south wing, 3rd floor south) and the hypermarkets (Big C, Carrefour, Lotus & Makro). Convenience takes precedence over ambience in such places, however. More worthwhile is the Galare Food Centre in the Night Bazaar (*163.X2*), where stalls sell food for coupons and diners can enjoy free shows of traditional dancing (*21:00–22:30*).

Several good shops serving food at local prices cater to a busy lunchtime clientele at the eastern end of Inthawarorot Road (*200.E8 mornings and lunchtime only*). These include some excellent noodle shops (*see noodles sidebar previous page*) as well as 'Kiat Ocha' (*Hrs. 06:00–13:00 or when the chicken runs out*), Chiang Mai's best steamed chicken on rice. Local vendors sell an array of tasty delicacies and desserts from carts on the street.

Thai Food to Order ผัดเปรี้ยวหวาน/ไก่ Help, there's no English menu!

Local restaurants and stalls away from tourist areas do not have English menus. This menu may help you order basic Thai dishes anywhere. The English words (mostly) appear in the same order as their Thai equivalents. Do not expect all dishes to be available. Happy eating!

How to order: combine items in the way you want; eg.

phat kraphao/nua/khai dao :
ผัดกระเพรา/เนื้อ/ไข่ดาว
 fried with basil/ beef/with fried egg
phat phrieo wan/kai : ผัดเปรี้ยวหวาน/ไก่
 sweet & sour/chicken

Choice of meat/prawn in stir-fried dishes

kai	ไก่	chicken
nua	เนื้อ	beef
mu	หมู	pork
kung	กุ้ง	prawn

Regular dishes

khao phat : ข้าวผัด
 fried rice (choose meat/prawn/fried egg)
phat phak ruam : ผัดผักรวม
 fried mixed vegetables
phat phak bung : ผัดผักบุ้ง
 fried morning glory
phat kraphao : ผัดกระเพรา
 fried with basil (choose meat)
phat phrieo wan : ผัดเปรี้ยวหวาน
 sweet and sour (choose meat/prawn)
phat phrik : ผัดพริก
 fried with chilli (choose meat/prawn)
mu thot krathiam phrik thai :
หมูทอดกระเทียมพริกไทย
 pork fried in garlic & pepper
khai chieo mu sap : ไข่เจียวหมูสับ
 Thai omelette with chopped pork
khai yat sai : ไข่ยัดไส้
 stuffed omelette
khai dao : ไข่ดาว
 fried egg
pla thot : ปลาทอด
 fried fish
tom cheut tao hu mu sap : ต้มจืดเต้าหู้หมูสับ
 mild soup with tofu and chopped pork

tom yam : ต้มยำ
 spicy soup (chicken, prawn or fish)
khao tom : ข้าวต้ม
 rice soup (chicken, pork, prawn or fish)
khao chan : ข้าวจาน
 plate of rice
khao to : ข้าวโถ
 bowl of rice for group

Serving style for dishes

chan : จาน
 on a plate
sai tuai : ใส่ถ้วย
 in a bowl
rat khao : ราดข้าว
 Individual portion on plate of rice
 (usually with stir-fried dishes and curries)

Drinks

nam plao : น้ำเปล่า
 water
kafe yen : กาแฟเย็น
 iced coffee with milk
oliang : โอเลี้ยง
 iced black coffee
cha manau : ชามะนาว
 ice tea with lime
Coke, Sprite : โค้ก สไปร์ท
 Coke, Sprite
nam khaeng : น้ำแข็ง
 ice

Local fruit and herbal drinks (sweet, and cooling)

nam bai buabok : น้ำใบบัวบก
 pennywort juice
nam farang sot : น้ำฝรั่งสด
 fresh guava juice
nam krajiap : น้ำกระเจี๊ยบ
 roselle juice
nam lam yai : น้ำลำไย
 longan juice
nam matum : น้ำมะตูม
 aegle marmelos juice
nam oi : น้ำอ้อย
 sugar cane juice
nam som khan : น้ำส้มคั้น
 fresh orange juice

Halal (Muslim)

Muslim restaurants (see locations of mosques) provide food good enough to be non-denominational.

Arabia Restaurant *163.Y2*
Anusarn Market. Hrs. 10:30–23:30.
Arabic,Pakistani, Indian, Thai
Muslim fare.
Tel: (0) 5381 8850

Gulf Restaurant *185/201.F9*
Arabian Indian & Muslim Thai Food
Chiang Mai Entertainment Complex,
Loi Khroh Rd. Hrs. 11:00–24:00.
Amongst the better sub-continental fare on offer in Chiang Mai.

Jen Pao Restaurant *169.H10*
Al Farooq Hotel: 341 Charoen Prathet
Rd. Hrs. 10:00–15:00 & 17:00–22:00.
Yunnanese food in the Muslim quarter in this area.
Tel: (0) 5382 1107

Khao Soi Islam *163.W2*
Charoen Prathet Soi 1 — satay stand
and single storey restaurant on north
side of lane. Hrs. 08:00–15:00.
Chicken and goat's meat is served in khao soi (ข้าวซอย) and with saffron rice — khao mok (ข้าวหมก). This is one of several good and inexpensive Halal res-

taurants found on Soi 1 which serve the Yunnanese community and visitors in Ban Haw.

Ruammit 1 &2 – Yunnanese-Thai
#1 at 170/2-3 Chang Khlan Rd.
Hrs:08:00-20:30 & #2 at Anusarn
market. Nice honey-grilled chicken and other meat dishes at the inexpensive and friendly diner at #2.
(163.Y2)

Sanga Choeng Doi *169 C7*
7/1 Charoensuk Rd., Santitham Hrs.
08:00–16:00. Don't go much later than 13:00 hrs for the excellent chicken on saffron rice (khao mok kai, ข้าวหมกไก่) and home-made yoghurt served beneath the sala of this local restaurant.

Vegetarian Thai

Many restaurants have vegetarian dishes on the menu, or will be able to prepare them to order. Dedicated vegetarian restaurants are usually very cheap, but tend not to be open in the evening. *Kin chae* กินเจ means 'I eat vegetarian food'.

Rock-bottom prices and ambience, but some of the tastiest vegetarian curries in town at the restaurant near the jail.

<www.Rejoicecharity.com> lists 35 vegetarian restaurants on a map that may be available at the Vegetarian Society. Many are worth going to whether you practise vegetarianism or not.

Aum – Thai *200.E9*
65 Mun Muang Rd. Hrs. 07:30–14:00
17:00–21:00 Serving veggies since 1993. Tel: (0) 5327 8315

Khun Churn – Thai *168.C5*
46/1 Rot Fai Rd. (west side of the
railway station). & Nimmanhaemin R
Soi 11 or 13.Hrs. 09:30–14:30 &
16:30–20:30. Vegetarian fare in more upscale setting. Tel: (0) 5324 5453

Thai Vegetarian Food Restauran
184.E7 55 Inthawarorot Rd. Hrs. 10:00–
15:00. Choose from trays of curries in their new shop-house location.

The Vegetarian Society *168.G6*
42 Mahidol Rd. Next to Lemon Green
gas station on Mahidol Rd. Hrs. 06:00
14:00. Best before 12:00. (E4)
Large palm roofed sala and non-refundable coupons. Very cheap.

Vihara Langsian – Thai *169.G10*
Chang Khlan Rd. Hrs. 09:00–18:00
weigh your loaded plate and pay before you eat.
Tel: (0) 5381 8094

Whole Earth Restaurant *185.F10*
88 Sridonchai Rd. Hrs. 11:00–14:00
17:00–22:00. Thai, Indian and vegetarian food in an upscale atmosphere at a wooden house.
Tel: (0) 5328 2463

Chiang Mai's Food Festivals

(Airport Park, Kat Choeng Doi or other— early December). Not to be outdone by the sponsor of the original 'Chiang Mai Food Festival', a second major brewer has sponsored a parallel event called the 'Chiangmai Food and Entertainment Festival' since 2000. The beer garden approach appears to be popular.

At both fairs lines of stalls contain temporary kitchens staffed by many of Chiang Mai's restaurants. Food is taken away and consumed at tables set before stages enlivened with song and dance performances.

The TAT has also sponsored 'food street' events during festivals by temporarily closing roads and creating a food market.

'Phat Thai — khon khoei ruai' on the apron translates as "Phat Thai — a person who was once rich". This is a reference to business-men who were forced to turn their skills to cooking and vending after the crash of '97.

ASIAN AND ORIENTAL

kathip – Chinese-Thai 168.B3
) Huai Kaew Rd. Hrs. 11:00–23:00.
ood for any occasion.
el: (0) 5389 3122

ia Tong Heng – Chinese 163.Z2
93/2 Sridonchai Rd. Hrs.
):00–22:00. Good food for couples
r large groups.
el: (0) 5327 5242

itchen Hush – Japanese 185.D10
awarat Bldg, Kaew Nawarat soi 3.
rs. 11:30–14:30, 18:00-21:00
el: (0) 5324 6432

e Gong Kum – Vietnamese 168.C5
an Doi House, 38/3 Soi Chantrasup.
f Huai Kaew Rd. Hrs. 11:00–21:00.
ood food in elegant leafy setting.
l (Fax): (0) 5322 1869

aan Mitr Mai – Yunnanese 184/
)0.E8 42/2 Ratchamankha Rd. Hrs.
:00–21:00. Shophouse atmosphere
·lies extraordinary fare. Try the 'fried
ilk'.
el: (0) 5327 5033

imping Restaurant Chinese-Thai
;9.C10 (Suki Rim Ping) 267/1
haroenrat Rd. Hrs. 10:00–23:00.
verside ambience for Chinese
eamboat - dinner boat trips offered.
l: (0) 5324 6486

iprakas Chinese 185/201.E11
·-49 Chiang Mai-Lamphun Rd.
·s10:00–23:00
l: (0) 5324 1241

uki Rot Yiam 168.D6
isement level. Kat Suan Kaew,
iai Kaew Rd.Hrs. 10:00–22:00
ther branches Mae Rim) Chinese
eamboat, Duck and other.
l: (0) 5389 4353

chu Do – Japanese 185/200.E9
· Loi Kroh Rd., soi 1. Hrs:11:00-
:00,17;00-21:00 closed Mondays
panese buffet evenings & lunch on Sats
d Suns, plus a la carte
l: (0) 5320 8086

ih Perng Yuan Sichuan 169.C9
5 Rattanakosin Rd. Hrs:11:00-
:00,17;00-22:00 closed Mondays
hinese food and Japanese noodles.
l: (0) 5323 4515

umi – Japanese 184/200.D8
/2-3 Si Phum Rd. Hrs:17:00-23:00
l: (0) 5322 2892

WESTERN AND INTERNATIONAL

Amazing Sandwich 184/200.D8
252/3 Prapokklao Rd Hrs. 15:00–02:00
After the sub, try the owner's home-made
cheesecake. Tel: '0' 5321 8846

Apocalypse Mexican Cantina–
Mexican 185/201.E9
80/2 Loi Kroh Rd. Hrs. 11:00–02:00.
Tel: (0) 5328 4288

Banrai Steakhouse 2 185/201.D10
94 Charoenrat Rd. (& #1 branch at 5 Soi
13, Prapokklao Rd.) Hrs. 11:00–01:00.
For beefeaters on a budget.
Tel & Fax: (0) 5330 2819

Bier Stübe – Euro-German
200.E9 33/6 Mun Muang Rd. Hrs. 07:30–
23:00. Reliable fare for local expats for
many years — pop in to the Blues Bar
next door for blues, beer and liquor
after the stübe closes. Tel: (0) 5327
8869

Chez Daniel – French 203.H8. 48/
15 Mahidol (Om Muang) Rd. Hrs.
12:00–14:00. & 18:00-23:00 Daniel
Le Normande prepares his own
Charcuteries. Set lunch menus.
Tel: (0)5320 4600

Coq Au Rico (Chez John) – French
168.G6 18/1 Airport Rd. Hrs. 12:00–
14:00 & 18:30–22:00. Chef John's fine
meats and wines.
Tel: (0) 5320 1551

Easy Diner – American/British 184/
200.E8. 27/29. Ratchadamnoen Hrs.
07:00–24:00/ 21:00 Sun & Mon
British breakfast & US burgers.
Tel: (0) 5320 8989 for orders.

Formula One North European.
163.Z2 149/23 Chang Khlan Rd.,
Anusarn Market. Hrs. 10:00–22:00.
Chef Eckard's fondues and vegetarian
dishes with satellite TV sports.
Tel: (0) 5327 4402

Giorgio– Italian 185.F10
2/6 Prachasamphan Rd, Chang Khlan.
11:30-14:30, 18:00-22:30 Highly rated.
Tel & Fax: (0) 5381 8236

Hilltribe Hemp Cafe – Thai &
Western 184/200.E9 19 Mun Muang Rd.
Hrs.07:00–till late. Healthy fare,
vegetarian friendly. Live music in the
evenings.

River Ping fare (Ban Suan)

Hotel Restaurants

Lunch is usually served between
11:30–14:00, and dinner between
18:00 to 22:00 (see pages 139-140
for locations). Prices are at the
higher end for Chiang Mai.

Ari-Rang – Korean (Hrs.06:30-
24:00 Star Inn, Tel: (0) 5327 0360)

Beefeater Steak House (Evening
hrs. till 23:00. The Empress Hotel,
Tel: (0) 5327 0240)

Castana – Italian & French
(Hrs.18:00-23:00 Westin Chiang
Mai. Tel: (0) 5327 5300)

China Palace – Chinese Restaurant
(Westin Chiang Mai, Tel: (0) 5327 5300)

La Gritta – Italian & International.
Lunch Buffet Hrs. 11:30-14:00
(Amari Rincome. Tel: (0) 5327 5300)

Miyuki – Japanese (Royal Princess,
Tel: (0) 5328 1033-4)

Phuping Chinese Restaurant
(Chiang Mai Orchid, Tel: (0) 5322
2099)

Riverside Terrace – International
buffet (Hrs.06:00-24:00 Westin
Chiang Mai. Tel: (0) 5327 5300)

Shabu-Shabu – Thai sukiyaki/Chi-
nese steamboat (Mae Ping Hotel. Tel:
(0) 5327 0160-80)

Western Grill – steak (Evening
hrs till 23:00. Chiang Inn Hotel,
Tel: (0) 5327 0070-6)

Cooking Courses

Since the Chiang Mai Thai Cookery School started in 1993, many other cooking schools have opened, and courses have become so popular that for a brief time mid-morning, foreigners may outnumber locals in Sompet market. This guide is unable to advise as to qualitative difference, if any, between different cooking schools.

Baan Thai, for example, runs a dedicated cooking school using two old houses conveniently located in the old city. The day starts with novice chefs sitting round a table with a recipe booklet planning which dishes they are interested in cooking. Certain dishes are cooked by all the group, but students may otherwise choose. This is an important preliminary as ingredients must be bought in the market. At the fresh market the teacher identifies herbs and points out other things, such as *kati* (coconut cream) and *khanom*—Thai desserts. The rest of the day follows a relaxed routine of first preparing ingredients and then cooking them. After each dish has been prepared, students may consume their creations, hopefully with relish. It is a good idea not to eat much breakfast as the day's cooking includes much tasting.

Baan Thai *200.E8*
11 Ratchadamnoen Soi 5. Hrs. 09:30–16:00. 3 days at 700 Bht/day
Tel: (0) 5335 7339. <www.CookInThai.com>

Chiang Mai Thai Cookery School *200.E9*
1-3 Mun Muang Rd. Course Hrs. 10:00–16:00. 5 days total 4,200 Bt or 900 Bht/day (E5)
Tel: (0) 5320 6388, Fax: (0) 5320 6387

Noi Cuisine (and catering service for parties)
75/1 Mu 7, Nong Chom, Sansai. (H1001 KM8 Soi 9 and right by Wat Sahakon)
Specialised courses (by arrangement) can make use of attached herb garden.
Tel: (0) 5335 4050. E-Mail: noi_cuisine@hotmail.com

How many cooks does it take to make a plate of 'phat thai'?

Irish Pub Restaurant *184/200.D8*
24/1 Ratwithi Rd. Hrs. 09:00–01:00.
Cakes & home-style cooking. Good for vegetarians.
Tel: (0) 5321 4554 📧 🌳

Italian Restaurant Babylon
168.B3   100/63 Huai Kaew Rd. Hrs. 11:00–14:00, 18:00–22:00.
Small shophouse, formidable Italian owner. *Granchi Gratinati* is a must.
Tel: (0) 5321 2180 📧 💬

Italian Restaurant Da Stefano
185/200.E9 2/1-2 Chang Moi Kao Rd. Hrs. 11:00–23:00.(Closed Mondays)
Popular with expatriates, clean.
Tel: (0) 5387 4189 📧 💬

Jerusalem Falafel – Mediterranean *200.E9 By Thaphae Gate. 35/3 Mun Muang Rd.. Hrs. 09:00–23:00.(Closed Fridays)* Popular Mediterranean fare.
Tel: (0) 5327 0208 📧 🌳

L'Auberge Chez Gibus Swiss European. *185/201.E9 42 Kamphaengdin Rd. Hrs.17:30–23:00.* Meaty fare.
Tel: (0) 5327 2712 📧 💬

La Gondola – Italian *185.D10 River bank in front of Rimping Condo 201/6 Charoenrat Rd. Hrs. 11:00–24:00.* Enjoyable food and location.
Tel: (0) 5330 6483 📧 🌳

Le Coq D'Or French *202.I10. 68/1 Koh Klang Rd. Hrs. 11:00–14:00, 17:00–23:00 Haute cuisine* in former residence of British Consul General.
Tel: (0) 5328 2024 📧 💬 🍸

JJ's Thai & International. *Chiang Inn Plaza W1., & Thaphae Rd. 163.V1 & 200.E9 Hrs. 06:30–23:00.* Esp.Good for breakfast. Tel: (0) 5321 1069-70 📧 💬

Pensione "La Villa" – Italian *184.E8 145 Ratchadamnoen Rd. Hrs. 11:00–23:00 high season.* Fine pizza from a wood-fired oven.
Tel: (0) 5327 7403 📧 🐘 💬

"Piccola Roma" Palace – Italian *163.Z3 144 Charoenprathet Rd. Hrs. 11:00-14:00, 17:00-23:00* Chef Angelo predominates. Call for free transportation.
Tel: (0) 5382 0297-8 📧 💬 🍸

Pumpui – Italian *184 E.8 Mun Muang Soi 1, Hrs. 12:00–24:00.* Sergio's popular place.
Tel: (0) 5327 8209 🐘 🌳 💬

To Nobody – German *168.E4 98/8 Mu 10, C.M. 50200, Soi beside Phayom Market off Suthep Road. Hrs 17:00-23:00* Residential dining.
Tel: (0) 5327 8794 📧 🐘 🌳 💬

ESTAURANTS CLOSE TO OWN (WITHIN 10KMS)

n Suan *80.C3*
Mu 3 Sanphisua CM 50300. 6kms rth of city on east bank of R. Ping. s. 11:00–22:00. Thai nouveau isine on a terrace overlooking bend river.
: (0) 5385 4169-70

n Suan Si Chiang Mai *80.D4*
/4 Sankamphaeng Rd. H1006 KM.4 ith turn — 400 m. Hrs. 11:30–22:00. iditional Thai buildings in a grove rain trees. Offers cooking classes.
/Fax: (0) 5326 2568-9

n Wang Tan Restaurant *80.E2*
08 Chiang Mai-Hang Dong Rd, east n just before KM9 — go straight, left

at T junction and enter housing estate *after 1.2 kms Hrs 11:00-22:00 Overlooks lake and parkland.*
Tel: (0) 5327 0830

Khrua Thai Samut Sakhon *M9 p.93. H106. West side — 200 m. south from Om-Muang intersection. Hrs. 10:30–22:00. Thai gourmet dishes in a simple sala setting.*
Tel: (0) 5327 7312

The Lagoon *80.C3*
Wong Waen That Mai Rd. Hrs. 11:00-24:00. Large restaurant overlooking ornamental lake. Good play area for children.
Tel: (0) 5324 6855

The Rainforest *80.E2*
H108 turn west at KM10 next to World Club Land (U-turn if coming from Chiang Mai). 181 Soi Khrui

Bungasingh.CM 50230. Modern and lively restaurant overlooking pond.
Tel: (0) 5344 1908, (0) 5343 2319

Sai Mok Kab Dok Mai *80.C3*
59 Wong Waen That Mai (Mae Rim-Mae Jo) Hrs. 17:00–24:00. H107 KM7 east turn by prison — 500m on north side of road Flower dishes as well as good northern and central dishes on the menu. Folk music in the key of gentle art. Tel: (0) 5335 7605

Sawai Riang – Lakeside Ville. *M9.p.93. 308 Mu 1, Noag Phung Soi 8, C.M. 50140. H106. West turn 2 kms. south from Om-Muang intersection — 700 m. Hrs. 10:00–22:00. StylishNorthern & Thai food overlooking a lotus pond. Rooms available.* Tel: (0) 5332 2061-2, Fax: (0) 5332 2062

Thai Fruits

Guava — *farang* (all year)

Sapodilla — *lamut* (Oct–Dec)

Pomelo — *som oh* (Aug–Nov)

Thailand is blessed with over thirty types of fruit, ranging from bananas to the exotic 'king of fruits', the durian. It may be hate at first whiff of the prickly durian, but love at first taste of the creamy yellow flesh that surrounds the hard seed. The banana is no less interesting, for several varieties are grown and other parts of the plant (the stem of the trunk and the flower head) are used for curries and spicy salads. The leaves serve as eco-friendly packing, and they are widely used as decoration for offerings.

The hot season is made particularly enjoyable by the arrival of the mango (March-May), which is often served in the markets as a dessert with sticky-rice and coconut cream. Lychees, which are grown in particular around Fang, are available in late April-May. The rainy season brings the most famous fruit of the valley, the longan. It is celebrated when Lamphun holds its *Lam Yai* festival for the first seven days of August. The festival ends with a colourful parade on the final Saturday.

The fresh markets provide the basis of Thai cuisine. So far they have survived the advent of the refrigerator and food packaging.

Longan — *lam yai* (Jul–Sep)

Sugar Apple — *noi na* (Jun–Sept)

Mangosteen — *mángkhut* (May–Sept)

Durian — *thurian* (May–August)

NIGHT-LIFE

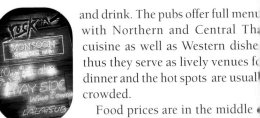

The night scene in Chiang Mai constantly changes as fickle revellers shift their preferences and popular bands come and go. Night spots tend to be localised, however; so if one place does not please, there is usually another not far away.

The Thais like to go out with friends to pubs where they can enjoy live music, food and drink. The pubs offer full menu with Northern and Central Tha cuisine as well as Western dishe thus they serve as lively venues f dinner and the hot spots are usuall crowded.

Food prices are in the middle the range of prices for restaurants. So drinks can cost around 50 baht, beers 10 baht, and cocktails 100-200 baht.

Popular Thai Pubs

Crowds of youths doing the boogie-woogie at their tables to live-music can make combining good food with conversation challenging if you are sitting near the stage of a popular pub. Most Thai pubs have quieter corners where you can enjoy the ambience of an evening out with friends and hear what they have to say.

DOWN BY THE RIVERSIDE

ENJOYING A SUNDOWNER while gazing out over the River Ping is a perfect way to enjoy the end of the day. Consequently, the roads along the east bank (*Charoenrat Road & The Old Chiang Mai-Lamphun Road G3 & H-4*), and to a lesser extent those on the west bank

The Night Bazaar

The Night Bazaar is a collection of side-walks and plazas crowded with stalls, shops and boutiques selling everything from fake watches to reproduction 'antiques'. The hours *(18:00–23:00; money changing till 22:00)* and variety make this the best one-stop shopping centre in town. Enjoy a good haggle at the stalls, for bargaining is the norm.

In the Nakhon Ping Night Bazaar Building, hill tribe products, woodcarvings and other handicrafts are sold at the basement level, while fabrics and antiques are found at the upper levels. Across the road, the Galare Food Centre, Beer Garden & Shopping Centre offers *(coupon system. Tel (0) 5327 2067)* free performances of classical dancing *(21:00–22:30)*. More handicraft stores as well as a good night-market for food can be found in the Anusarn Market Bazaar.

The Chiang Inn Plaza *(11:00–23:00)* and the smaller Chiang Mai Pavilion buildings contain up-market outlets, as well as Western fast food restaurants. The Chiang Inn Plaza also has restaurants at the basement level as well as a gallery, spa and bookshops at the upper levels. The Chiang Mai Centre *(12:00–23:00)* store sells handicrafts in the basement at back, but otherwise sells clothing found in most Thai Department stores. The Peak has become a fashionable spot to sit, drink and watch others going up the wall if you don't fancy it yourself.

Band on the river

(*Charoen Prathet & Wang Singh Kham*), have become Chiang Mai's premier locations for pubs and restaurants (*not all can be listed*).

Brasserie Restaurant & Bar
185.D10. 37 Charoenrat Rd. Hrs. 17:00–02:00. R&B guitar virtuoso Tu rocks the joint on most days. (For fo on the terrace see favourites p.153).
Tel: (0) 5324 1665

Consulate Park Pub & Restaurant *185/201.F10 127 Charoen Prathet Rd. Hrs. 16:00–01:00.* Queen Victoria's Statu once graced these grounds — now live music and food.
Tel: (0) 5327 8538

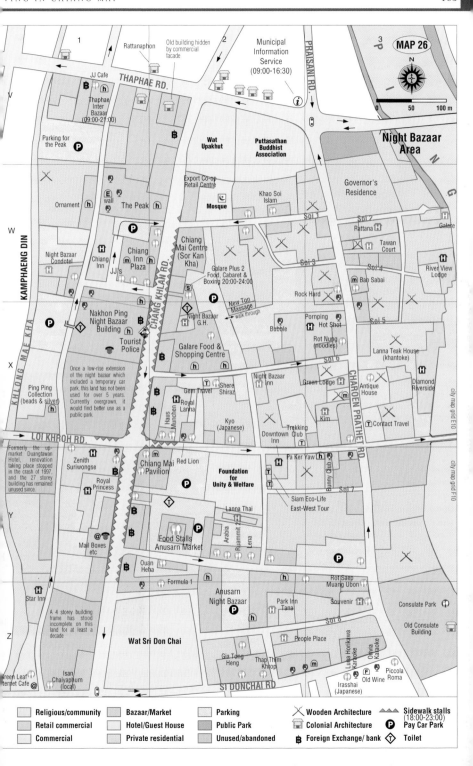

MAP 26

Night Bazaar Area

Legend:

- Religious/community
- Retail commercial
- Commercial
- Bazaar/Market
- Hotel/Guest House
- Private residential
- Parking
- Public Park
- Unused/abandoned
- ✕ Wooden Architecture
- Colonial Architecture
- Foreign Exchange/ bank
- ▲▲▲ Sidewalk stalls (18:00-23:00)
- **P** Pay Car Park
- ◇ Toilet

It's hard to keep good staff

Cottage and Decor *185/201.E11*
27 Chiang Mai-Lamphun Rd. Hrs.
18:00–02:00. The upwardly mobile
love the smooth jazz and latin rock.
Tel: (0) 5330 2225 ●■

The Good View *185/201.E10*
13 Charoenrat Rd. Hrs. 18:00–02:00.
Thais love this lively, jazzy pub-
restaurant, not only for its good food.
Tel: (0) 5330 2764 ●■

Huan Sontharee *169.B10*
46 Wang Sing Kham Rd. Hrs.16:00–
01:00. Northern folk songs from famed
Northern Thai singer Sontharee
Wechanon. Tel: (0) 5325 2445
●🏊■

The Resort *169.C10*
Faham Rd. Hrs. 11:00–01:00. (H4)
Dining on pleasant, spacious decks to
a variety of musical entertainment.
Tel: (0) 5326 2099 ●🏊■

The Riverside Bar & Restaurant
185/201.E10 9/11 Charoenrat Rd. Hrs.
10:00 –01:30. Bands at both ends of
this ever popular spot *(pictures p.146
& 164)* — standing room only when
the crowd starts to jump at the
northern bar. Very pleasant terrace.
Tel: (0) 5324 3239 ●🏊■

The River Terrace (Huan Boran 2)
*169.G11 154/1 Chiang Mai- Lamphun
Rd. (south of Kawila Memorial).
Hrs.16:00–02:00.* Good food & Thai
folk music for a local touch.
Tel: (0) 5324 0270 ●■

West Side Pub *169.C10*
Wang Sing Kham Rd. Hrs.17:00–02:00.
Country and Western on upper terrace.
Tel: (0) 5323 4431 ●🏊■

City-Side Pubs & Bars

A host of small bars are found
on Ratwithi Road between
Ratchaphakhinai and Mun
Muang roads *(200.E8-9)*. A
second area for night-life has
been growing along Nimmanhaemin Road *(168. C5)*, and a
third is found along Chiang
Mai Land *(Map 33.H9)*

  Though the closing time for
night clubs is officially 2 a.m.,
crackdowns and 'new social
orders' may be causing places
to close earlier, if not just pull
down their shutters.

Butterflies *184.D8*
21/3 Si Phum Rd. Hrs. 19:00–02:00.
lively folk/rock & blues.
Tel: (0) 5322 2235 ●

Darling *168.C5*
95/10 Nimmanhaemin Rd. Hrs. 17:00–
12:00. Tiny wine bar for quiet drinks (or
try nearby 'Drunken Flower' —*see* p.154)
Tel: (0) 5322 2235 ■🏊■

25 Satang Pub & Restaurant *184
D7. 157 Si Phum Rd. Hrs.17:00–*
02:00. Thai rock at this local spot.
Tel: (0) 5341 6159 ●🏊■

Fine Thanks *168.C5*
119 Nimmanhaemin Rd. Hrs. 18:00–
*02:00.*Polished music for the crowd at
this wooden house pub.
Tel: (0) 5321 3605 ●🏊■

The Pub *168.C5*
*189 Huai Kaew Rd. Hrs. 17:00–24:00.
Closed Mondays).* British country pub
style lounge bar & restaurant.
Tel: (0) 5321 1550 ■■

Rabiang *168.A4*
*108/11 Sanam Kila 700 Pi
Rd.(irrigation canal road) Hrs. 16:00–*
02:00. Plaeng phua chiwit - music for life.
Tel: (0) 5321 3605 ●🏊

The Red Lion *163.X2*
123 Loi Khroh Rd, Night Bazaar. Hrs.
12:00–24:00. British pub grub, or
sauerkraut from adjacent Haus
München.
Tel: (0) 5381 8847 ■🏊

The Smiling Monkey *185/200.F8*
*40/1 Bamrungburi Rd., Chiang Mai
Gate. Hrs. 09:00–02:00.* Wooden house

with long bar and terrace with waterfal
Tel/Fax: (0) 5327 7538 ●🏊

Sax Bar *200.E9*
35/2 Mun Muang Rd. Hrs.
17:00–01:00. Good contemporary
rock & jazz in Rudi's artistic venue.
Tel: (0) 5322 1140 ●

Thai German Brewery *202.C14*
*300m behind Carrefour on Chiang M
Lampang Superhighway. Hrs. 11:00–*
01:00. Einz, zwei, brüder lein ...
micro-brewery in a godown.
Tel: (0) 5324 4588 ■■

Touch *168.C5*
36/9 Huai Kaew Rd. Hrs. 17:00–01:0
Comfortable dining & armchair
drinking to live music.
Tel: (0) 5322 1140 ■■

Toy Ya Dong *184.D7*
4/2 Singharat Soi 3. Hrs. 18:00–02:00
Pickled herb liquors & other delight
served to locals beneath a thatch roo
Tel: (0) 5321 3227 ●

Uang Phung Chan Pha *168.C4*
69 Boriwen Kat Choeng Doi, Hrs
17:00-01:00. Country & Western Rock
Tel: (0) 5340 0505 ●🏊

Into the Night

THE MOST LIVELY SPOTS in
town are the
khrua tech
➼'kitchen
discos'

At these places, live bands get t
young crowd to jump up and
dance around their tables.

Singer in a 'Khrua Tech' ba

Blue Moon Nightclub *184/200.F8*
5/3 Mun Muang Rd. Hrs.21:00–02:00
Transvestite show and traditional
ballroom dancing — skilled taxi-
dancing partners available. Also offer
traditional massage *(10:00-02:00)*
Tel: (0) 5327 8818 ■■

nsadan *200. E8*
dard Hotel. 57-59 Ratchamankha
Hrs.20:00–01:00 Raucous khrua-
h. Thap Tim Karaoke in hotel.

: (0) 5327 0755 📠 🖃

ace Bubble Disco & Hot Shot
fé *163.X2 Pornping Tower Hotel, 46-*
haroen Phrathet Rd. Hrs 21:00–
00. Get down & dumb to the tech's
im machine, or move to the band at
Hot Shot Café. The complex also
ludes the **Pink Cocktail Lounge**
d the **Blue-Bat Barbecue Beer**
rden on the roof top *(18:00-24:00).*

: (0) 5327 0099 📠 🖃

ED LIGHTS & A-GOGO

OMEN, MEN AND IN-BETWEEENS
oke the desires of visitors,
pecially at bars along the
oats south of Thaphae Gate.
le masseurs in 'contempo-
ry' massage parlours *(ap op*
at อาบอบนวด *see warning*
195) work to relieve male
nsion, practising skills
ite different from those in
ditional massage *(nuat*
en boran นวดแผนโบราณ *p.183)*

lam's Apple *169.B7*
2/46-47 Soi Viangbua, Chotana Rd.
Lotus Hotel). Hrs. 22:00–01:00.
le a-gogo for gay. Tel: (0) 5322
80 📠 🖃

nny Club *163.Y3*
Khroh Rd. near Charoen Phrathet
Hrs 17:00–02:00. Leatherette
as, karaoke, whatever ....

: (0) 5381 8035 📠

n's Place & The Spotlight
.E9 Mun Muang & Kotchasan Rds.
s. 11:00–02:00. Across the moat
m each other, these two bars offer
gogo to go, TV and pool. (Jon's Tel:
) 5327 7964) 📠 🖃

ndora *202. E12*
/62-64 Charoenmuang Rd. Hrs.
00–04:00. Open the box in the
ssage parlour or karaoke. Tel: (0)
24 5740-1 📠 🖃

yuri Complex *202.E11*
oi 2 Bamrungrat Rd. Hrs. 12:00–
00. Coffee shop, karaoke, snooker
massage girls behind plate-glass.

: (0) 5324 2361 📠 🖃

Night Clubs

By local custom, nightclubs have the minimum of light, the maximum of aircooling and the maximum of noise from the band. Thus the first few minutes are spent groping around, like someone accidentally locked in a cold storage room with no lights and a blaring loudspeaker. After some minutes you may become acclimatised enough to realise the room is fairly full, and that there are dance partners at most tables. Groping may be observed to persist long after the eyes can see well enough to make this strictly unnecessary (Hudson's guide to Chiang Mai, 1973)

Things have changed, but then again they have not. The noise in the 'techs' will give people hearing problems, and when so many people jam tightly into a popular spot, you have to grope your way just to get to the bar. Taxi-dancers have become largely redundant, however.

'Suan aharn' — food gardens — or 'coffee shops' are different, though they may also be cold. At these places female singers entertain a generally older male clientele by singing while dressed in flamboyant outfits, if not swimming costumes. Attracted like insects to UV lighting, and despite the occasional painful tuning, the men lavish garlands on their favourite singers, often attaching banknotes to show their appreciation. When not singing, the women join the men at the tables and encourage them to drink up, not that this is really needed. Rotas of singers normally include one man, who never wears a swimsuit and who often sings better than most of the women.

Karaoke has largely taken over as the most popular entertainment, but 'coffee shops' can still be found in hotels such as the Pet Ngam (Diamond old wing), around the superhighway and near the red-light district in Santhitham.

New Chang Puek
112/12 Chotana Rd., C.M. 50300.
(H107 KM.7 E.side) Hrs. 17:00–02:00.
Tel: (0) 5389 1118-9 ☣ 🖃

Phitsamai Café *185/200.D9*
President Hotel, 226 Wichayanon Rd.
Hrs. 12:00–01:00.
Tel: (0) 5327 8704 📠 🖃

KARAOKE

THAIS LOVE TO DRINK AND SING, with the result that small Karaoke parlours are found throughout the city. Hostess karaoke parlours, which advertise themselves with female staff lounging around their entrances, may be less oriented towards 'family entertainment'. For the price of a lady-drink, hostesses will sit with you for half an hour and help you hold the microphone. They say that no holds are barred when big bills mount up and the white bird sings.

Several hostess karaoke bars are located near the eastern end of Sridonchai Rd, and in Chiang Mai Land (H9), where there are also restaurants serving *yakiniku* (Japanese barbecued meats), Chinese and Korean food as well as several bars and very loud techs for young Thais.

HANDICRAFTS OF CHIANG MAI

THE FOLK SKILLS used to produce the necessities of daily life have combined with the high arts of decoration used in temples and court regalia to form the basis of Chiang Mai's famous handicrafts industry. Whether an elegant celado vase, a length of homespun hem cloth, or a carved wooden elephan local artefacts make decorative sou venirs of the folk art of the regio

Looking for Handicrafts

ALMOST ALL HANDICRAFTS are available in the Night Bazaar area (see p.163), where the range of outlets — from humble street stalls to air-conditioned boutiques — should please anyone. More shops specialising in handicrafts are found in several areas downtown (see 'Lanna style' p180 for more listings), and the advertisements in the free magazines give a lot of additional information.

Outside of Chiang Mai the two main areas for handi-crafts are the Sankamphaeng Road to Bo Sang (see p.88-90), and the road from Hang Dong to Ban Tawai (see p.94)

With the descriptions of handicrafts that follow, the suggestions on where to go are not endorsements to buy at those places, as there are many other places selling all manner of handicrafts. Shops which have some form of demonstration that shows people making the products are marked with a **D**.

The Chiang Mai National Museum (09:00–16:00. Closed Mondays, Tuesdays & National Holidays) allows a look at handicrafts from a historical viewpoint, but collections of antiques are scattered and small (see

'small museums on p.115)

If you have a trade interest and want to see samples (or just buy something), a visit to the government run Northern Craft Centre (202.D13. 158 Thung Hotel Rd. 08:30–12:00, 13:00–16:30. Tel: (0) 5324 3494, (0) 5324 5361, Fax: (0) 5324 8315) may help.

BASKETRY

USING BAMBOO and other readily available materials, people throughout Thailand have been making house-hold objects such as baskets, hats, and traps for centuries.

In the north the most common woven objects are steamers and contain-ers for sticky rice, mats and traps for catching fish in the paddy. However, the skill used in making the older pieces is hard to match these days as demand for woven items has declined and young people no longer need the old skills.

Where to see basketry:
Different villages tend to specialise in a certain type of woven product such as mats or containers, but there is no special place to see the weaving. Around KM.13 on H108 (The Chiang Mai-Hot Road), a number of shops sell woven bamboo products. Some may also be found in Warorot Market and the Night Bazaar.

Nalakarn & Product Developmen Co. 163.W1 Both shops on Fl 2 Chia Inn Plaza.100/1 Chang Khlan Rd. Nalakarn Tel: (0) 5381 8193 E-m: nalakarn@hotmail.com & P.D.Co. Tel: (0) 5328 1364 E-m: PD@chiangmai.a-net.th

Basket weaving, tambon Pa Po

Thawan Somthan Map 7 p.88 78 Mu 4, Tambon Pa Pong, Saraphi C.M. 50140 . Pa Pong. Tel: (0) 5342 2899

Sumintar Bamboo Weaving Shop 204 Mu 3 T. Ban Wan, Hang Dong C.M. 50230. Export & wholesale. Tel: (0) 5342 2899

CERAMICS

THE FINEST POTTERY of the region is known as celadon, which has a distinctive glaze made with wood ash. The technique of producing these wares involves applying the aze before a second high mperature firing (1260°c in a duced atmosphere of carbon oxide). It was known to have en developed in China at ast 2000 years ago.

Traditionally the glaze is signed to 'run' (flow down e pot as the glaze becomes assy) as well as 'craze' and ke on a crackled appear-ce. Though a light green lour is considered ideal, d celadons could also be llow and brown and the aze matt and opaque if derfired. The main kilns Lan Na were at Kalong ear Wiang Papao), Phan etween Chiang Rai & ayao) and Sankamphaeng. st when and how the nsiderable skills required make this pottery came to n Na is uncertain.

It is generally accepted that oduction near Chiang Mai Sankamphaeng began early the 14th century, and, like her kilns, was helped by hinese potters who had oved south away from the ongols. However there is so the possibility that the cessary skills came from a therto undiscoverd kiln site d could be Thai in origin. ese kilns may have produced e wares, perhaps with help om earlier migrations of hinese potters, long before e establishment of the nkamphaeng kilns at the ginning of the 14th ntury.

The local industry thrived til the fall of Lan Na to the rmese. By the mid-17th ntury war and the mpetition from cheaper ue and white wares from hina had put out the fires in

Shopping for Antiques & Handicrafts

Few real antiques are available, and they are likely to be of Burmese or Lao origin. Most 'antique' shops, then, are selling reproductions, albeit as pieces that seem indistinguishable from old artefacts. Years of trade has dispersed much of the region's cultural heritage, but it has also encouraged high quality

reproduction as well as the adaption of traditional designs to create modern pieces. As a result visitors can buy attractive pieces for a fraction of the price of something genuinely old and increasingly scarce.

According to one local dealer, some tour operators take a percentage on monthly sales, and their tours only visit shops paying commissions. This can lead to visitors paying inflated prices and or getting inferior products. Shopping independently, unfortunately, may not bring cheaper prices, but it may help dealers who do not pay commissions.

13-15th century Sankamphaeng wares (private collection)

Borisoothi Antiques *Map 8. p.89*
15/2 Sankamphaeng Rd. KM.6 Hrs.
08:30–17:30.
Tel: 338460-2 Fax: 338462

Sanphranon Antiques
Chiang Mai-Hot Rd. (H108 KM.8 west side) 92/1 Mu 5, Tambol Mae Hual, Hang Dong. Hrs. 08:00–17:00.
Tel: (0) 5327 2898

Lanna kilns. Production began again at the beginning of the 20th century, bringing Lanna pottery to a new age.

Where to see ceramics:
Ban Muang Kung (see p.95) and Ban Kuan produce earthenware, and kilns are located on the Hang Dong-Ban Thawai Road (Map 6.p.80) and the Sankamphaeng Road (see p.89)

Ban Phor Liang Meun's Terracotta Arts — D *184.F8*
36 Prapokklao Rd., Soi 2, C.M. 50200 Hrs. 08:00–18:00. Bas-relief and figures in the round based on Indic iconography.
Tel:(0) 5327 8187 Fax: (0) 5327 5895

Baan Celadon — D *(Map 8.p.89)*
8 Mu 10, Chiang Mai-San Kamphaeng Rd.(H1006 KM.7) C.M.50130.Hrs. 08:30 –17:30. Tel: (0) 5333 8288, Fax: (0) 5333 8940 <www.chiangmai-online.com/baancel>

Earthenware production (Ban Muang Kung)

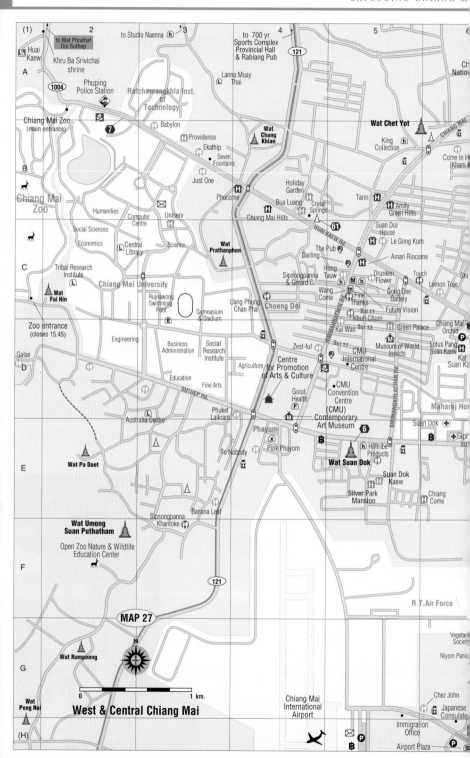

West & Central Chiang Mai

MAP 27

0   1 km.

(1) Huai Kaew
to Wat Phrathat Doi Suthep
Khru Ba Srivichai shrine
1004
Phuping Police Station
Chiang Mai Zoo (main entrance)
Babylon
Chiang Mai Zoo
Ratchamangkhla Inst. of Technology
to Studio Naenna
to 700 yr Sports Complex Provincial Hall & Rabiang Pub
121
Lanna Muay Thai
Providence
Ekathip
Seven Fountains
Just One
Phucome
Wat Chang Khian
Holiday Garden
Bua Luang
Chiang Mai Hills
Crysal Springs
HUAI KAEW Rd.
Tarin
Amity Green Hills
Suan Doi House
Le Gong Kum
Amari Rincome
The Pub
Darling
Wat Chet Yot
King Collection
Come In H (Kham
Humanities
Computer Centre
Uniserv
Social Sciences
Economics
Central Library
Science
Wat Prathanphon
Hong Tauw
Sipsongpanna & Gerard C.
Wang Come
Drunken Flower
Fine Thanks
Touch
Gong Dee Gallery
Soi 11
Future Vision
Lemon Tree
Shi
Tribal Research Institute
Chiang Mai University
Wat Fai Hin
Rujiawong Swimming Pool
Gymnasium & Stadium
Uang Phung Chan Pha
Choeng Doi
Kai Wan
Khun Churn
Soi 13
Green Palace
Chiang Mai Orchid
Zoo entrance (closes 15.45)
Galae
Engineering
Business Administration
Social Research Institute
Agriculture
Centre for Promotion of Arts & Culture
Zest-ful
Museum of World Insects
CMU International Centre
Lotus Pang Suan Kaew
Kat Suan Ka
Education
Fine Arts
Good Health
CMU Convention Centre
(CMU) Contemporary Art Museum
SUTHEP Rd.
Phuket Laikram
Phayom
Pink Phayom
Maharaj Hos
Suan Dok
Siph Su
Wat Pa Daet
Australia Centre
To Nobody
Hilltribe Products
Wat Suan Dok
Suan Dok Kaew
Silver Park Mansion
Chiang Come
Sipsongpanna Khantoke
Banana Leaf
Wat Umong Suan Puthatham
Open Zoo Nature & Wildlife Education Center
121
Wat Rampoeng
N
Wat Pong Noi
(H)
R.T. Air Force
Chiang Mai International Airport
Vegetari Society
Niyom Panic
Chez John
Japanese Consulate
Immigration Office
Airport Plaza
7
61
6

Potters walk around the vases beating them into shape with wooden paddles at Ban Kuan, near Hang Dong.(see map 6).

King Collection *168.B5*
70/5 Wat Chet Yot, C.M. 50300 Hrs. 09:00–18:00. Terracotta Indic figures from Isan. Tel/Fax : (0) 5341 4151. <www.kingcollection.com>

Mengrai Kilns *184.E6*
79/2 Arak Rd., C.M. 50200. Hrs. 08:00–17:00. Expensive Celadon. Tel: (0) 5327 2063, Fax: (0) 5327 8676

Korakot Stoneware — D *80.F1*
232/103 Mu2 Tambon Hang Dong. Hrs. 08:00–17:00.Large stoneware jars Tel: (0) 5343 4105 Fax: (0) 5333 1958

Siam Celadon — D *Map 8. p.89*
8 Mu 10, Chiang Mai-San Kamphaeng Rd. (H1006 KM.10) C.M.50130.Hrs. 08:30–17:30. A factory with a 'traditional kiln' on show at back. Tel: (0) 5333 1526, Fax: (0) 5333 1958

The Sankamphaeng Kilns — D
Map 8. p.89. 60/3 Mu 13, San Kamphaeng, C.M. 50130 (H1006 KM.11)Hrs. 08:00–17:00. Celadon, blue & white, Bencharong. Tel: (0) 5333 1034, Fax: (0) 5333 8034

(Left) 13th-15th century Earthenware (private collection)

Hand-woven Fabrics

WEAVING WAS ONCE a most important skill for Thai women. They wove plain designs for daily use, and more elaborate ones for rituals or ceremonies. In the north, cotton was woven by the Tai Yuan and Tai Leu, and silk was woven by the Lao. Thus silk usually had to be imported some distance and only high ranking families could afford it. Nowadays silk production is well established in the valley.

Women typically demonstrated their weaving skills on the tube skirt, known as *pha sin*. In the north the main parts of everyday *pha sin* are patterned with horizontal stripes and have separate waist-bands and hem pieces sewn on.

Ritual *pha sin* have much more detailed decoration and, like all *sin*, vary according to group. This is due to the fact that women stayed close to their place of birth and were less influenced by other styles. The young women would produce the most complex pieces to show their skills to attract husbands.

In the Chiang Mai valley, the favoured colours are red, green and yellow, with red and black being used in the waist band and hem pieces. The decoration is put in the hem piece in a style of weaving known as *tin chok*, which is characterised by diamond shaped patterns.

Where to see hand-woven fabrics:
Traditional weaving of cotton is found in the villages south of Pa Sang, south of Chom Thong and near Mae Chaem (*see pages 102,105,107, 112*). Silk production can also be seen at the emporiums on San Kamphaeng Road (**Jolie Femme, Piankusol, Le Bombyx** — *see p. 88*). Many shops in town sell hand-woven cotton garments.

Ban Rai Pai Ngam *184.G7*
206 Thiphanet Rd., C.M. 50000. Hrs. 08:00–16:00. Hand woven cottons (Factory: H108 KM.69-70. Fax: (0) 5336 1230) Shop Tel: (0) 5327 3625

Golden Thai Silk *185/201.E9*
27 Thaphae Soi 3. C.M. 50100

Tin cho

Hrs.08:00-18:00 Woven pieces of silk as well as silk cloth by the yard. Tel: (0) 5327 1563 Fax: (0) 5327 5422 E-mail: thaisilk@cm.ksc.co.th

Shinawatra Thai Silk — D
Map 8. p.89. 145/1-2 San Kamphaeng Rd. (H1006 KM.7) Hrs. 08:30–17:30. A local house with branches in town (Huai Kaew Rd. 168.C6) and on Sankamphaeng Rd. (H1006) Tel: (0) 5333 8054-5, Fax: (0) 5333 8475

Studio Naenna — D *168.A3*
138/8 Soi Changkhian – off Huai Kaew Rd.Hrs. 8:30–17:00. Call first. Hand-woven tube skirts and natural dyeing Tel: (0) 5322 6042, Fax: (0) 5321 770 <www.infothai.com/naenna>

ILL TRIBE ARTEFACTS

E HILL TRIBES are famous for
eir bright costumes and
vellery, but other artefacts
ch as pipes, knives, basketry
d musical instuments also
ake desirable souvenirs.
owadays much of the hill
be production is aimed at
e tourist market.

The unique designs have
ade their silver jewellery
iongst the most desirable
hill tribe artefacts.
aditionally, the hill tribes
ve valued silver as a
isted measure of wealth
d the amount worn at
remonies would show the
itus of the family. Wearing
'ge amounts of silver
vellery is still the custom at
iportant rituals and
stivals. Silver ornamenta-
n could also have a
iritual value to protect
ainst evil spirits. The
gest pieces of jewellery are
e neck rings, silver buckles
d heavy bracelets, while
e most decorative are the
ains with silver pendants.
The silver originally came
om coins which were either
elted down or used directly
decoration on women's
thing. Each group had their
'n designs, which came
om individual silversmiths
ho would only make a few
nilar pieces. Most of these
d pieces have long been
ld, and the formerly
iportant village silversmiths
ve all but vanished.
wland silversmiths now
oduce modern jewellery
sed on a mix of traditional
signs.

Traditional Dress

Northern women usually wear traditional dress when taking part in temple ceremonies during festivals.

"*The Lao females.. wear the Lao petticoat...ornamented...and embroidered... The married women are moreover dressed in a jacket or spenser, closely fitting as far as the waist, and from thence expanding more amply until it reaches the knee... Those who can afford it, have rich necklaces, and rings in their ears and on their fingers;... a silk shawl or scarf of red or rose colour is thrown loosely over their shoulders. The latter refers to the married women — young ladies, unmarried, do not dress above their waste.*

Black and shining their hair is, the racemes of the white flowered Moringa or the fragrant Vateria, or if such be not in blossom, those of any other tree or plant similar in colour, set it off much more by the great contrast, when these flowers are placed in their raven tresses. The mouth of the young girls is formed exquisitely. But few of the Lao women indulge in betel chewing, hence they do not render that organ, so fairly formed by nature, hideous by the prevailing custom of the Thai; and their teeth remain as white as nature made them"

Sir Robert H. Schomburgk. Kt. F.R.S., British Consul at Siam on a visit to Chiang Mai in 1860.

Since King Chulalongkorn's admonitions for women to cover up their breasts, blouses have been worn with tube skirts. The use of silver belts is also recent as belts would have been hidden by folds of cloth and used for support.

Men used to be naked except for a cloth wrapped around the loins that was either short or long. Short cloths would reveal more of the tattoos, which covered their bodies from the waist down to the knees. Men began to wear round necked shirts at the same time as women began to wear blouses.

Indigo cotton cloth known as *mohom* came to be used for shirts and loose fitting trousers for working in the fields. In a relatively new development, this cloth has become symbolic of northern Thai dress for men

Dressed in 'mohom', artist Lipikorn Makaew plays the 'pin pia'

Lanna Artisans

Lanna art originated from the desire of leaders to embellish religious structures to legitimise their majesty. Power depended on the control of people, and so skilled artisans were ranked very highly, and they would be brought in from neighbouring principalities, either as a result of political negotiation or military campaign. Retaining their ethnic identity, they would be settled in communities close to the city walls. Thus it was that the wars against the Burmese and the raids for manpower of the 19th century formed the basis of the handicraft *mubans* in Chiang Mai today (see city walk 3).

Early artisitic styles were therefore heavily influenced by those of

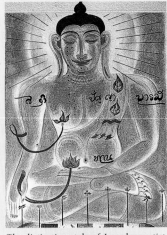

The distinctive style of Lamphun artist Prasong Leumuang in panels between windows of the viharn of Wat Chang Khun, Saraphi.

neighbouring states like Pagan and Sukhothai, with later influences to come from Burma and the Shan States. Last but not least has been the Rattanakosin influence from Bangkok.

The artisans who worked on the temples were anonymous however, for the merit accumulated to the sponsors, as it does today (their names can often

be found written on the parts of the temple building they paid for).

While the Fine Arts Department of Silpakorn University takes charge of historical restorations, the abbots of temples often determine how new temple structures should look, and monks sometimes work as artisans themselves. The monks of Wat Phuak Taem, for example, *(see City Walk 1 or 3)* make metal filligree for stupa finials for many temples in the country in a small workshop on the south side of the temple compound. Phra Bun Prasert (1925-1987) was well known for his designs of wooden panels and stucco decorations in the Lanna style, but the execution of the designs depended on the artisan doing the work (examples may be seen on the shutters of Wat Buppharam, the scripture library at Wat Rampoeng and the stucco work of the *ubosot* which sits above the *viharn* of Wat Phan On).

Though art in Thailand has become commercial, local artisans still embellish temples, and even well-known artists may illumine temple walls with murals in the anonymous tradition of their forbears.

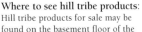

Phra Anan Rattanako — monk and woodcarver at Wat Pang Hai, Tambon Thepsadet

---

Where to see hill tribe products:
Hill tribe products for sale may be found on the basement floor of the Night Bazaar building (Chang Khlan Rd.) and at the Galare Centre. In the daytime, try the places below.

Hill Tribe Products Promotion Centre *168.E5 21/17 Suthep Rd., C.M. 50200. Hrs. 09:00–17:00.* Tel: (0) 5327 7743

The Lost Heavens (Tribal & Primitive Art) *185/201.E9*
234 Thaphae Rd., C.M. 50100. Hrs. 09:30–18:00/21:00. Tel: (0) 5325 1555-7, Fax: (0) 5323 5151

Thai Tribal Crafts *169/202.D11*
208 Bamrungrat Rd., C.M. 50000. Hrs. 09:00–17:00. Tel: (0) 5324 1043 Fax: (0) 5324 3493

Sop Moei Arts *185/201.D10*
31-35 Charoenrat Rd, C.M. 50000. Hrs. 10:00–22:00. Except Fridays (10:00–17:00) and Saturdays (18:00–22:00). Karen weavers produce modern designs. Tel & Fax: (0) 5326 0844 <www.sopmoeiarts.com>

dant worn by bridegroom (Hmong)

acquerware

ACQUER was originally used to provide a smooth, eather-proof finish that uld preserve the life of an tefact. As lacquer provided a se for gilding and glass or arl inlay, it was widely used r decoration in temples.

Its most common use was to umine wood panels on doors d windows, and especially r cabinets that were used to ep palm leaf manuscripts. e lacquer came from a tree *Melanorrhea usitata* Anacaraceae) found in Northern ailand and Burma.

The main design was in ack and gold, a style known *lai rot nam*. The designs were

Khoen lacquerware betel set

two dimensional (no perspective was used) and created a fine balance of gold and black with numerous flower designs round the main motifs.

The technique used to do this has been applied to modern production. A pattern in a yellow water soluble gum is painted on the piece and covered with a thin layer of lacquer. Gold foil is put onto to the sticky lacquer. When the piece is washed, the yellow paint and foil above it dissolve to reveal the black of the pattern underneath.

Laquer was also used to seal baskets and Chiang Mai used to be the centre of a style of *khoen* ware that was red and black. This was used on household objects, but the style went out of fashion and is no longer widely produced. Modern designs using coloured lacquer on lines etched into a black base are Burmese in style.

Where to see lacquerware:
Lacquerware production is dispersed, and therefore can most easily be seen at the handicraft emporiums. Real lacquer from the tree is also increasingly scarce, and modern work often uses petroleum base mixes.

Lanna House *Map 18. p.117*
Entrance to Regent Resort, Mae Rim,
Hrs. 09:00–18:00 Closed Wednesdays.
Antique Burmese lacquerware, woodcarvings and other hand-crafted work.
Tel: (0)5386 1257
E-m: information@lannahouse.com

Living Space *185/201.E9*
267-8 Thaphae Rd. CM 50300. Hrs:
08:00-21:00 Modern interpretations in lacquerware.
Tel: (0) 5387 4299.
<www.livingspacedesigns.com>

P Collection *Map 8. p.89*
2 Mu 1, San Kamphaeng Rd., C.M.
50000 (H1006 KM.3) Hrs.
08:30–17:00. Tel: (0) 5324 0222-5
Fax: (0) 5324 0231

(right) Preparing 'lai rot nam' at a San
Khamphaeng Road emporium

Prathuang Khruang Khoen — D
169.G7 101 Nantaram Rd. Hrs.
08:00–17:00. Consider buying something at this last surviving small producer in the former centre of this industry. Tel: (0) 5327 2186

SILVERWARE

IN THE NORTH, silverware goes back at least to the time of King Mangrai, who imported artisans from Burma, and Chiang Saen period silverware has been found in burial mounds. Despite this long tradition, antique silver from Chiang Mai is usually no older than 100 years.

The modern silver industry has Burmese origins that began with the resettlement of people from the Shan States by Chao Kawila. King Chulalongkorn also settled Burmese craftsmen in Chiang Mai in the Wualai area, which has remained the centre of silver working ever since.

Bowls are created entirely from repeated hammering of silver nuggets. Once the basic shape has been achieved, repoussée patterns are

hammered in. Local demand and the tourist market has given new life to the industry, and wealthy businesses have revived the production of large silver bowls.

Where to see silverware:
Silver shops line Wualai Road, the traditional centre of Chiang Mai's silversmiths. Prices are calculated by the weight of a piece, making the skilled handiwork seem cheap.

Ban Makbanwang -D *184.F7*
28 Wualai Rd. Soi 2, C.M
Hrs. 09:00–17:00. Traditional silversmith in Chang Lor area (on City Walk 3). Tel: (0) 5320 0142

Sherry Silver Jewellery
59/2 Loi Khroh Rd., C.M. 50100. Hrs. 09:00–21:00.
Modern silver jewellery.
Tel: (0) 5327 3529
Fax: (0) 5327 3196

Sipsong Panna
168.C5 95/19 Nimmanhaemin Rd., C.M. 50200 (C2) Hrs. 10:00–18:00.
Antique & new silver jewellery.
Tel: (0) 5321 6096
Fax: (0) 5321 6022

Parading a silver vessel to be presented Their Majesties (19

Northern Music

In addition to cymbals and drums, the most important instruments in a typical northern Thai band are the *sung,* stringed instruments resembling lutes, bamboo reed flutes known as *khlui,* and two to four stringed fiddles with long necks and small bulbous sound

Lai Muang - a traditional Northern Thai ensemble

chambers known as *salor.* The *pin-pia* is similar in shape but has a sound chamber made from a half coconut and the strings are plucked while the chamber is held close to the breast *(photo p.171).*

In past times, single men wandered around the village in the evening, flirting with the young women sitting beneath their houses and entertaining them with whatever skills they could muster. The *pin-pia* was a particu-

larly suitable instrument to charm a lady's ears, for it is best played against the naked breast and the listener must get close to hear its gentle tones.

A story goes that players of a *sung, salor* and *pin-pia* came to blows when competing for the same lass, and the *sung* player was killed by the *pin-pia* player. By way of punishment, the *chao* banned the playing of the *pin-pia,* with the result that the tradition of playing this instrument was only preserved in remote areas.

Northern ensembles may still play at parties celebrating such events as marriages, completion of new houses and temple buildings. Their instruments are also used to back up a form of music known as *sor,* in which a male and female sing impromptu verse in a form of repartee that can get quite ribald.

More formal occasions such as funerals and important rituals may be attended by a larger percussion group common to all of Thailand. In this music the sound is dominated by notes from wooden xylophones and circles of gongs.

Somboon Kawichai
38 Muang Sat Rd, Nong Hoi, C.M. 50000 (202.I12) Hrs. by appointment. Northern Thai musical instrument maker. Tel: (0) 5380 2880

the sung

WOODCARVING

THIS ART FORM originated from the tradition of carving religious objects such as Buddha images, pulpits, royal regalia and household objects for the court and nobility. The doors, shutters, gables and triangular brackets supporting the overhanging roofs of temples are often intricately carved with animal and plant motifs. Some of the best examples of carvings in Chiang Mai are at Wat Buang Di, Wat Saen Fang and Wat Inthrawat (Wat On Khwen).

Nowadays craftsmen specialise in just one type of carving used in the decoration of a *viharn*. The modern wood-carving industry itself is a development of only the last few decades. Traditionally only a few artefacts were commissioned, the wooden elephant being the most common carved object. The popularity of temple carvings imported from Burma as souvenirs encouraged dealers to get local craftsmen to reproduce them using aging processes which included burning and baking in urine. The methods are now so good that experts can have difficulty deciding whether an object is genuinely old.

The scarcity of teak has forced modern carvers to use other woods, and staining to hide the light colours of the woods has become more common. The carving itself is usually done in the rough in

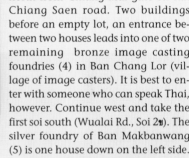
Artisans making decorative figures using repoussée technique may be seen at Wat Si Suphan.

City Walk 3. Handicraft Walking Tour

Two routes begin at Chiang Mai Gate Market *(see map below and page 184-185)* (1), the first taking Prapokklao Lane 6, passing Ban Phor Liang Meun's terracotta works and Wat Phan Waen (2). From there the route heads west on Samlan Soi 7 to Wat Phuak Taem (3), where a monastic workshop turns out filigree used on the finials of stupas. From there you may either cross the moats to (5), or continue on the Old City Walking Tour *(page.42)*

The second, shorter route goes north from Chiang Mai gate on Rat Chiang Saen road. Two buildings before an empty lot, an entrance between two houses leads into one of two remaining bronze image casting foundries (4) in Ban Chang Lor (village of image casters). It is best to enter with someone who can speak Thai, however. Continue west and take the first soi south (Wualai Rd., Soi 2฿). The silver foundry of Ban Makbanwang (5) is one house down on the left side.

Continue straight at the junction to Wat Si Suphan (6), where the viharn is decorated with ornate murals in gold and beaten panels on the shutters.

Cross Wualai Road and enter Soi 3, walking down past silverware shops to Wat Meun San (7). Note the unusual tigers built into the corners of the chedi. These refer to a legend in which monks in the temple could transform themselves into tigers and protect the city from malevolent forces. Walk west and then turn east on Wualai Soi 5. On Nantaram Rd. turn left and look for Prathuang Khruang Khoen (8) on the opposite side of the road. This is the sole lacquerware maker to remain in what was once the centre of this craft in the area around Wat Nantaram, where a shrine is dedicated to them. The return route via Suriyawong Rd. passes three old chedis.

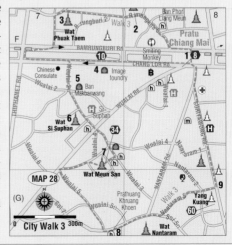

Seup San Lanna

The *Honghian Seup San Phum Pannya Lanna*, (Lanna Wisdom Heritage School), a school dedicated to preserving and propagating the traditional art and culture of Lan Na, is at the forefront of a revival of local culture. The school usually stages events show-casing Lanna culture for the Lanna Arts and Culture festival held at the beginning of April, either at the school itself *(202.C11)*, at the Three Kings Monument, or at the Art Museum.

The cast of Khru Ba Sivichai before removal of imperfections and polishing. The finished image now resides in front of the 'honghian'.

Casting an image of Khru Ba Sivichai (above) at 'Seup San Lanna', a three-day fair held in April 2001. On this occasion a team of founders from Ban Chang Lo waited till the cool of evening before melting down old radiators and pans in charcoal burning crucibles. Two men holding special clasps (centre) lifted the crucibles to pour the molten contents into the mold (off the picture).

Best has been a fair called *Seup San Lanna*, which has been held more or less annually, though not necessarily at the same

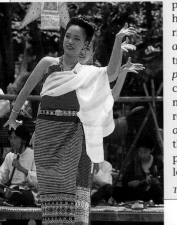

place or time of year. The fair has been a delightful mix of ritual, stage performance and artistic demonstration, with a traditional food market *(photo p.156)* and stalls selling local clothing. While the *honghian* may not stage such fairs with regularity, it is worth going to any event being organised by this school if you want to experience the undercurrent of local culture.

Traditional dancing at Seup San Lanna

outlying villages, before the pieces are sent for detailed work in the woodcarving centre at BanTawai.

Where to see woodcarving:

Pech Viriya—D *Map 7. p.88*
56/1 Mu 1, Ban Buak Khang, Sankamphaeng Hrs. 08:00–18:00. closed Sundays. Pech Viriya leads a team specialising in carving elephants. Tel: (0) 5333 2578

Ratana House *203.J5*
284 Mu 6, Hang Dong Rd., C.M. 50000 (H108 KM.6) Hrs. 08:30–16:30.
The carvings on the building itself are as interesting as the contents. More such buildings are at Ban Tawai *(see p.94)*. Tel: 274356, 271734 Fax: 270922.

SA PAPER & UMBRELLAS

The tourism industry has made the once small craft thrive in the area around Bo Sang. Frames for umbrellas are produced in stages, and it is common to see men or women underneath houses working on a batch of umbrellas at one stage of the production process. Different households may specialise in a certain stage of the process

Driven by increasing local and tourist demand for decorative paper, sa paper production has been through a similar transformation. The paper is produced by drying the woody stems of the sa plant (a kind of mulberry). Then they are soaked and pulverised into a mush in a mill. Colour is added and the mix is placed in tubs where it is suspended in water. By drawing a fine mesh grill through the tub, sediment accumulates on the grill in thin sheets. In drying the sediment coagulates to form

A Traditional House

The twin gabled house was typical of houses built from the 1920's through 1960's in the Sansai-Doi Saket area. Occupying spacious compounds containing various out-buildings such as a rice barn and a toilet (or latrine),

Floor Plan

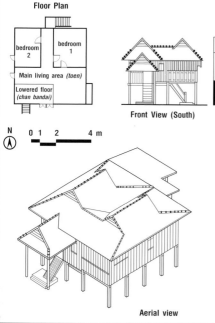

Front View (South)

Aerial view

Information from "The study of Styles and Usages of the vernacular timber houses in Chiang Mai" by Wichulada Nilmuang (MA Thesis, Silpakorn University, 1998).

the houses were oriented north-south to allow prevailing winds to pass through. Floors were a little over 2 metres above ground, and side walls between 2.5 and 3 metres in height. Roofing covered the entire floor area to protect against rain and heavy dews in the cold season.

The area beneath the house (*thun ban*) would be used for practical activities such as weaving. A slightly lowered platform at the top

of the front stairs gives entry to the main living area (*thoen ban*), which would typically take up about 50 percent of the upstairs floor space. The auspicious east side of this area would contain the Buddhist shrine.

A passage between two or more bedrooms leads to a smaller kitchen and washing area at back. Bedrooms would be small, with the senior family members sleeping on the east side, and others sleeping on the hotter western side. With male children often finding work elsewhere, the youngest daughter would normally take care of her parents in old age and inherit the house upon their passing. When she married, her husband would come to live with her. Other children who married might build houses in the same compound if they had not gone to live elsewhere with their wives. Thus it is that women in northern Thailand traditionally have the greatest power in a household.

(photos and illustration) A twin gabled house in San Sai district. The style reflects early symptoms of a timber shortage.

---

e sheets of paper. These are en sold, or fashioned into uvenirs such as cards and tebooks.

LEISURE ACTIVITIES

ART

Except for the Art Museum, galleries in Chiang Mai are small and do not always have exhibitions on display.

(Chiang Mai University Contemporary) Art Museum (หอศิลปวัฒนธรรม มหาวิทยาลัยเชียงใหม่) *Nimmanhaemin Rd. Hrs. 09:30–17:00. Closed Mondays.* Tel: (0) 5394 4833 This recently built concrete complex is Chiang Mai's main venue for exhibitions. Shows are usually changed on a monthly basis, and other events such as concerts are staged on an ad hoc basis. Regular events include puppet performances at the Chiang Mai Playhouse 'Hobby Hut' as well as free showings of 'art films' at 15:00 hrs every Sunday. The complex houses a gift shop, snack bar, health food shop and multi-purpose halls.

Where to see Art: Apart from listed galleries selling paintings and the **Gallery Bar & Restaurant** (*see p. 153*), several shops on the road between Hang Dong and Ban Tawai hang pictures for sale.

Traditional Houses

The compound of the Centre for Promotion of Arts and Culture (easily reached by walking directly west in the grounds of the art museum. (Tel: (0) 5394 3628, Fax (0) 5322 2680) contains five reconstructed houses (listed clockwise from the north-west corner)
1. The small, single-gabled Kalae (photo) House was built in the Chom Thong district in the 1910's.
2. The Phaya Wong House is a medium sized twin gabled Kalae house dating from the 1890's. It belonged to descendants of Lamphun's ruling family in Pasang district. The house was dismantled and reconstructed in Wat Suwanachedi in Lamphun, before being sold and donated to the University.
3. The Vichai Laohavad Rice Granary was originally built in the compound of the Phaya Wong House. The large size of the granary (10 poles) is in keeping with the owner's status.
4. The Ui Kaew House was built in the 1940's near Hua Rin corner. Structurally similar to local farm houses, it was modified with new techniques of wall panelling and openings.
5. Built in the 1910's in Ban Muang Luang in Doi Saket District by people of Tai Leu ancestry, the Thai Lue house is a Lue style modified to suit the environment of Chiang Mai.

'Kalae' are decorative finials using buffalo horns as a motif.

Chiang Mai Playhouse "Hobby Hut' *Contemporary art museum. Shows: Fri, Sat, Sun 18:30. 45 min. Adults 250 Bt/Children 100 Bt.* Combining puppets and performance. Thai folktales are presented in a modern format that can be readily understood by non-Thai speakers. Reservations Tel: (0) 5389 2450

Fine Arts Faculty Gallery *168.D3. Chiang Mai University, Hrs. 08:30–18:00.* Exhibitions by students, staff and invited artists Tel: (0) 5322 1699 ex. 48507-9

Gong Dee Studio & Gallery *168.C5. 12 Soi 1, Nimmanhaemin Rd. Hrs: 09:00-19:00.* Shop and gallery are separated by a few metres. Exhibitions, performances & sales. Studio Tel: (0) 5322 2230 and

Chiang Mai University's Faculty of Fine Arts (Tel:(0) 5321 1724) organises events of installations and performance with names like 'Eukabeuk' and 'Week of Co-operative Suffering'. Foreign artists are welcomed — inquire at the Art Museum to find out more.

showroom (0) 5322 5032 <www.gongdee.com>

Lotus Fine Art Studio *184.E7 1/65 Arak Rd (Soi Yoga Centre).* Introduction to the Lanna art world by appointment. Tel: (0) 5381 4253 (0) 1603 6792 <www.lotus-art-studio.itgo.com>

Tita Gallery *Map 18 p.117. 68 Mu 6, Old Mae Rim-Samoeng Rd (next to Regent Resort). 09:00–18:00* Tel: (0) 5329 8373

Yin Dee Art Gallery *163.W1 3rd Floor Chiang Inn Plaza, Chang Khlan Rd. C.M. 50000. Hrs. 12:00–17:00.* Sales of paintings, sculptures & prints. Tel: (0) 5328 1340

CINEMA

Chiang Mai has modern th atres with surround-sour showing the latest forei movies with Thai subtitles

same movie is showing at
ore than one theatre in the
me complex, one version
ay be dubbed). Less commer-
al movies may be enjoyed at
e Alliance Française, at the
deo library of the AUA, and
the Art Museum.

Though Thai cinema has
oduced outstanding movies
er the years, only very few
oductions are given English
btitles, and these versions
most never reach Chiang Mai.

iance Francaise *185. F10*
nch soundtrack, English subtitles.
aroen Prathet Rd. Tuesdays 16:30 &
days 20:00. except Nat. Holidays.
nthly programmes are published
he free magazines.
(0) 5327 5277

ture Media *168.C5*
limmanhaemin Rd. (Hrs 10:00-
00 entry for last showing. 200 Bt/
m for 4 people, extra persons 50 Bt.
h). Rent private AC room with
ne theatre and watch a DVD/laser
c of your choice from an extensive
llection. Tel: (0) 5321 3055,
5321 3095

jor Cineplex
ntral Airport Plaza. 168.H6)
(0) 5328 3939 for programme
ormation. First & last showing
00&22:00. 7 theatres with capacity
(screens 1-3), 300 (4-5),600 (6-7).
sdays 70-80 bt, Fri-Sun 100-120
other days 90-100.Bt.)

sta Cinemas
di theatres show soundtrack
eign and Thai movies. To find out
at is playing at any Vista theatre,
the cinema, or call the Vista
el (252 Phapokklao Rd. Tel:
0663-4, Fax: 214563. Prices: 70 Bht.
n-Thu, 90 Bht. Fri-Sun)

ta 1-7. Kat Suan Kaew *168.D6*
ai Kaew Rd. Tel: (0) 5389 4415
ta 1&2, *168.C6*
Huai Kaew . Tel: (0) 5340 4374.
ta 1&2 *202.E12. 459/5 Charoen*
ang Rd. Tel: (0) 5326 0372
ta Thiphanet Cinema *169.G7*
ai soundtrack. 124-6 Thiphanet Rd.
(0) 5327 5682

movie information try Raintree
mmunity Services movie line Tel:(0)
6 2661 or <www.movieseer.com>

CULTURAL LEARNING

For cooking course, see p.160

**Honghian Seup
San Phum-
pannya Lanna**
*202.C11 35
Rattanakosin Rd.*
Courses in Lanna
arts at Lanna
Wisdom Heritage
School (in Thai).
Tel: (0) 5324
4231-2

**The Lanna
Vernacular Art
Museum &
Chiang Mai Terracotta Gallery**
80.B2 (H1260 KM2. See p.115)
lessons in terracotta sculpture by
arrangement.Tel: (0) 5329 8897

Mae Sa Valley Craft Village
*Map 18 p.117 Mae Sa Valley Resort (H
1096 KM13) approx 600-1200 Bt/
course includes return transfer, 150
minutes of activity with basic materials
supplied & one meal. Call for times of
morning, mid-day and evening
courses).* Parasol, fan & ceramic
painting, batik dyeing, sa paper making,
& cooking in a very pleasant setting.
Tel: (0) 5329 0051-2, Fax: (0)5329 0017

Nova *185/201.E9*
*201 Thaphae Rd. class hrs 10:30-16;30
Mon-Fri. 5 day course 4000 bt. approx.*
Workshops in silver jewellery, stone
carving & leather working.
Tel: (0) 5327 3058
E-mail: info@nova-collection.com

Thai Language Courses:

AUA *184/200.E8*
73 Ratchadamnoen Rd., C.M. 50200
Tel: (0) 5327 8407. E-mail:
aualanna@loxinfo.co.th

Australia Centre *168.D3*
*75 Soi Wat Pa Daeng (Soi 5) Suthep
Rd., C.M. 50200.* Tel: (0) 5327 6269,
(0) 5381 0552-3

**Baan Pasa (NES) Institute of
Languages** *185/200.D9*
*4 branches in the city. #1 & 4 are
opposite Sompet Market on
Chaiyaphum Rd.* Tel: (0) 5323 3050
E-mail: baanpasa@loxinfo.co.th

YMCA *168.C6*
*11 Mangrai Rasmi, Sermsuk Rd.,
Santitham, C.M. 50300.*
Tel: (0) 5322 1819

What can I do with the children?

The movie theatres
and video game
machines of Kat
Suan Kaew shop-
ping centre can be
fun for the young
on rainy days. The
complex also of-
fers bowling and
ice-skating,
though call to con-
firm the latter is
operating *(see 'shopping').*

On clear days the zoo and
elephant camps will appeal
to all the family. Boys might
like go-karting and climbing
(see sports below) and girls
may like the Chiang Mai
Dolls Museum *(see p.106).*

Swimming seldom fails
and children usually enjoy
splashing around near a
waterfall, but keep them
away from slippery rocks
and cascades. However,
higher National Park fees for
foreigners *(see p.83)* now
mean that for the entrance
price to a national park for a
family of four, you can go to
a resort, get a meal and use
their pool if they have one.

Tour Route 2 *(p.88-90
listings p.191)* requires the
shortest time in a car. Both
The Wang Tarn Resort *(Map
7 p.88)* and the Bua
Restaurant *(Map 8 p.89)*
have pools where the kids
can play while adults relax
at the table. The Sankam-
phaeng Resort has paddle
boats for a small lake, the
Muang On cave is an
adventure for all, and the
spacious gardens at the hot
springs are good for open-
air relaxation.

READING & RESEARCH

Bookshops

Bookazine *163.W1*
Basement, Chiang Inn Plaza, Chang Khlan Rd. C.M. 50000. Hrs. 10:00–21:00.

Back Street Books *200. E9*
2/8 Chiang Moi Kao Rd. Hrs. 09:00–20:00. Second-hand books
Tel: (0) 5387 4143

The Book Zone *200.E9*
318 Thaphae Rd. hrs: 09:30-21:30
Tel&Fax: (0) 5325 2418

D.K. Book House *185/200.E9*
*79/1 Kotchasan Rd., C.M. 50100 (F4) Hrs. 09:30–21:00. daily.*Large Thai bookstore with English selection Tel: (0) 5320 6995, Fax: (0) 5320 6999.

Gecko Used Books *200.E9*
Chiang Moi Kao Rd. Hrs. 09:30–21:00. daily. Tel: (0) 5387 4066

The Lost Bookshop *200.E8*
34/3 Ratchamankha Rd. Hrs. 09:00–14:00 & 17:00–20:00. (F4) Very good for second-hand books.

Shaman Bookstore *201.E9*
250/1 Thaphae Soi 2. C.M. 50300 Hrs. 09:00–20:00. Second-hand books.
Tel: (0) 5323 5652

Suriwong Book Centre *185.F9*
54/1-5 Sridonchai Rd., C.M. 50100 Hrs. 08:00–19:30. Suns. 08:00-12:30 . Large store of Local English language publisher. Tel: (0) 5328 1052-5

Libraries

Chiang Mai University Library
168.C2 Chiang Mai University, C.M. 50200. Hrs. 08:00–21:00. weekdays; 08:30–16:30 weekends and semester breaks. Tel: (0) 5322 1699 ex 4528
<www.lib.cum.ac.th>

Thai-American Library
184/200.E8 AUA 24 Ratchadamnoen Rd. C.M. 50200. Hrs. 12:00–18:00 Mon-Fri. 08:30-18:00 Sat. 09:00-13:00 Adults 400 Bt. annually, students 200 Bt., visitors 50 Bt./month. Periodicals, children's, reference & videos. Tel: (0) 5321 1377, Fax: (0) 53211973
E-mail: aualanna@loxinfo.co.th

Payap University Archives
169.C11. Kaeo Nawarat Campus (opp. McCormick Hospital) on Kaew Nawarat Rd. Mon-Fri. Hrs: 08:00-12:00, 13:00-16:30. Archives for local history. Tel&Fax: (0) 5330 6125

Payap University Library
202.C14. Mae Khao (main) Campus (near Carrefour on Superhighway) on Kaew Nawarat Rd. Mon-Fri. Hrs: 08:00-19:30, 10:00-19:30 weekends) Tel & Fax (0) 5330 4085-13 ext 386

Tribal Research Institute Library
168.C2 Chiang Mai University C.M. 50200. Hrs. 08:30–12:00, 13:00–16:30, weekdays only. Tel:(0) 5322 1933

SHOPPING

Foreign Foods

Buonissimo *169. A11*
111/5 Mu 3 Chiang Mai-Phrao Rd (H1001 KM1) Hrs. 09:00–20:00. Delicatessen and wine cellar
Tel: (0) 5385 3098-9

Kasem Store *185/201.D9*
19 Ratchawong Rd. Hrs. 08:00–20:00. Bakery & imported foodstuffs
Tel: (0) 5323 4986

Rimping Superstore *169. C7*
Chotana Branch. *171/1 Chang Phuak (West of Novotel) , Hrs. 10:00–21:00.* Best supermarket for foreign foodstuffs. Tel: (0) 5321 0007-8

The Old Wine, Wine Gallery
163.Z3 98/7-8 Sridonchai Rd. Hrs. 09:00–21:00. closed Sundays.
Tel: (0) 5327 9099

Herbal Health

Good Health (foods) *168.D4*
Art Museum, Nimmanhaemin Rd. Hrs 10:00-20:00. Tel: (0) 5320 6888

Kat Ban Nua (health foods)*185/200.D9* Off Wichayanon Rd (opp. First Hotel) Aden & others, Thai Orchid (Vegetarian Restaurant) and 'Pyramid Power' meditation centre.
Tel: (0) 5323 2053

J - Imbun (vegetarian supermarket)
169. C10. 188/1-3 Ban Imbun, near Kham Thien market. Hrs 08:00-18:00.
Tel: (0) 5323 5487
E-mail: j_imboon@hotmail.com

Mungkala (Chinese herbal) *184/200.E8* 21 Ratchamankha Rd. CM. Tel: (0) 5327 8494, (0) 5320 8431 Fax: (0) 5320 8432
Hrs.09:30-12:30,14:30-19:00
<mungkala@cm.ksc.co.th>

Chip Aun Tong (Chinese herbal & western pharmacy)*201.D10* 48-52 *Chiang Moi Rd. CM 50300. Hrs 08:00-*

18:00. A Chinese doctor trained in Western medicine diagonoses and dispenses Chinese herbal treatmen *(Hrs. 09;30-14:00).* Also sells silica gel by the kilo. Tel: (0) 5323 4187, Fax: (0) 5325 1561.

Gems

Clever, well-mannered English-speaking people still befriend touri and fool them into paying high pri for poor quality or fake stones — t price for greed and stupidity. All reputable dealers sell genuine stone but beware of the 'ghost guide'!

Ornament/Princess Gems
163.W1 Chiang Inn Hotel (Fl 2) & 5 5 Thaphae Soi 1. Hrs 09:00-21:00. Small, reliable jeweller will design order. Tel: (0) 5382 0811, Fax: (0) 53 8748 E-mail: ornament99@hotmail.c

Lanna Style

The term 'Lanna style' is used loose to indicate shops selling modern

interior decor, furniture and clothi in styles that may have been influenced by local and ethnic traditions *(also see listings pages 166-175).*

Shops around Tha Chang on Charoenrat Road near Wat Ketkaram — *see city walk p7.*

Fai Tor Ngam *201.D10*
86/1-2 Charoenrat Rd. Hrs 09:00-21:00 Teak furniture & cotton & interior design.
Tel: (0) 5330 6175

Khampan *201. E10* (Gourmet)
9 Charoenrat Rd. Hrs 10:00-23:00 Furniture & hoe products.
Tel: (0) 5326 2419. E-mail: khampan_chiangmai@hotmail.com

Oriental Style *185/201.E10*
36 Charoenrat Rd., Hrs: 08:30-23:00 Furniture and decor. Tel: (0) 5324 5724. E-mail: oriental@loxinfo.co.

Paothong *185/201.D10*
66 Charoenrat Rd., Hrs: 10:00-22:0

(0) 5330 2072. Stylish cotton
hing. E-mail:
nongshop@hotmail.com

a Cini *185/201.E10*
2,34 Charoenrat Rd., C.M. 50000.
: 10:00-22:00 Silk & cotton.
(0) 5324 4025 or contact through
ntal Style <www.vilacini.com>

ddition to shops listed above,
napa (decor), **Mei Wen Su**
inese antique furniture) **Regina**
cor) & **Sop Moei Arts** (*see p.170*)
other small shops are located in
Tha Chang area.

**ps on Nimmanhaemin Road
r the Amari Rincome Hotel:**

signone (decor) *168.C5*
immanhaemin Rd Soi 1 CM 50200
: 09:00-18:00 Furniture, ceramics
nail: designone@hotmail.com
(0) 5322 5833

ard Collection *168.C5*
3-24 Nimmanhaemin Rd. Soi 1 CM
00 Hrs: 09:00-18:00. Bamboo
niture/decor. Tel: (0) 5322 0604
ww.thaibamboo.com>

ne of the other shops in the
nmanhaemin Road area which are
listed above include **Alter Decor,**
dha, **Tawan Decor** and **Gongdee**
Arts) — all sell decor. **Sipsong-**
na (*see p 173*) sells silverware and
ndakhwang cotton products.

**ps on Loi Khroh Road and
aphae Road:**

Ker Yaw *163. Y3*
-4 Loi Khroh Rd, C.M. 50000. Hrs.
30–19:00. Cottons & hilltribe
rics & baskets. *Closed Sundays.*
(0) 5327 5491

ps in malls:
rt from The **Chiang Mai Pavilion**
Chiang Inn Plaza** and **Night**
aar (*Map 26 p.163*) buildings,
ps are found in the **Suriwong**
za (*Kotchasan Rd. opposite*
phae Gate 185/E9*) and **Kat Muang**
ound floor Zone B, Kat Suan Kaew
see below*).

n Ngualai *168.D6*
Kat Muang, Kat Suan Kaew
rthern Thai artefacts & old
otographs. Tel: (0) 5327 4928

alls & Hypermarkets

ough of questionable architectural
rit, two large shopping malls with
lti-storey car parks provide the
nt mix of department stores, fast
, boutique shopping and

---

entertainment to represent the face of
modern Thailand.

Central Airport Plaza *168.H6*
*Airport Intersection. (Tel: (0) 5328
1661-8, 10:30-21:00, 10:00-21:00
weekends)* Five floors of shops and
restaurants include the **Robinson
Department Store** (*Tel: (0) 5320
3640-59 Hrs 11:00-21:00 weekdays*),
Tops supermarket and 'Junction X'
for teenagers (basement). A food
centre and **Major Cineplex** (*Tel: (0)
5328 3939 - see Cinema*) are on the
4th floor. A new wing with more
shops and restaurants is under
construction

Kat Suan Kaew *168.D6*
*Huai Kaew Rd. (Tel:224444 hrs 10:00-
21:00).* Zone A (*Huai Kaew entrance*)
contains the **Central Department
Store** (*Tel: (0) 5322 4999*), a Tops
supermarket (basement)and four
floors of restaurants and stores. On
the fourth floor are 7 **Vista Cinemas**.
The **Kat Theatre** (*Tel ext 50078*) and
gallery are on Floor 5. At ground level
of Zone B in the wing west of the
central atrium, **Kat Muang**, consist of
shops selling Lanna handicrafts. The
upper levels contain function halls
and the main car park. Zone C east of
the central atrium contains a food
centre (Fl.3), **Bully Bowl** (*09:00 -
02:00 Fl.4*), **Bully Sky Ice** (*ice-skating
11:00-02:00 FL5*) and family karaoke
(*21 rooms 11:00-02:00 Fl.5*). Zones
B&C give access to the southern
block which contains the **Pang Suan
Kaew Lotus Hotel**, a fitness centre
(Fl 2) and traditional massage (Fl.6).

    With ATM's, food centres and
personnel on skates, the hypermarkets aim to be super convenient
for shopping by car. Breadth of
choice is not necessarily matched by
depth, however, as some items can be
limited to one or two (house) brands.

Big C *202.H14*
*Chiang Mai-Lampang Superhighway.
Hrs. 09:00-23:00* Tel: (0) 5326 2300

Carrefour. *202.C13*
*Chiang Mai -Lampang Superhighway
Sun-Thurs 09:00-22:30, Fri-Sat 09:00-
24:00* Tel: (0) 5385 0670-7

Makro *202.E14*
*Chiang Mai-Lampang Superhighway
Hrs.06:00-22:00* Tel: (0) 5326 1200

Tesco Lotus *203. I5 & 169. A9*
*Chiang Mai-Hang Dong Rd. Hrs.
09:00-24:00* Tel: 807478-97 & *Chiang
Mai-Lampang Superhighway.*

Spa & Beauty

Ban Laplae *202.110*
*55 Koh Klang Rd., Nong Hoi Hrs.
09:00-20:00.* Traditional massage and
beauty treatments. Massage 100 bt./
hour to a 1500 Bt. skin master in
long established Thai beauty salon.
Tel: (0) 5327 8167, (0) 5380 1453-4

Ban Sabai *185/201. E10*
*17/7 Charoen Phrathet Rd. Hrs. 12:00-
24:00.* Stylishly converted downtown
shop-house. Prices from 350 Bt. for
herbal steam sauna to 1500 Bt. for
body masque wrap (2 hrs). Tel: (0)
5328 5204-6 <www.ban-sabai.com>

The Lanna Spa *M18. p.117*
*The Regent Resort, Chiang Mai. Old
Chiang Mai -Samoeng Rd, Mae
Rim.Hrs 09:00-21:00.* A range of
indulgent treatments in luxurious
private suites offering tubs, steam
rooms and 'rain-shower massage
beds' for 40-50 US$/hour. Tel: (0)
5329 8181 <www.regenthotels.com>

Padma Aroma Spa *185/201.D10*
*204-206 Charoenrat Rd. Hrs. 09:00-
22:00.* Compound of wooden houses
converted into a boutique spa.
Treatments from 650 bt. (foot
massage 1 hr) to 6000 bt. (All day
spa ritual). Call for transportation.
Tel: (0) 5324 8358

Siam Spa Health & Beauty
*163.W1 Chiang Inn Plaza Fl 2, 100/1
Chang Khlan Rd. Hrs. 11:00-21:00.*
Massage for beauty service,
aromatherapy, hair care, facials,
waxing. 200 Bt. for a head and
shouder massage to 1600 Bt.for a
permanent. Tel: (0) 5381 8208

Siamese Traders' Garden Spa
*80.C3. 85 Sukasem Rd. Hrs. 10:00-
22:00. (Enter Soi Lanna Hospital from
super-highway and turn right at Soi 2)*
Small, friendly spa in a garden setting
offers steam and massage treatments
at local prices. Siamese Traders also
sells natural products in adjacent
shop. Tel: (0) 5340 9705
E-m: nikolahs@siamesetraders.com

Suan Bua Garden Spa *Map 17
p.114 Suan Bua Resort & Spa (H1269
KM19) Hrs: 10:00-20:00.* Single and
combinations of treatments given in
wooden Lanna-style house cost 300
to 2500 Bt. (excluding tax ++) for
90-150 min. programmes. Longer spa
packages available. Tel: (0) 5336
5270-8.
E-m: suanbua1@loxinfo.co.th.

SPIRITUAL HEALTH

For churches see p.194.

Buddhist Meditation

Virtually all monks are in favour of visitors studying dhamma, but due to logistic difficulties they may be unable to help in practice. **Wat Umong Suan Phutthatham** (*see p 61*) is a good place to begin enquiries. Two temples have established procedures (by advance arrangement only) for receiving serious students of dhamma. **Wat Rampoeng Tapotaram** *Soi Wat Umong, Tambon Suthep. C.M. 50200* (A5) One month residential meditation courses. Tel: (0) 5327 8620, (0) 5381 0197. **Wat Phrathat Si Chom Thong** (*see p 107*)runs 21 day initial courses. Tel: (0) 5382 6869.

Hatha Yoga Centre 203.I9

129/79 Chiang Mai Villa 1 Mon-Fri 08:00-10:00, 17:00-19:00 Weight control, stress management, meditation, healing through exercise. Tel/Fax: (0) 5327 1555 <www.hathayogachiangmai.com> Email<marcelandyoga@hotmail.com>

Raja Yoga Meditation Centre

169.A7 Tel: (0) 5321 8604 evenings. Thai Main Centre Tel: (0) 5321 4904)

Tai Chi Chuan 202.B11

Naisuan House, Rattanakosin Rd Soi 1. Hrs. Sessions: 07:00-09:30, 13:00-14:00, 17:00-19:30. Residential 10 day courses at 'ashram' on rooftop of apartment block. Meditation & Chi Kung. <www.taichithailand.com> Tel: (0) 5330 6048

Tao Garden Health Resort

M7 p.88. 274 Mu 7, Luang Nua, Doi Saket, Chiang Mai 50220. 'Longevity & cosmic healing' with guru Mantak Chia. Tel.(0) 5349 5596 to 9, Fax: (0) 5349 5852. <www.universal-tao.com> E-m: universaltao@universal-tao.com

Yoga Centre Chiang Mai 184.E7

65/1 Arak Rd (Soi Chanwirot') Ten-day and five-day(advanced) workshops in Astanga/hatha yoga for serious students. Tel: (0) 5327 7850 E-mail: yogacntr@loxinfo.co.th

SPORTS

Aerobics

Classes are held in the evenings from around 18:00 at the gymnasium on Hassadisewi Rd., as well as by the fitness park on Nimmanhaemin Rd. *(10 Bt./session).*

Bowling

UFO Bowling *Map 9 p.93 (Nong Hoi)* Hrs 09:30-02:00. Prices from 50-70Bht per game. Tel: (0) 5380 1446, Fax: (0) 5380 1451) is south of town, but **Chiang Mai Bowl** *(Si Phum Road) &* **Bully Bowl** *(Kat Suan Kaew —see Shopping Malls.)* are both close to Chaeng Hua Lin *(40.D7).* Games cost 80Bt. Lanes close around 02:00 hrs.)

Bungy Jumping *Map 18 p.117*

Jungle Bungy Jump *(229 Mu1 Mae Ram. H1096 KM4. Hrs: 09:00-18:00 daily.Insured jumps 1000 Bt. Transfer from hotel 100 Bt. Tel: (0) 5329 8442, (0) 1894 7698)* offers jumps above a pond.

Climbing

The Peak *163.W1 (Night Bazaar, Chiang Khlan Rd. Hrs 12:00-24:00 Instruction 2 hrs 1000 Bt. Climbs 150-250 Bt.for non-members.Tel: (0) 5382 0776-8)* has a 15m wall surrounded by bars, and offers tours to bolted climbs in Mae On district (*elementary, advanced and children groups. 08:00-17:00 departure from the peak. 1500 bt. includes all equipment and lunch. Contact Khun Phichai for details Tel: (0) 1951 6529)* E-m: thepeak99@hotmail.com

Golf & Sports Clubs

Non-members welcomed

Chiang Mai Green Valley Country Club *80.B2. (H108 KM 15 east turn) Closed Tuesdays.* Flat ground and water by the river. Angsana spa in club-house. Tel: (0) 5329 8220-3, (0) 5329 8249-51 Fax: (0) 5329 7386

Chiang Mai–Lamphun Golf Club *M7 p.88 (H1147 KM.24 — east turn 3 kms.)* Course in a small side valley (Official venue for 1995 SEA Games). Tel: (0) 5388 0880-4 Fax: (0) 5388 0888.

Chiang Mai Sports Club *80. B2 (H07 KM.7 — east turn 1 km.)* Badminton, squash, horse riding, **Club-House Inn** Tel: (0) 5329 8326 Fax: (0) 5329 7897

The Gymkhana Club (*see p.71*) *41.G11 Chiang Mai-Lamphun Rd.* Tennis, squash and 9 holes of golf at the second oldest sports club in SE Asia. Hosts Chiang Mai Cricket Sixes. Tel: (0) 5324 1035 Fax: (0) 5324 7352

Lanna Sports Club – Golf *80.C2 (H107 KM.6)* 27 holes, driving range, horse riding, tennis, badminton, fitness and shooting. Tel: (0) 5322 1911, Fax: (0) 5322 1743

Royal Chiang Mai Golf Club *M21 p.123 (H1001 KM.26 east turn 4 kms.)* Par 72 course set in low hills. Modern clubhouse, & hotel. Tel: (0) 5384 9301-6, Fax: (0) 5384 9310

Flying - microlight/paraglide

Soar above the paddy with **Chiang Mai Sky Adventure Club** *North turn from H118 to Doi Saket near Km12 (Map 7 p.88). Hrs. 06:00-12:00,15:00 15/30 minute flights 1,200-2,200 Bht includes transportation plus training courses).* Tel: (0) 5386 8460 Fax: (0 5386 7646 E-m:flying@cmnet.co.th

Fitness & Jogging

The **Chiang Mai Orchid Hotel** and the **Hillside Condominium** (*Huai Kaew Rd*) have fitness centres open the public. Public fitness parks are found on Nimmanhaemin Rd (168.D5), and Huai Kaew Road nea the zoo (168.B2). Jog around the

Put your bicycle on a red minibus by the zoo and ride up to Phuping Palace. From there you can go to the Hmong villages of Ban Meow Doi Pui, Ban Chang Khian or Ban Mae Sa Mai. The routes involve pedalling up and down sealed and dirt roads, pushing up steep paths and riding the brakes on long descents (photo: the east side of Doi Pui on the path to Ban Mae Sa Mai).

iversity or the Rama IX park on
otana Rd. To run with the local
apters of the Hash House Harriers
ntact the **Hash House Pub** *200.E9*
un Muang Rd. Soi 2, Tel: 206822
s. 09:00–02:00).

orse Racing
07 KM.5 after Lanna Gardens —
st turn through arch 400 m.
urday afternoons see Map 6 detail
4) The army run racetrack offers
al betting, but the punters seem
ore interesting than the horses.

orse Riding
e **Lanna Sports Club** (*Riding*
ntre Tel: (0) 5321 7956), and the
iang Mai Sports Club (*see*
osite) offer riding facilities, as
es **The Royal Thai Army Pack**
uadron *80.B2 (H107 west side just*
ore KM.12. Mon-Fri after 16:00;
t-Sun all day. Needs Thai speaker.)

ountain Bicycling
club organises events from
aphae Gate at 07:00 on Sunday
ornings. Learn more from
ww.chiangmaicycling.com>
Click and Travel *158/60 Chiang*
ai- Hod Rd. T. Paded CM 50100. Tel:
) 5320 1194. Fax: (0) 5328 1554
ww.ClickandTravelOnline.com>)
ers tours in the valley on good
ountain bikes. **Contact Travel** (*see*
ting' below) arranges longer tours
season and rents out quality bikes.
Velocity (*next to Novotel 169.C7*
s. 10:00-21:00 Tel: (0) 5341 0665
m: velocity@thaimail.com) rents
ality bicycles. **Lung Gaew**
ountain **Bike & Mr. Mechanic**
0.E9 (both Mun Muang Soi 5) rent
eaper machines. **Top Gear** (Chiang
oi Rd tel: (0) 5323 3450), and
aithawat (75/4 Ratchaphina Rd.
l (0) 5327 9890) sell bicycles.

afting
ntact Travel/Thai Adventure
fting *163.X3 73/7 Charoen Prathet*
. CM. 50100.Tel: (0) 5327 7178,
x: (0) 5327 9505. Pai Office (0)
69 9111. E-mail:
o@activethailand.com
ww.ActiveThailand.com>
ofessionally run day trips to Mae
eng and very good overnight trips
om Pai to Mae Hong Son.
Mae Sot Conservation Tour also
ganises raft trips on the River Mae
aem (listing p. 199).

hooting
d Dev. Battalion Range *80.C2 (H107*
M8) 09:00-18:00 Tel: (0) 5321 1828

.22-.45 calibre 30 shots 1700 Bt.

Snooker
The **Thaphae Place Hotel** and the
Kum Kaew Snooker Club (Ratwithi
Rd. near the prison) have good tables
for the game James Wattana
popularised in Thailand.

Speedway/karting
Chiang Mai Speedway. *80.E2. 254*
Mu 11, Chiang Mai-Hod Rd. H108
KM.12. Riding Hrs. 10:00-19:00. Bt.
150 for 10 min. Tel: (0) 5343 0059-
60.) Beat the lap-record and celebrate
at the Turkey & Steak House.

Swimming & Tennis
Several hotels including the **Amari**
Rincome (90 Bt.), **Diamond**
Riverside (100 Bt.), **Prince Hotel**
(40 Bt.), **Top North Guest House** (50
Bt.) offer swimming/tennis to non-
residents. **The Chiang Mai Land**
Sports Club *203.H9 (hrs 09.30-21:00*
Tel: (0) 5327 2821) offers swimming,
tennis & aerobics to non-members.
Anantasiri *168.B6 (06:00-21:00 Tel:*
(0) 5322 2210) offers tennis only.

*Breaking a clinch at a Thai-Myanmar bare
hands' boxing tournament held at the Winter
Fair in the mid 90's.*

Thai Kick Boxing
Boxing bouts for tourists are put on
at Chiang Mai's entertainment (bar-
beer) centres, but to see professional
bouts, go to the **Kawila Boxing**
Stadium (*Kawila camp 169.E11*
Every Friday 19:30hrs-24:00. Tickets
300 Bt.Tel: (0) 5320 1899 ext 101).
   To seriously study the art, take a
training course at **Lanna Muay Thai**
(*64/1 Soi 1, Chang Khian, Huai Kaew*
Rd., C.M. 50300. Tel: (0) 5389 2102)
<www.lannamuaythai.com>

Pai style

Traditional Massage

Nuat Phen Boran (นวดแผนโบราณ)

   A full Thai massage usually
takes two hours (100-300 Bt./
hour). The masseurs appreciate tips as welcome additions
to their percentage of the
hourly rate you pay.

International Training Massage
169.C7   17/7 Morakot Rd.
10 day courses & longer start
Mondays. Tel: (0) 5321 8632 see
<www.infothai.com/itm/>

Let's Relax *163 W1&Y2*
Chiang Inn Plaza & Chiang Mai
Pavilion, Chang Khlan Rd. Hrs. 10:00-
24:00. Prices from 100bt/15min arm
massage to 600 Bt/165 mins of
'heavenly relax'.

Old Medicine Hospital *169.G6*
78/1 Wualai Rd. Hrs. 08:30–17:00.
Long-established school offers
traditional massage at 100 Bt./hour
and 10 day courses twice a month.
Tel: (0) 5327 5085 (E5) E-mail:
thaimassageschool@hotmail.com

Suan Samoonphrai *169.C10*
8 Wang Sing Kham Rd. Hrs. 08:00–
22:00. Tel: (0) 5325 2716, (0)5323
2664. An original location for massage.

Thai Massage Conservation Club
168.C6   9 Ratchadamri Rd, Chang
Phuak. Hrs. 08:30–09:00. Tel: (0) 5340
6017. Masseurs trained by the Thailand
Caulfield Foundation for the Blind also
work at several other downtown
parlours.

Wang Come Massage *168.C5*
301/2 Nimmanhaemin Rd. Hrs. 09:00–
10:30. (G2) Tel: (0) 5322 2770.

The Diamond Riverside, the Pornping
Tower and the Lotus Pang Suan Kaew
are some of the hotels offering a massage
service to non-resident customers.

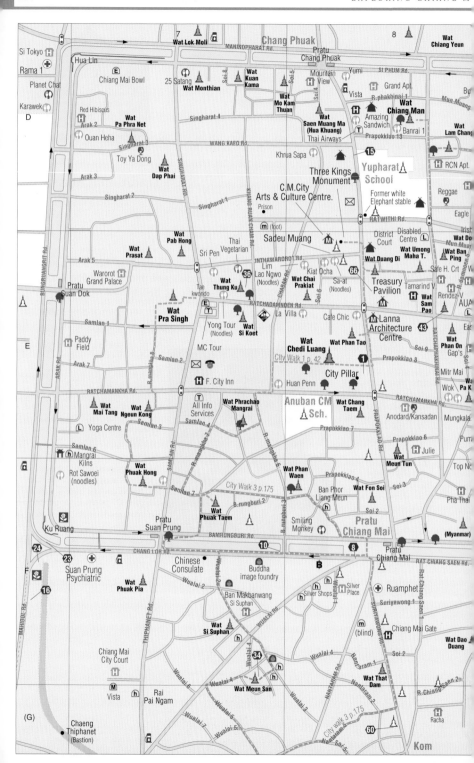

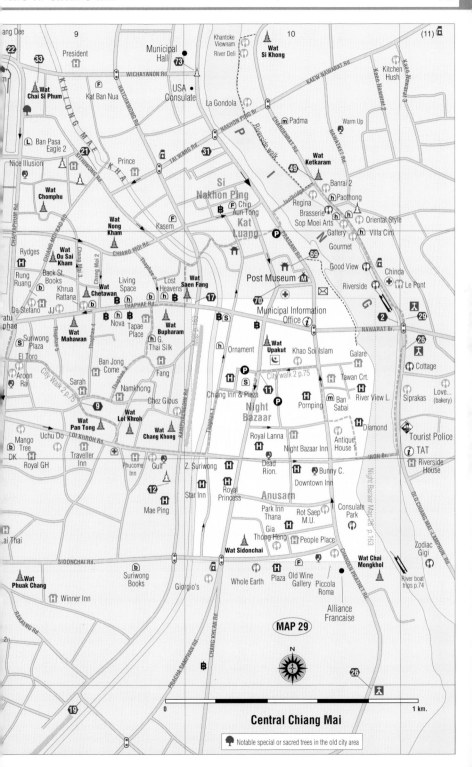

Central Chiang Mai

N

0   1 km.

MAP 29

Notable special or sacred trees in the old city area

PRACTICAL INFORMATION

Getting to Chiang Mai

Chiang Mai's modest size makes it an excellent first stop destination in Thailand. Few flights from overseas land directly at Chiang Mai, but Thai Airways runs a frequent shuttle on the 50 minute domestic flight to Chiang Mai from Bangkok International Airport. After arriving, airport taxis will take you on the 15-20 minute journey to anywhere downtown for 100 baht. They will also pick you up for your departure upon request *(tel: (0) 5320 1307).*

Waiting at Bangkok International Airport

If you want to rest near Bangkok airport, day rooms are available in the international transit lounge. Rooms are also available at the Amari Airport Hotel *(Tel: (0) 2566 1020-1 Fax: (0) 25661941. E-mail: airport@amari.com. Access by covered walkway from between upper departure and lower arrival halls of Terminal 1. Less expensive daytime rates between 08:00-18:00),* and the Comfort Suites Airport Bangkok *(Tel: (0) 2552 8921-9, Fax: (0) 2552 8920 — call for transportation 2kms south of international terminals). Warning: Thieves target small bags in the airport area. Never turn your back on your luggage!*

Trains and Buses

Don Muang (Bangkok International Airport) station is on the main line from Bangkok to Chiang Mai. Air-conditioned trains make the 750 kilometre journey overnight to Chiang Mai (from Hualamphong Station in Bangkok), arriving in the early morning *(see transportation for schedules).* Buses to Chiang Mai depart regularly from Mor Chit 2 (Northern) bus station, as well as from main provincial towns in Central and North-Eastern Thailand.

Currency & Credit Cards,

The unit of Thai currency is the baht, and the exchange rate appears to fluctuate between 42-46 baht to one US dollar. Baht coins are worth 1, 5 and 10 baht, and smaller brass alloy coins are worth a quarter baht and a half baht each. Notes are in denominations of 10, 20, 50, 100, 500 and 1000 baht.

Banking hours are 08:30-15:30, but exchange booths are open longer in tourist centres. Visa, Master, American Express, Diner's Club and JCB credit cards are widely accepted and can be used to draw cash at ATM machines or exchange booths. Many businesses levy a 3-5% surcharge if you pay by credit card, and Thailand has a high rate of 'credit card abuse'. Always monitor what is being done with your card.

Telephone and Time

If in-country dial 0 before the eight digit number (for Chiang Mai these always begin with 53). If calling from abroad, dial 66 (Thailand country code) and the eight digit number. Local time is seven hours ahead of GMT.

ACCOMMODATION: CITY

HOTELS & GUEST HOUSES are located throughout the city, and the city is blessed with numerous inexpensive places to stay (not all are listed in this guide). These usually offer comfortable rooms at reasonable prices.

The most convenient area to stay without your own transport is between the east side of the old city (Mun Muang Rd.) and the river, but outlying hotels usually offer some kind of minibus transportation downtown.

In general, downtown hotels are in high or medium-rise tower blocks and do not have much in the way of gardens — what space there is being used for parking. However, for open-air relaxation, these hotels generally offer pool-side sun bathing areas with some greenery on an upper floor.

Hotels indicated as low-ris in the listing have four or les floors, and where there is some genuine green space, this is given special mention

Recommendations(— R) are those of the author, who prefers quiet, low-rise, place with a bit of garden and reliable service.

Hotel Listing Symbols

Price ranges are categorised according to the rack rate for the least expensive type of oom offered at each hotel. At best rack rates show where the hotel places itself in the market, for most hotels usually charge 20-60% less than their posted rates according to demand and occupancy rate. *Always* ask for a discount, which will be quoted over the phone, or book through an agent.

85/202.G11. = Map on page 185 or page 202 grid reference G11
car+ = own transport an advantage

PRICE RANGE INDICATIONS

	(Thai Baht)
B	= 250-500
BB	= 500-1000
BBB	= 1000 to 2500
BBBB	= 2500 to 4000
BBBBB	= above 4000

FACILITIES & SERVICES

- ➡ = Accepts credit cards
- 🏢 = Business Centre
- 👥 = Conference Facilities
- 🏃 = Fitness Centre
- 🏊 = Swimming pool
- 🎾 = Tennis court
- 🛎 = 24 hr room service
  (most hotels and resorts offer room service in normal hours)
- ➡ = Air-conditioned
  (economy accommodation)
- B = rooms with fan only
  (economy accommodation)

Superior Hotels

Superior hotels offer luxurious rooms decorated in a northern style, often in some of the tallest buildings in the city. Large closets, satellite TV and mini-bars are the norm. Bathrooms have bath and shower units, and western-style toilets. Most hotels offer suites at higher prices than those indicated in the listing.

Main restaurants serve ThaiChinese and Western food and many hotels have another restaurant serving specialised cuisine (*see* p.157 for a listing). Most hotels offer some live music in the lobby lounge if not an in-house night club (*all hotels in this range are air-conditioned*).

Amari Rincome Hotel 168.C5—R
1 Nimmanhaemin Rd., C.M. 50200 Pleasant medium-rise hotel with garden areas and two pools. Good for families. Tel: (0) 5322 1130, (0) 5322 1044, Fax: (0) 5322 1915
E-m: rincome@amari.com>

Amity Green Hills C.M. 168.B5
24 Chiang Mai-Lampang Super Highway, C.M. 50300 High-rise hotel with pleasant rooms. car+. Tel: (0) 5322 0100-9, Fax: (0) 5322 1602
E-m: amity@loxinfo.co.th

Chiang Mai Hills Hotel 168.B4
18 Huai Kaew Rd., C.M. 50200 Comfortable medium-rise hotel with facilities including a Japanese restaurant & contemporary massage. car+ Tel: (0) 5321 0030-4, (0) 5340 0601-5, Fax: (0) 5340 0610
E-m: cmhills@cm.ksc.co.th

Chiang Mai Plaza Hotel 185.F10
92 Sidonchai Rd., C.M. 50100. Medium-rise hotel with spacious rooms and facilities. Tel: (0) 5327 0036-50, Fax: (0) 5327 9457

Chiang Mai Orchid 168.D6
23 Huai Kaew Rd., C.M. 50200 Medium-rise hotel located next to Kat Suan Kaew shopping complex. Tel: (0) 5322 2099, Fax: (0) 5322 1625
E-m: chiangmaiorchid@loxinfo.co.th

Empress Chiangmai Hotel
169.G10 199 Chang Khlan Rd., C.M. 50100. Popular high-rise hotel with pleasant rooms and pool bar. Tel: (0) 5327 0240, Fax: (0) 5327 2467
<www.empresshotels.com>

Imperial Mae Ping Hotel 185.F9
153 Sidonchai Rd., C.M. 50100 High-rise hotel with a conference wing & an open-air entertainment area containing a beer-garden & Khantok dining area. Tel: (0) 5327 0160-80, Fax: (0) 5327 6486
<www.imperial.hotel.com>

Novotel Chiang Mai 169.C7
171 Chang Phuak Rd., C.M. 50300 Comfortable newer medium-rise hotel. Tel: (0) 5322 5500, Fax: (0) 5322 5505 <www.hotelweb.fr>

The Park Hotel 202.H10
444 Chang Khlan Rd., C.M. 50100 High-rise hotel with top-floor pool car+ Tel: (0) 5328 1997, (0) 5327 9948, (0) 5328 0080, Fax: (0) 5327 9979 <www.empresshotels.com>

Royal Princess 163.Y1
112 Chang Khlan Rd., C.M. 50100 Older medium-rise hotel with good restaurants at the Night Bazaar. Tel: (0) 5328 1033-43, Fax: (0) 5328 1044 <www.royalprincess.com>

Rydges Tapae Chiangmai Hotel
185/200.E9 22 Chaiyaphum Rd., C.M. 50300 Chiang Mai's newest high-rise hotel offers views over the moats and the old city. Tel: (0) 5325 1531, Tel/Fax: (0) 5325 1465
<www.rydges.com>

Suriwongse Zenith Hotel — R
163.Y1/185.F10 110 Chang Khlan Rd., C.M. 50100 Older medium-rise hotel with light, spacious rooms overlooking the Night Bazaar. Tel: (0) 5327 0051-7, Fax: (0) 5327 0063

Tamarind Village — R 184/
200.E8 50/1 Ratchadamnoen Rd, Sri Phum, C.M. 50200. Stylish low-rise boutique hotel built around mature trees — green ambience downtown. Tel:(0) 5341 8896-9, Fax: (0) 5341 8900. <www.tamarindvilllage.com>

The Westin Chiangmai — R

202.H10. 318/1 Chiang Mai-Lamphun Rd., C.M. 50100 Palatial facilities and rooms in riverside high-rise. Good restaurants. car+ Tel: (0) 5327 5300 Fax: (0) 5327 5299 E-m: westincm@loxinfo.co.th

Mid-Range Hotels

Many of Chiang Mai's second class hotels offer near equal room quality to superior hotels, and in some cases comparable if not nicer ambience. However, they may lack the range of guest facilities and have a subtly lower level of luxury. Nevertheless, they can offer very good value, especially with discounts *(all hotels in this range are air-conditioned).*

Chiang Inn Hotel *163.W1/185.E10*

10 Chang Khlan Rd., C.M. 50000 Older medium-rise hotel at the heart of the Night Bazaar. Good for business travellers. Tel: (0) 5327 0070-6, Fax: (0) 5327 4299 E-m: chianginn@chiangmai.a-.net.th

Chiang Mai Gate Hotel *184.F8*

11/10 Suriyawong Rd., C.M. 50100. Medium-rise hotel that included former Chatri Guest House. Tel: (0) 5327 9179, (0) 5320 3895-9 Fax: (0) 5327 9085

Chiang Mai Phucome *168.B4*

21 Huai Kaew Rd., C.M. 50200 (B2) This large medium-rise hotel is good for conferences and contains a contemporary massage parlour. car+ Tel: (0) 5321 1026-31, Fax: (0) 5321 6422

Diamond Riverside Hotel — R

163.X3/185.E10 33/10 Charoen Prathet Rd., C.M. 50100. A high-rise tower overlooks the river and pleasant pool-side area. A cheaper old wing contains a nightclub with singers *(see p.165).* Khantok dinners are staged in an old mercantile house. Tel: (0) 5327 0080-5, Fax: (0) 5327 1482

Downtown Inn *163.Y2/185.F10*

172/1-11 Loi Khroh Rd., C.M. 50000 Pleasant rooms near the Night Bazaar — use of the facilities at the Empress

Mature trees and low-rise development at the Tamarind Village have created superb ambience

Hotel. Tel: (0) 5327 0662-70, Fax: (0) 5327 2406 E-m: empens@samart.co.th

Eurasia Hotel *202.D13*

1 Likhasith-Ratwithi Rd., C.M. 50000 Bungalows in a garden are combined with attractive rooms in a renovated low-rise building. Recommended if you have a car. Tel: (0) 5324 7790-6, Fax: (0) 5324 7797. E-m: eurasia@chmai.loxinfo.co.th

Felix City Inn Hotel *184.E7*

154 Ratchamankha Rd., C.M. 50200. Older four-floor hotel rise in old city. Tel: (0) 5327 0710-6, (0) 5327 5396, Fax: (0) 5327 0709.

Lanna Palace Hotel *169.G9*

184 Chang Khlan Rd., C.M. 50100. Facilities include pleasant rooms and a sauna for guests. Tel: (0) 5327 0722-40, Fax: (0) 5328 2175

Lanna View Hotel *169.A9*

558 Superhighway soi Lanna., C.M. 50300. Medium rise hotel with a small garden area. car+ Tel: (0) 5321 7784-6, Fax: (0) 5321 7749

Lotus Pang Suan Kaew Hotel

168.D6 99/4 Mu 2 Huai Kaew Rd., C.M. 50200 A large medium-rise hotel with a cavernous atrium, it offers good value for large rooms. Vast conference facilities and easy access to Kat Suan Kaew shopping mall *(see p.179)* Tel: (0) 5322 4333, Fax: (0) 5322 4493 E-m: lotus.htl.psk@chiangmai.a-net.net.th

Palms Springs Lodge *202.I13*

120 Mu 5, Om Muang Rd., C.M. 50000 Set in an open grassy parkland fronting a housing estate. Car+ Tel: (0) 5324 2910, Fax: (0) 5324 2641 <www.cm-online/palm>

Pornping Tower *163.X3/185.E10* 46-48 Charoen Prathet Rd. C.M. 50000 High-rise hotel with a brash style and popular city night spots (see p.165). Tel: (0) 5327 0099, Fax: (0) 5327 0119

River View Lodge *163.W3/185.E10* 25 Charoen Prathet Rd., Soi 2, C.M. 50000 The prices are commanded for the small garden and riverside location rather than the rooms. Tel: (0) 5327 1109-10, Fax: (0) 5327 9019 <www.riverviewlodgech.com>

Royal Lanna *163.X2/185.E10* 119 Loi Khroh Rd. C.M. 50100 Newer high-rise towers right over the Night Bazaar. Tel: (0) 5381 8773-5, (0) 5381 9002-13, Fax: (0) 5381 8776 E-m: royal_lanna@yahoo.com

Suan Doi House — R *168.C5* 38/3 Soi Chantrasup. off Huai Kaew Rd., C.M. 50000 This small low-rise hotel has a unique leafy atmosphere and a good Vietnamese restaurant. Tel: (0) 5340 6091, (0) 5322 1869, Fax: (0) 5322 1869

Star Inn Hotel *163.Z1/185.F10* 36 Soi 4 Loi Khroh, C.M. 50100 Medium rise hotel includes the use of Suriwongse Zenith facilities across the road. Tel: (0) 5327 0360-70, Fax: (0) 5327 0371

Tarin Hotel *168.B5* 10/7 Mu 2, Chiang Mai-Lampang Superhighway., C.M. 50300. Medium rise. Car+ Tel:(0) 5340 0131, Fax: (0) 5340 0140. <tarin@ch.cscoms.com>

Economic Hotels

This category includes more expensive guest houses as well as inexpensive small hotels which provide a comparative service. Room facilities often include a TV with satellite programming *(all hotels in*

his range offer air-conditioned rooms,
ut some have fan rooms available).

aantai Hotel 169.G7
1/10 Sipingmuang Rd., C.M. 50200
arge two-floor teakwood building in
nusual setting. car+ Tel: (0) 5327
938, (0) 5327 2301, Fax: (0) 5320
946

alare Guest House 163.W3/
85.E10 7 Charoen Prathet Rd., Soi 2,
M. 50100. Attractive low-rise
uilding in riverside location. Tel: (0)
382 1011, (0) 5381 8887, Fax: (0)
327 9088

hiang Mai President 185/200.D9
26-8 Wichayanon Rd. C.M. 50300.
ld medium rise hotel recommended
r those with a taste for Thai
ntertainment for males. Tel: (0)
325 1025-31, (0) 5325 1032
ax: (0) 5327 1982

oliday Garden Hotel 168.B4
6/16 Huai Kaew Rd., C.M. 50300.
his high/medium-rise hotel is
voured by tour groups and contains
pleasant grassy poolside with
alms. car+ Tel: (0) 5321 1333, (0)
321 0901-4, Fax: (0) 5321 0905

ai Thai Guest House 185/200.F9
4/4-5 Kotchasan Rd., C.M. 50000
el: (0) 5327 1725, (0) 5327 1414,
) 5327 1534, Fax: (0) 5327 2724

ontri Hotel 185/200.E9
haphae Gate Medium-rise hotel
ith attractive lobby lounge — Tel:
) 5321 1069-70, Fax: (0) 5321
16

ight Bazaar Inn 163.X2/185.E10
Charoenprathet Rd. Soi 6, C.M.
100. Medium rise business hotel.
el: (0) 5381 8096-100, Fax: (0)
382 0639

ark Inn Tana Hotel — R 163.Z2/
85.F10 10 Charoen Prathet Rd., Soi
C.M. 50100. Medium-rise hotel
ell located for the Night Bazaar. Tel:
) 5327 0191-2, Fax: (0) 5327 0193

rince Hotel — R 185/201.D9
ai Wang Rd., C.M. 50300 Low-rise
d-style hotel. Good pool. Tel: (0)
325 2025-32, Fax: (0) 5325 1144

Rim Ping Garden Hotel 202.H10.
411 Charoen Prathet Rd., C.M. 50000
A low-rise hotel with nice rooms,
considerable green ambience, and the
pleasant Rachawadi riverside
restaurant. The nearby orchard is
currently being used as a bar-beer
entertainment area. Car+. Tel: (0)
5320 4500-1, Fax: (0) 5328 1060

Sri Tokyo Hotel 184.D6
Bunruangrit Rd., C.M. 50000.
Comfortable rooms in medium rise
overlooking old city. Tel: (0) 5321
1100-1, Fax: (0) 5321 1102

Tapae Place 185/201.E9
2 Thaphae Rd., Soi 3, C.M. 50100
Medium rise — snooker. Tel: (0)
5327 0159, (0) 5340 0131-9, Fax: (0)
5327 1982

Top North Hotel — R 185.E9
41 Mun Muang Rd.., Soi 3, C.M.
50100. Refurbished medium-rise
hotel. Tel: (0) 5327 9623-5, Fax: (0)
5327 9626

Traveller Inn 185/200.E9
66 Loi Khroh Rd., C.M. 50100
Medium rise hotel. Tel: (0) 5320
8484-6, (0) 5328 0977-81, Fax: (0)
5327 2078

Vista Hotel 184/200.D8
252 Prapokklao Rd., C.M. 50200.
Comfortable and quiet low-rise hotel
offers Khantok dinner at Khum Kaew
Palace. Tel:(0) 5321 0663-4, (0) 5321
4315, Fax: (0) 5321 4563.

Warorot Grand Palace 184.E7
64 Inthawarorot Rd, C.M. 50200.
Medium-rise hotel.Tel & Fax: (0)
5341 6102-3

Winner Inn Hotel 185.F9
19/1 Sidonchai Rd. Soi 2, C.M. 50100.
Medium-rise hotel. Tel:(0) 5327
2377, (0) 5327 4508, Fax: (0) 5320
8769

YMCA 168.C6
11 Soemsuk Rd. Soi Mangrairatsami,
C.M. 50300. Medium rise hotel.
Tel:(0) 5322 1819-20, (0) 5322 2366,
Fax: (0) 5321 5523

Guest Houses

Many good guest houses in Chiang
Mai are more like small hotels,
offering air-conditioned rooms and a
coffee shop. All guest houses listed
here are of reasonable standard and
are centrally located. They offer
rooms with attached bathrooms with
hot running water, a surprisingly
useful facility in the cold season.
Prices range from around 250 baht
for a fan room to 350-500 baht for an
air-conditioned room. Most do not
accept credit cards. Reservations, if
accepted at all, are best made in the
morning on the day of arrival (Guest
houses that offer fan rooms at less than
200 baht are marked ¢)

Ban Jong Come 185/201.E9
47 Soi 4 Thaphae Rd., C.M. 50000
Tel: (0) 5327 4823

Duang Dee House 185.D9
14/23-24 Soi Insuan, Maninopharat
Rd., C.M. 50200 Tel: (0) 5321 9361
E-m: duangdee@iname.com

High rise struc-
tures are banned
within the moats
and may not be
built directly
over-looking
temples.

(Photo: View
NW over the old
city towards Doi
Suthep)

Fang Guest House *185/201.E9*
46-48 Kamphaengdin Rd., Soi 1, C.M.
50100 Tel: (0) 5328 2940,
(0) 53272500 🛏 ♿ 🛏

Gap's House *185/200.E8*
3 Ratchadamnoen Rd., Soi 4, C.M.
50100 Tel: (0) 5327 8140, (0)5327
0143. Cooking school <www.thai-
culinary-art.infothai.com>

Mountain View *184/200.D8*
105 Si Phum Rd., C.M. 50200.
Tel: (0) 5321 2866, Fax: (0) 5322 2635
🛏 ♿ 🛏

Namkhong Guest House *185/*
201.E9 *55-57 Thapae Rd. Soi 3 C.M.*
Tel: (0) 5327 5556, Fax: (0) 5341
9150 🛏 ♿ 🛏 🛏

Nice Apartment *184/200.E8*
15 Soi 1 Ratchadamnoen Rd., C.M.
50200 Tel: (0) 5321 0552,
Fax: (0) 5341 9150 🛏 ♿ 🛏

Northlands House Hotel *185/200*
D9 *2 Soi 7 Mun Muang Rd., C.M.*
50200 Tel/Fax: (0) 5321 8860
🛏 ♿ 🛏

Pathara House *184/200.E8*
24 Soi 2 Mun Muang Rd., C.M. 50200
Tel: (0) 5320 6542-3, Fax: (0) 5320
6543 🛏 ♿ 🛏

Pha Thai Guest House *184/200.F8*
48/1 Ratchaphakhinai Rd., C.M. 50000
Tel: (0) 5327 8013, Fax: (0) 5327 4045
🛏 ♿ 🛏

Rendezvous Guest House *184/*
200.E8 *3/1 Soi 5 Ratchadamnoen Rd.,*
C.M. 50100 Tel: (0) 5321 3763
Fax: (0) 5321 7229 🛏 ♿ 🛏

Riverside House *185/201.F11*
Old Chiang Mai-Lamphun Rd., C.M.
50000 Tel: (0) 5330 2121,
Fax: (0) 5330 2122 🛏 🛏

Rung Ruang Hotel *185/201.E9*
398 Thaphae Rd., C.M. 50000 Tel: (0)
5323 2017-8, Fax: (0) 5325 2409
🛏 ♿ 🛏

Royal Guest House *185/201.E9*
5 Soi 4 Kotchasan Rd., C.M. 50100
Tel: (0) 5328 2460, Tel/Fax: (0) 5320
6404-5 🛌 🛏 ♿ 🛏

Safe House Court *184.E8*
178 Ratchaphakhinai Rd., C.M.
50200. Tel: (0) 5341 8955-7, Fax: (0)

Getting a Down-town Guest House

Touts and some *songthaeo* drivers waiting at the stations may try to take you to guest houses that pay them commission. These are likely to be in locations away from the main centre. The best central locations (*see* map 30 p.200-201) are on the sois south of Thaphae Rd. *(201.E9)* and west of Mun Muang Rd. (ถนนมูลเมือง) *(200.E&D8)*. From the stations *songthaeo* should cost 10 baht per head (*see* page 198 for guidelines), so fix clear destinations and prices with drivers before getting in their vehicles. Expect the *Songthaeo* to take other passengers

Some guest houses are known to pressure guests to take their trekking tours, a *modus operandi* that may begin on Khao San Road in Bangkok. There are plenty of guest houses and certainly enough trekking companies, so just quietly move to another guest house if there are problems.

5341 9031 <www.thainice.com/
safehousel> 🛏 ♿ 🛏

Sarah Guest House *185/200.E9*
20 Thaphae Rd., Soi 4, C.M. 50000.
Tel: (0) 5320 8271, Fax: (0) 5327
9423 E-m: jack21@loxinfo.co.th
🛏 ♿ 🛏

S.K.House *184/201.D9*
*30 Mun Muang Rd., Soi 9, C.M.*Tel: (0)
5341 8396, Fax: (0) 5321 0675
🛌 🛏 ♿ 🛏 🛏

Top North Guest House *200.F8*
15 Mun Muang Rd., Soi 2, C.M. 50000
Tel: (0) 5327 8900, (0) 5327 8684 Fax:
(0) 5327 8485 🛌 🛏 ♿ 🛏 🛏

The White House *184/200.E8*
12 Soi 5 Ratchadamnoen Rd., C.M.
50200 Tel: (0) 5335 7130 🛏 ♿ 🛏

Your House *184/200.D8*
8 Soi 2 Ratwithi Rd., C.M. 50200 Te
(0) 5321 7492 <www.siprog.com/
your house> ¢ 🛏 ♿ 🛏

Hotel/Apartments

The following offer monthly and
nightly rates. For more places, see
<www.chiangmaiinfo.com>

**Le Pont Restaurant & City
Residence** *201.E10 14 Charoenrat
Rd. Wat Ket, C.M. 50000* Tel: (0) 53
1712, Fax: (0) 5324 3673
🛏 🛏 🛏

Paddy Field Rooms & Apartment
184.E6 49/1-8 Arak Rd, CM.50200
Tel: (0) 5381 4558, Fax: (0) 5381
4560 🛏   🛏 🛏

Tawan Court *163.W3/185.E10*
15/1 Charoen Prathet Rd., C.M. 5010
Tel: (0) 5328 4212 -20, Fax: (0) 53
4221 <www.tawancourt.com> 🛏

ACCOMMODATION: VALLEY & MOUNTAINS

There are many resorts
offering quiet ambience in
cooler uplands. The level of
service may not match that
a good city hotel, but their
lovely natural settings are
unbeatable. Many are less
than an hour's travel from t
downtown area of the city.

Some resorts cater more t
local trade and may be very
quiet during the week. At
weekends they can become
busy with block bookings a
well as with day visitors
coming to relax in the
gardens. (🛈 08:00-17:00 =
restaurant service hours).

Doi Saket-San Kamphaer
pp.81-91

San Kamphaeng Hot Springs
*Map 7 p.88 Sahakon Village, Mae On
H1317 KM.29 west turn — 2.5 kms.*
🛈 08:30 –20:00. Cabins near mine
pool. Tel: (0) 5392 9077, Fax: (0)
5392 9099 🛌 🛏   🛏 🛏

nkamphaeng Resort *Map 7 p.88*
8 Mu 10, Sankamphaeng C.M.
130. H1006 KM.8 🕐 08:00–17:00.
try fee to gardens 20 Bt. Wood
bins in a copse by a small lake with
ddle boats. Tel/Fax: (0) 5388 0587-8
≋ Ⓑ Ⓑ

ong Arun Hot Springs Resort
7 p.88 H1317 KM.29 west turn —
5 kms. 🕐 08:00–20:30. Bungalows
th mineral baths. Visitors can enjoy
hs, jacuzzi and traditional massage
: (0) 5324 8475, Fax: (0) 5324
91 🏃🏊 ≋   ☁ Ⓑ Ⓑ

ang Tarn Resort *Map 7 p.88*
18. KM.17 north-west turn along
led road by irrigation canal — 6
s. 🕐 06:00–22:00. Rooms, cabins
d houses. Gates to nearby dam and
e close at 18:00. Tel: (0) 5386
55-7, Fax: (0) 5386 5655
≋   ☁ Ⓑ Ⓑ

mphun - Li, pp.100-108

hiang Mai Lakeside Ville *80.E3*
'Sawai Riang' (p.161)for details.

ll Moon Resort *80.F3*
nna style hideway near Saraphi—
y suit long stays. Tel: (0) 5342
78 <www.fullmoonresort.com>

un Tan Viewpoint Resort
p 11 p.102 222 Mu 4 Tha Sop Sao,
e Tha, C.M. 51040. H11 KM.56
st turn — 3.5 kms. 🕐 07:00-23:00.
ngalows in field overlooking small
nd. Chiang Mai off. Tel: (0) 5380
22, Fax: (0) 5327 8396. Resort: (0)
60 4913 ≋   ☁ Ⓑ Ⓑ

ae Ping National Park *Map 16*
13 Park HQ (0)5351 9031 or
2579 5734. Privately owned rafts
rented from Tha Nam/ Tha Phae by
ng Dok (0) 5351 9232 or Khun
aroen (0) 5397 9068

npatong - Doi Inthanon
ational Park, pp.106-8

thanon Highland *Map 14 p.109*
009 KM7 north turn 500m. Various
ngalows/houses in orchard.
.office Tel/Fax: (0) 5327 8396.
≋ Ⓑ Ⓑ Ⓑ

More modest places down the
same lane are **Inthanon Tharnthong**
(Tel: (0) 1436 4192) & **Inthanon
Paradise Resort** (Tel: (0) 1603 6084).
Service is uncertain, however.

Inthanon Riverside Resort *M10
p.97* 4 Mu 4 Nong Long, Wiang Nong
Long, Lamphun. 🕐 07:00-20:00.
Bungalows in fields — the river must
have moved. Tel: (0) 5350 5166
Fax: (0) 5325 1751 ☞   Ⓑ Ⓑ Ⓑ

Kao Mai Lanna *Map 10 p.97*
1 Mu 6 Chiang Mai-Hot Rd (H108
KM.29), Sanpatong C.M. 50120. 🕐
07:00-23:00. Leafy setting includes a
shop selling traditional cottons. Tel:
(0) 5383 4470-5, Fax: (0) 5383 4480
<www.kaomailanna.com>
☞   Ⓑ Ⓑ Ⓑ

Little Home Guest House *Map 14
p.109* 11/Mu 10 Nam Tok Mae Klang
(H1009 KM6+), Chom Thong, C.M.
50160. Practical huts in a row. Tel:
(0) 1224 3446. ☢   Ⓑ

Doi Inthanon National Park, Mae Chaem, OmKoi
pp.108-13

Hod Resort *Map 14 p.109*
239 Mu 1, Hot-Mae Sariang Rd (H108
KM.4). 🕐 08:00-22:00. Rooms and
cabins overlook riverside pasture.
Tel/Fax: (0) 5346 1070
≋ ☢   Ⓑ Ⓑ

Khao Krairat Resort *Map 14 p.109*
237 Mu 1, Ban Luang Dong, Hot-Mae
Sariang Rd (H108 KM.17). Nice
rooms close to Ob Luang gorge.
Tel: (0) 5322 9285, (0) 5338 4542-3.
☢   Ⓑ Ⓑ

Mae Chaem Plantation *M14 p.109*
FIO Suan Pa Mae Chaem Mu 3 Kong
Khaek, Mae Chaem. H1088 KM16.
Comfortable wooden A frames,
mountain bikes & even rafting. Call
C.M. OfficeTel: (0) 5324 5356

Navasoung Resort *Map 15 p.112*
165 Mu 9 Thapha, Mae Chaem, C.M.
50270. H1192 KM19. Cabins.
Tel/Fax: (0) 5382 8477. ☢   Ⓑ Ⓑ

Om Koi Resort *Map 16 p.113*
*Turn right at intersection in Om Koi
where H1055 turns sharply east for
Mae Tun. 500m. Cabins in orchard.*

*The gardens of the Regent Resort,
Chiang Mai*

Offers trekking, mountain bike & off-
road. Call first Tel: (0) 1950 7789,
Fax: (0) 5333 8493 ☢   Ⓑ Ⓑ

Mae Sa & Samoeng, pp.114-119

Botanic Residence *Map 18 p.117
(H1096 KM12) Opp. Queen Sirikit
Botanic Gardens, Mae Rim C.M. 50180.*
Spacious, somewhat institutional
ambience, nice pool. Spa. Tel: (0) 5329
0029, Fax: (0) 5329 0021
🏃🏊 ≋   ☁ Ⓑ Ⓑ Ⓑ Ⓑ

Hmong Lodge *Map 17. p114*
H1096 KM.4 north turn 17 kms.
Package resort — no walk in. C.M
Off. Tel: (0) 5321 6780, Fax: (0)
5321 5072 ☢   Ⓑ Ⓑ

Kangsadan Resort — R *Map 18
p.117 H1096 KM.18 south turn — 1.5
kms.* 🕐 07:00-22:00. Wooden
buildings on terraces overlook a gully
and torrent Tel: (0) 5327 4789, (0)
5387 2263 🏃☢   Ⓑ Ⓑ

Mae Rim Lagoon Hotel *Map 18
p.1175/1 Mu 6, Mae Rim-Samoeng
Old Rd. C.M. 50180.* 🕐 07:00-22:00.
Low-rise hotel in parkland. Tel: (0)
5329 7288-9, Fax: (0) 5329 7290
🏃🏊 ≋ 🍴≋   ☁ Ⓑ Ⓑ Ⓑ

Mae Sa Valley Resort *M18 p.117*
H1096 KM.13 🕐 06:00–21:00.
Cabins above well-tended gardens
and craft learning centre (see p.179).
Tel: (0) 5329 0051-2, Fax: (0) 5329 0017
🏃🏊 ☢   Ⓑ Ⓑ Ⓑ

Mount & Sky (Mon Doi Ing Fa)
*Map 18 p.117 24/32 KM.15 Mae Rim-
Samoeng Rd. (H1096) Mae Rim, C.M.
50180.* Wooden chalets in garden.
Tel: (0) 5387 9312-3, (0) 5387 9334-
5, Fax: (0) 5387 9313 ☢   Ⓑ Ⓑ

The Paradise *Map 18 p.117*
43/1 Mu 6 Mae Rim, C.M. 50180.
Bungalows in garden. SPA. Tel: (0)
5386 0464-5, Fax: (0) 5386 0463

Pongyang Garden Resort — R
Map 18 p.117 H1096 KM.14 49/3 Mu
2, Pong Yang, Mae Rim, C.M. 50180.
🕐 *08:00–21:00.* Bungalows in very
attractive valley setting. Tel: (0) 5387
9151-2, Fax: (0) 5387 9153

**The Regent Resort
Chiang Mai — R** *Map 18 p.117*
(H1096 KM.2 south turn — 400 m.)
Mae Rim-Samoeng Old Rd., C.M. 50180
Electric carts, bathrooms with
gardens, videos on command, private
salas, pro tennis coach, luxury spa —
in a class of its own. Tel: (0) 5329
8181-9 Fax: (0) 5329 8190
<www.regenthotels.com/
regentchiangmai>

Samoeng Resort *Map 17 p.114*
*(2 kms. from market on road to Wat
Chan)* *79 Mu 2, Samoeng, C.M. 50250.*
🕐 *07:00–20:00.* Large grounds &
'Tea for Two' restaurant Tel: (0) 5348
7072-5, Fax: (0) 5348 7075

Sanctuary Point Resort
*Map 18 p.117 H1096 KM.1 99 Mu 7,
Tambon Rim Tai, Mae Rim, C.M.
50180.* Ruan Mai Home Restaurant
🕐 *08:00–22:00.* Spacious apartment
suites in high-rise recommended for
longer, comfortable stay. Tel: (0) 5386
1511-3, Fax: (0) 5386 0322
<www.thaisanctuary.com>

Samoeng Villa and **Samoeng/
Nantima Guest House** are located on
the road between the Samoeng Resort
and Samoeng.

Hang Dong - Samoeng Road (H1269)

Ban Klang Doi Hotel & Resort
*Map 17 p.114 (H1269 KM.23) 190
Hang Dong-Samoeng Rd., C.M. 50230.*
🕐 *07:00–17:00.* Peak Pub hrs. 17:00-
22:00. Lanna style lodges in park. Tel/
Fax: (0) 5336 5350, Tel/Fax: (0) 5336
5306-7

Belle Villa *Map 17 p.114*
(H1269 KM.19) 135 Mu 5, Tambol Ban

Pong, C.M. 50230. 🕐 *06:30–23:00.*
Resort & houses in attractive setting.
Tel: (0) 5336 5318-21, Fax: (0) 5336 5322

Golden Orchid Hill B&B *Map 17
p.114 (H1269 KM.23) 159 Hang
Dong-Samoeng Rd., C.M. 50230.*
Rooms in country style houses. Tel:
(0) 5336 5104, Fax: (0) 5336 5105

Krisda Doi *Map 17 p.114*
*(H1269 KM.25) 90 Mu 4, Hang Dong-
Samoeng Rd., C.M. 50230.* 🕐 *07:00–
21:00.* Swiss chalet style and popular
flower gardens. Tel: (0) 5336 5231-4,
Fax: (0) 5336 5235

Lanna Resort *Map 17 p.114*
*(H1269 KM.28) 1 Mu 4, Hang Dong-
Samoeng Rd., C.M. 50230.* 🕐 *08:00–
20:00.* Thai-style chalets in pretty
resort. Tel: (0) 5336 5222-3, Fax: (0)
5336 5224 <www.lannaresort.com>

Suan Bua Hotel & Resort *Map 17
p.114 (KM.22 158) Mu 3, Tambon
Banpong, C.M. 50230.* 🕐 *06:00–
22:00.* Extensive low-rise buildings in
gardens. Spa & full hotel service.Tel:
(0) 5336 5270-9, Fax: (0) 5336 5280
<www.chmai.com>

Yord Doi Resort *Map 17 p.114*
*(H1269 KM.25) 186 Mu 4, Hang Dong-
Samoeng Rd., C.M. 50230* 🕐 *07:00–
22:00.* Balcony restaurant with a view
& cabins. Tel: (0) 5336 5253, Fax: (0)
5336 5254

Mae Rim to Pai pp 120-122

For recommended guest houses in
Pai see Map 20. p122.

Hut Ing Pai — R *Map 20 p122*
*(H1095 KM.102+ south turn — 300m.)
29 Mu 4 Mae Na Toeng. M.H.S 58130.*
🕐 *07:00–22:00.* Comfortable chalets
in landscaped garden setting. Chiang
Mai Off. tel: (0) 5369 9781-2.
<www.hutingpai.com>

Muang Pai Resort — R *Map 20
p.122 (KM.101 south turn — 4 kms.
on road to Mo Paeng Waterfall) 94 Ban
Mo Paeng, MHS. 58130.*🕐 *06:00–
24:00.* Comfortable chalets. C.M.Off.
tel: (0) 5327 0906, Fax (0) 5327 2895
Resort: (0) 5369 9988

Pai Mountain Lodge *Map 20
p.122 (KM.101 south turn — 4.2 km
on road to Mo Paeng Waterfall) 84 M
4, Ban Mo Paeng, MHS. 58130* 🕐
06:00–21:00. Huts in a dell.
Tel: (0) 5369 9995

Rim Pai Cottage *Map 20 p.122
17 Mu 5, Pai, M.H.S. 58130* Dark
cabins, but pleasant riverside
location. Tel: (0) 5369 9133

Spa Exotic Home — R *Map 20
p.122 86 Mu 2, Ban Mae Hi, MHS.
58130.* 🕐 *07:00–22:00.* Cabins in
garden with open air mineral tubs.
tel: (0) 5369 8088.

Thaphai Spa Camping *Map 20
p.122 84/1 Mu 2, Mae Hi, MHS.
58130.* 🕐 *07:00–22:00.* Rooms in r
houses in garden with extensive
open-air mineral bathing. tel: (0)
5369 9695. C.M. Off Fax: (0) 5321
9610

Mae Taeng, Chiang Dao Phrao, pp.124-129

Chiang Dao Hills Resort — R *Ma
21 p.123 (H107 KM.100) 28 Mu 6,
Tambon Ping Khong, Chiang Dao, C.
50170.* 🕐 *07:00–22:00.* Comfortab
cabins in pretty woods around a
small lake. Tel: (0) 5323 2434, Fax
(0) 5325 1372

Chiang Dao Inn Hotel *Map 21
p.123 (H107 KM.72) 20 Mu 6, Chia
Dao, C.M. 50170* 🕐 *07:00–01:00.*
back from high street. Tel: (0) 5345
5134, Fax: (0) 5345 5132

Doi Farang Bungalow *Map 22
p.126 203 Mu 1, Tambon Pa Nai,
Phrao, C.M. 50190.* 🕐 *08:00–20:30*
Rooms in converted rice barns/
custom cabins in rural location.
Mountain bikes. Tel/Fax: (0) 5347
4392
<www.doifarangbungalow.com>

Mae Rim Lodge Resort *80.A2
(H107 KM.19+ right turn 2.5 kms.)
124/1 Mu 10, San Pong, Mae Rim,
C.M. 50180.* 🕐 *07:00–21:00.*
Cottages in unusual rural village
location. Tel: (0) 5337 6105, Fax: (
5337 6314
E-m: maerimlodge@yahoo.com

yal Ping Garden & Resort
⊅ 21 p.123 (H107 KM.52)110/2-14
3, Ban Pao, Mae Taeng, C.M.
'50. ⊕ *06:00–22:00.* Luxury
ising development on the banks of
River Ping.Tel: (0) 5326 3386-90,
:: (0) 5326 3385 🏇 🏊 🎿 ➤
● 🛢 🛢

n Doi Resort *Map 21 p.123*
178 KM1) 46 Mu 4, Muang Ngai
e night cafe and A-frames.
, (0) 5337 5028-9 ➤ ⊛ 🛢
ww.rimdoiresort.com>

ntarn Floating Bed/Breakfast
Restaurant *Map 21 p.123 (sales*
) 535 Rimtai, Mae Rim, C.M.50180.
'ts on Mae Ngat Lake, Sri Lanna
ional Park. Fishing, boats, and
als. Tel: (0) 5329 7060, Fax: (0)
29 7283. ⊛   🛢 🛢

g Khang, Fang &
aton, pp.130-133.

gkhang Nature Resort *Map 23*
t. p130 1/1 Mu 5, Ban Khum,
nbon Mae Ngon, Fang, C.M. 50320
07:00–14:00, 18:00–21:00. Amari's
urious chalets in the highlands.
, (0) 5345 0110-19, Fax: (0) 5345
20 <www.amari.com>
➤ 🛢 🛢 🛢

g Khang Villa *&*
ha Garden Home *M23*
t. p130 Ban Kum, Ang
ng, Chaiprakan, C.M.
20 ⊕ *07:00–23:00.* Basic
rames. Tel: (0) 5345 0010
ng Khang Villa), (0) 5345
8 (Naha) ⊛   🛢 🛢

n Suan Riverside
sort M25. p132 134 Mu
Thaton C.M. 50280.
's by the river. Tel: (0)
37 3214-5, Fax: (0) 5337
5
⊭ ⊛   🛢 🛢

e Kok River Village
5. p132 121 Ohotana
Thaton C.M. 50280
07:00-23:00 Chalet-cabins
riverside centre for
tural and adventure
rism. Tel: (0) 5345
28-9
:: (0) 5345 9329.
ww.track-of-the-tiger.com>
➤ ⊛ ➤ 🛢 🛢 🛢

Thaton Chalet *Map 25 p132*
192/1 Mu 14, Thaton, Mae Ai, C.M.
50280 ⊕ *06:30–23:00.* Medium rise
hotel on the river bank. Tel: (0) 5337
3155-7, Fax: (0) 5337 3158   ➤
➤ 🛢 🛢

Thaton River View Hotel
Map 25 p.132 Thaton, Mae Ai, C.M.
50280 ⊕ *06:00–22:30.* Pleasant
cabins by the river, gourmet dishes at
the restaurant. Tel: (0) 5337 3173-5,
Fax: 459288 ➤   ➤ 🛢 🛢 🛢

AIRLINES

Call for latest schedules:

Air Mandalay
107 Doi Ping Mansion, 148 Charoen
Prathet Rd. Yangon & Mandalay, Thu &
Sun . Tel: (0) 5327 6884 Ext. 107,
Fax: (0) 5381 8051
<www.myanmars.net/airmandalay>

Bangkok Airways
Chiang Mai Airport, Fl.2, C.M.50000
Sukhothai & Bangkok daily (onward
connections to Koh Samui & Phuket),
Jinhong, Yunnan: Tue, Thur, Sat. Tel:
(0) 5328 1519, Fax: (0) 5328 1520

Lao Aviation
Nakorn Ping Condo Fl 1, 2/115
Ratchapluak Rd. C.M. 50200
Luang Phabang & Vientiane
Thu & Sun. Tel: (0) 5340 4033

LTU International Airways
Huai Kaew Rd. Berlin, Munich,
Dusseldorf & Hamburg via Abu Dhabi
Tel: (0) 5321 8715-19, Fax (0) 5322 2013

Mandarin Airlines
Chiang Mai Airport Fl.2, C.M.50200
Taipei Tue, Wed, Sat Tel: (0) 5320
1268-9, Fax: (0) 5392 2237

Silk Air
Imperial Mae Ping Hotel, 153
Sidonchai Rd. C.M. 50100.
Singapore Tue, Fri, Sun
Tel: (0) 5327 6495

Thai Airways International
184/200.D8 240 Prapokklao Rd.
C.M.50200
Bangkok 8-13 flights daily from
07:00-21:30 according to season
Mae Hong Son 10:00, 13:05, 15:55
daily
Chiang Rai 08:05, 18:50 daily
Mae Sot 16;20 Mon, Tue, Thur, Sat
Nan, Phrae & Phitsanulok 10:15,
Mon, Tue, Thur, Sat
Phuket 11:15 daily
Tel: (0) 5321 1044-7, (0) 5321 021
(outside office hrs: (0) 2628 2000)

Chiang Mai's Climatological Data: Means for 1990-1999

Northern Meteorological Office, Chiang Mai. <www.geocities.com/north_met>
For weather reports 24hrs call (0) 5327 7919

Month	Jan	Feb	Mar	Apr	May	Jun	Jul	Aug	Sep	Oct	Nov	Dec
Max Temp °C	30.2	32.2	35.4	36.1	34.4	33.0	31.9	31.3	31.6	31.2	30.0	28
Min Temp °C	14.2	15.5	19.3	22.6	23.8	24.1	23.9	23.5	23.2	21.9	19.0	15.6
Relative Humidity %	68	57	51	57	70	76	79	83	83	80	76	72
Rainfall (mm)	5.6	16.1	26.3	53.5	154.3	85.3	156.3	224.9	179.1	105.0	43.7	14.4
Rainy days	.9	1.3	2.2	6.3	14.8	15.3	18.7	21.5	18.0	11.6	4.9	1.4
Wind (knots) Direction	1.6 S	2.3 S	3.0 S	3.6 S	3.8 SW	3.8 SW	3.2 SW	2.8 SW	2.6 S	2.5 N	2.2 N	2.1 N
Cloudiness (0-10)	2.1	2.1	2.4	4.0	6.0	7.5	8.4	8.6	7.4	5.8	4.4	3.3
Visibility (kms)	7.1	7.3	7.1	8.7	12.0	12.9	12.7	12.1	11.2	9.6	9.2	8.6
No of days with haze	28.3	26.0	29.2	20.8	2.3	0	0	0.7	2.4	11.6	13.9	21.2

BUSINESS HOURS

Government Office hours

are from 08:00–12:00, 13:00–16:30 on weekdays except national holidays.

Business Service

All Info Services

179 Ratchamankha Rd.(opp. Felix City Inn. 184.E7). C.M. 50200. Hrs. 09:00–17:00. Mon-Fri, 09:00-12:00 Sat)
Tel/Fax: (0) 5381 4152
E-m: allinfo@loxinfo.co.th

CLIMATE

Chiang Mai's northern latitude (18°47') and mountain location ensure a wide seasonal variation in the weather (*see means on p.193*)

Cool Season

(November–February) Surprisingly low temperatures at night make warm clothing necessary, especially if you plan to travel in the mountains where temperatures can drop to near freezing at higher altitudes.

Hot Season

(February–May) Heat and haze reach their maximum at the end of March. Short, violent storms in April and May can bring high winds and welcome rain.

Rainy Season

(May–October) Days often begin bright, but darken as clouds gather above the mountains. Short intense rainstorms usually occur in the afternoons, clearing again by evening. Sustained rain occurs when tropical storms hit the region. This has been common in recent years.

COMMUNICATIONS

Cyber cafés

These are numerous and inexpensive in the downtown area.

Post Office hours

08:30–16:30 weekdays; 09:00–12:00 on Saturdays.

Overseas Telephone Services

International phone and mail facilities are offered by the Post Office from 08:30 through 18:00 at:

Airport Post Office (*terminal building*)
    Chiang Mai Post & Telegraph Office (*Sanpakoi, Charoen Muang Rd. E12*)
    Phra Singh Post Office (*Samlan Rd. 184.E7*).
    Calls may be made from the **Mail Boxes Etc** (*124 Chang Khlan Rd 09:00-23:00 163.Y1*) and from the basement of the Night Bazaar (*till 23:00*). The cheapest rates are from the **Telecommunications Authority Office** on the Chiang Mai-Lampang Superhighway (*24 hrs.202.F14*). For international calls, dial 001 + country code & number. The minimum charge for a call is one minute; then the call is priced in units.

Useful Phone Numbers:

Telephone Services:

Directory 1133,
Emergency 191,
Fire 199,
Telephone Problems? 1177
International Operator 100
Immigration
(0) 5327 7510
Tourism Authority of Thailand
(0) 5324 8604, (0) 5324 8607
Tourist Police
1155 (free) or (0) 5324 8974, (0) 5324 8130

Answering Machines in Thai

If you do not know the extension number, try pressing 0, this will usually (not always) get the operator.

COMMUNITY

Chiang Mai Disabled Centre

184/200.E8 133/1 Ratchapakhinai Rd. opp. Wat Ban Ping. Hrs 08:00-20:00
Foundation to encourage the potential of disabled people. Offers internet, graphic services and support for disabled.
Tel: (0) 5321 3941.
Fax: (0) 5324 0935

Churches

For full listings see 'Chiang Mai Info' <www.chiangmaiinfo.com>
Catholic Church *202.G11*
255 Charoen Phrathet Rd.
Tel: (0) 5327 1859
Chiang Mai Community Church
1 Charoenrat Rd. Tel: (0) 5324 2469
Chiang Mai First Church/Church of Christ *202.E11* 10 Charoenrat Rd.
Tel: (0) 5330 2530-1

'Free Magazines'

Several magazines giving news, cultural and social information are freely distributed in the city. Some also have websites. These are:
<wwwchiangmainews.com>
<www.chiangmai-online.com/gmcn
<www.chiangmai-chiangrai.com>

Raintree Community Services

201.E11 Charoen Muang Rd, near Nawarat Bridge. Mon-Sat 10:00-12:00 Sun 15:45-16:45 Children's storytelling media library, info for new residents counselling by arrangement. Payap University Info-line Tel: (0) 5326 26 Movie line (0) 5326 2661

DIPLOMATIC REPRESENTATIVES

Consulates

China, *184.F7 111 Chang Lor Rd.*
Tel: (0) 5327 6125
India *169 C11 344 Charoen Rat Rd.*
Tel: (0) 5324 3066
Japan *169.H6 90 Airport Business Park* Tel: (0) 5320 3367
USA *185.D10 387 Wichayanon Rd.*
Tel: (0) 5325 2629

Honorary Consulates

Australia, *Lotus Hall, Sirimang-khlachan Rd. 168.C5* Tel: (0) 5322 1083
Austria, *15 Mu 1 Huai Kaew Rd.*
Tel: (0)53 40 0231
Canada, *151 Superhighway (Highwa 11)*, Tel: (0) 5385 0147
Finland *163.V2, Rattanaphon, 104-1 Thaphae Rd.* Tel (0) 5323 4777
France *185.F10 Alliance Française Charoenrat Rd.* Tel: (0) 5328 1466
Germany, *Club House, Nai Fan 2 Housing Estate, Mae Hia.*
Tel: (0) 5383 8735
Great Britain *202.D11 British Counc 198 Bamrungrat Rd.*
Tel: (0) 5326 3015
Sweden *168.C6 YMCA (14:00-16 Mon & Tues only)* Tel: (0) 5322 08

HEALTH

Pharmacies in Thailand readily dispense a wide rang of drugs for all manner of ills. Light ailments such as minor stomache problems can occur if you have built up no local immunity,

"How we don't catch AIDS" (Village sign near Chiang Dao in mid 90's)
   Eating and drinking together
   Sharing a bathroom and toilet
   Working together

specially in the hot season, but they are seldom serious. Serious threats to health are s follows:

Dengue Fever

This may occur 5-8 days after a bite by the aedes mosquito in the day, specially in the rainy season. Symptoms are sudden chilly sensations, severe headaches, pains in the joints, and severe tiredness. Fevers can get high, but the disease is seldom fatal. Treatment is by rest, lots of fluid and paracetamol. Hospitalisation is recommended in severe cases.

HIV/AIDS (& STD's)

Though positive action by the government has improved the situation, and though there is little visible evidence of the suffering, the problem remains *extremely serious* in the area. Whatever the relationship between risk behaviour (unsafe sexual practice, sharing intravenous needles, etc.), HIV and AIDS, *no one should ignore the warnings.*

Malaria

The disease is rare in Chiang Mai, but it is endemic in border areas, and can only truly be protected against using repellents and nets. The mosquitoes are mainly a threat in the hours before and after dusk and dawn. Expert consultation is available from Centre for Malaria Control (Mahidol U., in the grounds of Maharaj Hospital)

Rabies
Some 40-50 cases are reported annually in Thailand. If you are bitten by an animal, consult a doctor and begin a course of injections immediately.

Road accidents
All the main hospitals are well-equipped to deal with trauma, but the Maharaj (government) and Chiang Mai Ram (private) hospitals are considered the best.

HOSPITALS AND CLINICS

Out-patient consultation is best done in the mornings, but all hospitals have a 24 hour service.

Chang Phuak Hospital *169.C8*
1/7 Soi 2, Chang Phuak Rd. 24hr. Emergency. Dental. Hrs. 08:00–20:00. Small private hospital. Tel: (0) 5322 0022, Fax: (0) 5321 8120

Chiang Mai Central Memorial Hospital *169.G9*
186/2 Chang Khlan Rd., C.M. 50100. 24 hr Emergency & Dental. Private hospital. Tel: (0) 5327 7090-3, Fax: (0) 5327 1621

Chiang Mai Dental Hospital
169.A7 1/42 Mu 3, Chiang Mai-Lampang Super-highway. Hrs. 09:00–24:00. Tel: (0) 5341 1150

Chiang Mai Ram Hospital *169.D6*
8 Bunruangrit Rd. 24hr. Emergency. Dental: Hrs. 09:00–20:00. Favoured by an international insurance company for its accident victims. Tel: (0) 5322 4861, Fax: (0) 5322 4880

Chiang Mai Ram 2 *Map 33. A11*
99 Superhighway. 24hr. Emergency. Tel: (0) 5385 2590, Fax: (0) 5385 2999

Children's Hospital *169.C7*
722/2 Mu 3, Hassadisewi Rd. Hrs. 07:00–08:30, 20:30–23:00. Private clinic of respected pediatrician Dr. To Phong. Tel:(0) 5322 3108

Global Doctor Clinic *168.D6*
102 Huai Kaew Rd (opp. Kat Suan Kaew) Hrs. 09:00–20:00. Mon-Fri, Sat 09:00-13:00. Dr Phanu makes house/hotel calls on a 24hr basis. Office Tel: (0) 5321 7762, Fax: (0) 5321 7763 (After hours (0) 1952 9722)

Defensive Driving in Thailand

Nothing spoils a holiday like an accident! A red *tung* by the roadside shows that a death from a road accident has occurred near that spot. Pay attention to the following on Thai roads.

• Vehicles entering from side roads onto main roads may not stop.

• Buses and heavy vehicles may overtake regardless of oncoming traffic – the latter must pull onto the hard shoulder *or else!*

• Watch out for oncoming traffic overtaking on blind corners or hills — be ready to pull onto the hard shoulder at any time.

• Watch your off-side — people overtake on the inside too!

• Let impatient drivers overtake you before they take unreasonable risks.

• Motorcycles, bicycles, tractors and carts without lights are common at night, particularly during the early part of the evening. Statistically this (17:00-20:00 hrs) is the most dangerous time on the roads.

• Gravel and sand on roads can cause motorcycles to slide easily when braking or going around corners.

Lanna Hospital *169.A8*
1 Sukkasem Rd. 24hr. Emergency. Private hospital with a good outpatient service. *(Dental clinic by appointment. Hrs. 08:00–20:00 closed Mon.)* Tel: (0) 5321 1037-41, Fax: (0) 5321 8402

Maharaj Hospital *168 E6*
Suan Dok Hospital. 110 Suthep Rd. 24hr Emergency.

The largest government medical/ teaching institution in the north. Excellent facilities, but suitable for visitors only in emergencies. Go to the Sriphat Clinic for private treatment in this hospital.
Tel: (0) 5322 1122

McCormick Hospital *169.C11*
133 Kaew Nawarat Rd. 24hr
Emergency. Dental Hrs. 08:00–16:00.
Older Christian hospital with a good, reliable service. Tel: (0) 5324 1311
Fax: (0) 5324 1177

Special Medical Service Centre (Siphat Clinic, Chiang Mai University Faculty of Medicine)
168.E6 110/392 Sriphat Bldg. (in grounds of Maharaj/Suan Dok Hospital) The clinic offers both in and out patient treatment. 24hr in patient service includes ICU, operation and labour rooms. For

emergencies refer first to the Maharaj facility (Suan Dok Hospital) and request a transfer to the clinic after initial processing. Call betweeen hrs. 08:00-20:00 for appointment with specialists. Tel: (0) 5394 6900-1 Fax: (0) 5389 4901

INFORMATION

Chiang Mai Municipal Tourist Information Centre *201.E11*
135 Praisani Rd. Hrs. 08:30–12:00, 13:00–16:30. C.M. 50000. Provides useful information about events in the city area. Tel: (0) 5325 2557

The Tourism Authority of Thailand *201.E10*
105/1 Chiang Mai-Lamphun Rd., C.M. 50000 . Hrs. 08:30–16:30 daily)
Located 300 m. south from the Nawarat Bridge, the TAT and Tourist

Police offices are in the same building. Tel: (0) 5324 8604, (0) 5324 8607, Fax: (0) 5324 8605

<www.Chiangmaiinfo.com>
Comprehensive listings are found o the on-line companion to the printe "Chiang Mai Info". For other useful websites, go to <http://dmoz.org/ Regional/Asia/Thailand/Provinces/ Chiang_Mai/>

RENTING VEHICLES

Walk-in rental agencies offe very competitive prices. Agencies may be found alon Chaiyaphum and Mun Muang Rds. Rental cars mus be fully insured by law, but check provisions carefully. For mountian bikes see p.18

Long Distance Buses from Arcade (no 2) Bus Station Tel: (0) 5324 2664 **Northern Destinations**	Air-conditioned first class (reclining seats) Air-conditioned second class ordinary
Chiang Khong via Phayao (6hrs.)	06:30, **08:00**, 12:30
Chiang Rai (4hrs.) Frequent buses from 06:00 to 17:30	All Mae Sai/Golden Triangle buses plus 08:15, **08:30**, **10:00**, 11:10, **11:30**, 13:30, **14:00**, 15: 00, 17: 30
Chiang Saen and Golden Triangle	12:00, **12:15** (or take bus to Chiang Rai and change – 6 hours)
Lampang & Phrae only (5hrs.)	All Nan via Phrae buses above + 06:00, 09:00, 11:30, 12:0 **12:30**, 13:00, **15:30**, **16:00**
Li via Lamphun	10:30, 12:30, 14:30
Mae Hong Son via Mae Sarieng & Khun Yuam (8hrs.) *Mae Sariang only	**06:30**, 08:00, **11:00**, *13:30, *15:00, 20:00, **21:00**
Mae Hong Son via Pai (8hrs.)	07:00, 09:30, 11:30, (16:00 Pai only)
Mae Sai via Chiang Rai (5hrs.)	06:00, **07:45**, **09:15**, 10:30, 11:30, 13:10, **15:30**, **17:00**
Mae Sot via Tak (6hrs.)	11:00, **13:10**
Nan via Lampang & Phrae (6hrs.)	07:00, **08:00**, 08:30, **10:00**, 11:00, **14:00**, **15:00**, 07:00, **22:00**, **22:30**
Nan via Phayao & Chun (6hrs.)	09:00, 10:00, **11:00**, 13:30, 15:00
Phayao (3hrs.)	All buses to Chiang Khong & to Nan via Chun plus: 06:00, 07:00, **11:00**, **13:30**, 17:30
Phitsanulok (6hrs)	06:30, **10:00**, 14:15,
Sukhothai (5hrs) & Phitsanulok (*Sukhothai only)	*05:00, *06:00, 07:00, **08:00**, *09:00, *10:15, *11:00, **12:00**, 13:30, 15:00, 18:00, **20:00**

Other destinations: First class a/c buses (+ no of other buses, first departure) Bangkok **09:00**, **18:30**, **19:00**, **19:30**, **20:0** **20:30**, **21:00** (+11, 06:30); Khon Kaen **21:00** (+3, 05:00); Korat **18:45**, **20:30** (+8, 03:30); Ubon Ratchathani **12:15**, **16:20**, **17:00**, **18:00** (+2); Rayong (via Pattaya) **13:15**, **16:15**, **17:45**, **18:30** (+4, 05:00): Udon Thani **20:30** (+2,12:20)

Further Exploring in Northern Thailand with Budget

This guide-book is a start for self-drive exploration into Northern Thailand beyond the

area covered by this book. You can get more maps and information produced by this author by renting a car from Budget Rentacar

and going on any of their 'WorldClass Drives' for Thailand.

Routes from Chiang Mai go to the Golden Triangle via Mae Salong, Chiang Rai and Phayao; to Mae Hong Son via Pai and Mae Sariang, and to Mae Sot, Tak and Lampang. You may go farther afield and drive off to Isan (North-East Thailand) via Phitsanulok and Loei, or you can venture south to explore the coastline of Thailand in three separate drives. Strip maps for the main north-south trunk routes as well as a Bangkok environs highway map are available.

Budget's competitive rates are for vehicles which are purchased new, maintained to international standards and replaced after a fixed amount of use. The company has over 26 branches nationwide which offer one-way rentals for greater convenience. Call 1-800-BUDGET or visit <www.budget.co.th>

Local Buses and *songthaeo* minibuses from Chang Phuak, (No.1) Bus Station. Tel: (0) 5322 1586, **Kat Luang** (Warorot, Lam Yai & Si Nakhon Ping Markets) and **other places.**

Destination	Frequency	Departure Point
Doi Saket (yellow pick-up), Mae Cho & San Sai (green pick-up)	05:30 -21:00 (according to demand)	East side of Si Nakhon Ping market (north of Lam Yai market)
Bo Sang & Sankamphaeng (white songthaeo)	06:00–21:30 (Every 30 min. according to demand)	From lane south of Warorot Market off Wichayanon Rd.
Lamphun (white bus; some AC, + blue pick-ups)	06;30 every 10 min till 18:00 Pick-ups 04:30-20:30 according to demand	No 1 Bus Station (buses) Praisani Rd. opp Lam Yai Market (pick-ups & buses)
Lamphun, Lampang (& onwards to Phayao, Phan, Chiang Rai, Mae Sai)	05:40-17:30 frequent service	Old Chiang-Mai - Lamphun Rd. in front of Sriprakas Hotel.
Sanpatong, Chom Thong (blue buses & yellow pick-up) Hot via Chom Thong (blue bus) Doi Tao (blue bus) - all buses go to Chom Thong & Hot Om Koi via Hot & Chom Thong	06:30 every 20 min. till 18:00, pick-ups according to demand 06:10 every 20 min. till 16:10 04;30, 05:30, 07:30, 09:30, 10,30, 12,30, 14:30, 15:30 08:10, 18:30	Chang Mai Gate Market (all buses originate from No 1 Bus Station
Samoeng (yellow pick-up)	06:30–18:00 (approx. according to demand)	West end of Si Kakhon Ping Market near Ratchawong Rd.
Bo Kaeo via Samoeng (yellow pick-up)	09:00-16:00 (approx. every two hours according to demand)	Empty lot near Bangkok Bank, Chang Phuak Rd.
Mae Rim (yellow pick-up), Mae Taeng (white - pick up) Phrao (red bus)	06:30–18:00 (according to demand) 06:00 hourly till 16:10	East side of Si Nakhon Ping market (north of Lam Yai market) Buses from No. 1 Bus Station.
Fang (a/c vans) via Chiang Dao Fang (buses) via Chiang Dao Mae Ai & Thaton (orange buses) via Chiang Dao Piang Luang via Chiang Dao	07:30 and hourly till 16:30 05:30 and every 30 min. till 19;30 06:00 07,20, 09:00, 11:30, 13:30,15,30 08:10, 18:30 08:00, 12:00, 15:00 (5hrs.)	Buses from No 1 Bus Station.

Avis Rent A Car
Airport Terminal Bldg. Hrs.
08:00–21:00. cars/jeeps
Tel: (0) 5320 1798, Fax: (0) 5320
1799 <www.avisthailand.com>

Budget Rent a Car Co., Ltd.
168.H6 Golf range Business Park,
Mahidol Rd. opp Airport Plaza. Hrs.

07:30–19:00. Cars, jeeps, vans, pick-ups.Tel: (0) 5320 2871-2 Fax: (0) 5320 2873 24 hr toll free customer service 1-800-BUDGET (land-line), 1 401 BUDGET(283438) (mobile) <www.budget.co.th>

Dang Bike Hire *200.E9*
23 Kotchasan Rd. Hrs. 09:00–20:30.

motorcycles. Tel: (0) 5327 1524

Lek Big Bike *200.D9*
74/2 Chaiyaphum Rd., 250-850 cc
motorcycles can be reserved.
Tel/Fax: (0) 5325 1830, (0) 1784 6956
E-m: lekbigbikes@hotmail.com

Songthaeo (red minibuses) & Tuk Tuks

Chiang Mai has no bus service in the city area. Public transport is provided by converted red pick-ups *(songthaeo — so named because of the two rows of seats in the back)*. Some keep to preferred routes and others go according to demand, rather like a taxi. Local people pay a flat fare of 10 bt. for downtown journeys. If the driver has to go down a side lane, or your destination is beyond the downtown area, fix a price before boarding.

You have to flag a *songthaeo* down, and then ask if the driver is prepared to go to your destination. Be prepared to pay more if travelling with a bicycle or large bags. *Songthaeo's* may be rented *(half-day 400-800 Bt., whole day 1000-1500)*.

Tuk Tuks operate like taxis and are more expensive. Expect to pay 40-50 baht for a journey from the middle of town to a destination near the 'super-highway' ring road.

The State Railway of Thailand

(Reservations & Information Tel: (0) 5324 2094). Sleeping berths and seats on rapid (**Rap**), express night trains (**Exp**), and special express trains (**Exp S**) and reclining seats on the 'sprinter' (**Drcx**) service may be booked using the SRT's computerised reservation system. Bookings cannot be made for local (**Loc**) trains.

The lower sleeping berth in second class (air-conditioned or fan) is a little wider and more comfortable than the upper. Rapid and express trains have dining cars, and vendors sell drinks, snacks and food. Reservations can be made through agents or at advance booking offices at main stations.

Trains	Rap	Drcx	Rap	Exp	Drcx	Exp S	Rap	Loc
Bangkok	06:40	08:25	15:00	18:00	19:25	19:40	22:00	
Don Muang (Airport)	07:31	09:16	15:50	18:50	20:11	20:32	22:53	
Ayutthaya	08:10		16:33	19:29		21:11	23:36	
Lopburi	09:11	10:35	17:50	20:25	21:32		00:39	
Nakhon Sawan	10:50	11:49	19:50	21:55	22:51	23:35	02:25	05:00
Phitsanulok	12:51	13:24	22:00	00:08	00:59		05:14	07:29
Uttaradit	14:24	14:35	23:44	01:34	02:14		06:46	09:26
Den Chai (Phrae)	15:56	15:27	01:05	02:40	03:13	04:09	07:58	10:55
Lampang	18:03	17:27	03:30	04:48	05:15	06:20	10:27	13:42
Khun Tan	19:18		04:25	05:39		07:20	11:20	14:42
Lamphun	20:05	18:58	05:11	06:21	06:51	08:05	12:01	15:37
Chiang Mai	20:30	19:20	05:35	06:50	07:10	08:30	12:20	16:10

	Rap	Loc	Drcx	Rap	Exp	Exp S	Drcx	Rap
Chiang Mai	06:25	07:35	08:35	15:45	16:25	18:00	20:10	21:30
Lamphun	06:50	08:06	08:57	16:09	16:49	18:25	20:30	21:53
Khun Tan	07:48	09:09		16:56	17:37	19:17		22:36
Lampang	08:42	10:16	10:26	18:10	18:43	20:08	21:57	23:27
Den Chai (Phrae)	10:50	13:20	12:25	20:25	21:48	22:25	23:54	01:30
Uttaradit	12:02	14:47	13:02	21:43	21:55		00:50	03:10
Phitsanulok	13:42	16:42	14:36	23:34	23:10		02:12	04:33
Nakhon Sawan	15:46	19:30	16:18	01:58	01:16	02:34	03:52	06:37
Lopburi	17:47		17:35	03:50	02:58			08:15
Ayutthaya	19:04			04:46	03:57	05:08		09:22
Don Muang (Airport)	19:52		19:07	05:35	04:42	05:57	06:48	10:09
Bangkok	20:45		19:50	06:25	05:30	06:50	07:45	11:05

guar Motorcycle Hire *200.D9*
Mun Muang Rd. Hrs. *08:00–18:30.*
torcycles, mountain bikes & jeeps.
: (0) 5341 9161

e's Bike Team *200.E9*
'1 Soi 2, Chiang Moi Rd. Big bike
air specialists & reliable 250 cc trail
es for rent. Tel: (0) 5325 1186
For information on motorcycle
ring, maps and publications,
sult <www.Gt-Rider.com>

rth Wheels *200.D9*
7/1-2 Mun Muang Rd. Hrs. *07:00–*
00. cars/jeeps, English speaking
des & drivers. Tel: (0) 5321 6189,
5341 8233-4, Fax: (0) 5322 1709
bile (0) 1952 6160
ww.northwheels.com>

i Enduro Team *M20 inset p.122*
Mu 1 Tambon Viangtai, Pai M.H.S.
130. motorcycles trekking and
duro school. Tel/Fax: (0) 5369 9395

een Bee Car Rent *200.E9*
Mun Muang Rd. cars/jeeps + travel
: (0) 5327 5525, (0) 5320 8135
x: (0) 5327 4349

RAVEL, TREK & TOUR
OMPANIES

ntact Travel (Thai Adventure
fting) *163.X3 73/7 Charoen Phathet*
. C.M. 50100. Rafting, bicycling,
kets, etc Tel: (0) 5327 7178 Tel/Fax:
0) 5327 9505
ww.activethailand.com>

hiang Mai BIS Travel *200.E9*
'1 Loi Khroh C.M. 50100 Myanmar
vel specialist. Tel: (0) 5320 6738
/Fax: (0) 5327 9111 E-m:
ni@chmai.loxinfo.co.th

hiang Mai Adventure Tour
0.E8 131 Ratchadamnoen Rd. C.M.
200 Local Tours. Tel/Fax: (0) 5327
10 E-m: cmat@loxinfo.co.th

hiang Mai Green Alternative
ur *201.E11 31 Chiang Mai-*
mphun Rd. Eco-friendly city and
ral cultural & natural tours.
: (0) 5324 7374, Tel/Fax: (0) 5324
04 E-m: cmgreen@cmnet.co.th

ick & Travel see p.182 or
ww.ClickandTravelOnline.com>

st-West Tour *163.Y2*
wntown Inn. *1721-11 Loi Khroh Rd.,*
M. 50100. Tours visit Lisu Lodge
ww.lisulodge.com> & Lanna Farm

Tel: (0) 5328 1789, Fax: (0) 5328 1788

Edelweiss Princess Co
4 Hassadissewi Rd. Mae Ping Lake Tour.
Tel: (0) 5340 4717, Fax: (0) 5322 1852

Erawan PUC Tours
211/14-15 Chang Khlan Rd. Local
tours to Mae Kamphong Tel: (0) 5327
4212-3, Fax: (0) 5327 6548 E-m:
erawanpu@loxinfo.co.th

Gem Travel *163.X2*
Soi 6 Charoen Prathet Rd. Hrs. *07:30–*
21:30. Local Tours. Tel: (0) 5327 2855,
(0) 5381 8932, (0) 5381 8744, Fax: (0)
5327 1680 E-m: info@thaifocus.com

Mae Ping Riverside Tour *201.F11*
101 Chiangmai-Lamphun Rd. Hrs.
07:30–18:00. Local Tours. Tel: (0)
5330 2121, Fax: (0) 5330 2122
<www.vacations.to/chiangmai>

M.C. Tour (Mae Sot Conservation
Tour) *184.E7 175/18 Ratchadamnoen*
Rd. C.M. 50200. Action tours to army
camp in Mae Rim & rafting on Mae
Chaem. Tel: (0) 5381 4424, Tel/Fax:
(0) 5381 4505 E-m: msc@loxinfo.co.th

Pon & Annette Trekking *200.D8*
Eagle House #1, *26 Ratwithi Rd. Soi 2.*
C.M. 50200. 4 day/3 night treks.
Tel: (0) 5387 4126, Fax: (0) 5387
4366 <www.eaglehouse.com>

Thana Guest House *200.E9*
27/8 Soi 4 Thaphae Rd. C.M. 50100.
Suzuki Caribian convoys into the hills.
Tel/Fax: (0) 5327 9794, Fax: (0) 5327
2285

Travel Shoppe *200.E9*
2/2 Chaiyaphum Rd. Hrs. *08:30–17:30.*
Air tickets. Tel: (0) 5323 2352,
(0) 5387 4091, (0) 5387 4280
Fax: (0) 5323 2300

The Trekking Club *163.X2 41/6*
Soi 6 Loi Khroh Rd. Licensed guides.
Tel/Fax: (0) 5381 8519
E-m: t_tanpidcha@hotmail.com

The Trekking Collective *200.E8*
25/1 Ratwithi Rd. Hrs. *09:00–18:00.*
Alternative treks & travel.
Tel/Fax: (0) 5341 9079-80
E-m: trek-collective&cm.ksc.co.th

Third Eye
220 Mu Chang Khian Soi 9. Chang
Phuak, C.M. 50300. alternative & eco-
tours by special arrangement.
Tel/Fax: (0) 5389 2405
E-m: thirdeye@loxinfo.co.th
www.3rdeyetravel.com

Security & Safety
The Chiang Mai area is
much safer than most parts
of the world, especially the
cities, and most people are
very honest. You must, however, take normal precau-
tions as for any place. Bag
snatching in dark sois at
night has been reported, and
things can go missing from
rooms, even from safety de-
posit boxes. The incidence of
such crimes is not frequent
enough to warrant any un-
due concern, however.

You should monitor your
credit card when using it —
credit card use is now widespread, but play it safe.

Misadventure from acci-
dents can be reduced by
standard measures such as
wearing motorcycle helmets
and fastening seat belts. Misadventure can also occur
through being caught taking
illegal drugs. Penalties are
extremely severe!

Certain types of visitor
regularly switch off their
brains when they meet seemingly friendly 'ghost guides'
who skillfully lead them to
'great deals' (for the guides,
that is) on gemstones!

Finally, just as some
foreigners may think that all
Thai women are of loose
virtue, so a few Thai men
may have misperceptions
about foreign women. In the
unlikely event of being
harassed, seek trusted
company and be careful.

Kirsty Jones. R.I.P.
<www.chiangmainews.com/
kirstyjones>
Tourist Police call 1155
toll free, or (0) 5324 8974,
(0) 5324 8130

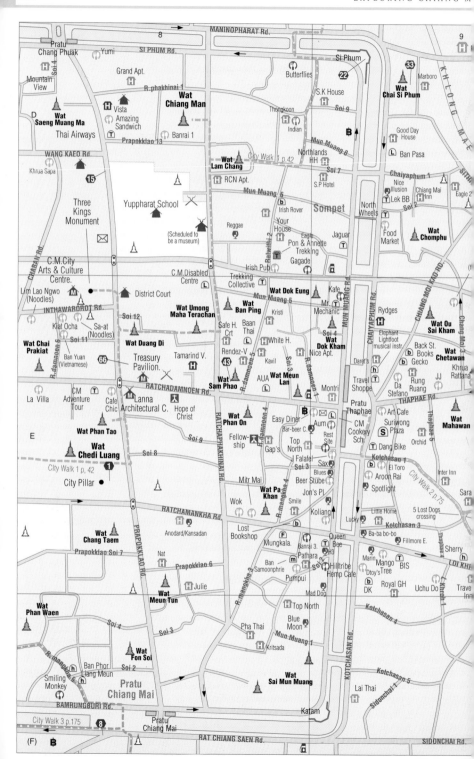

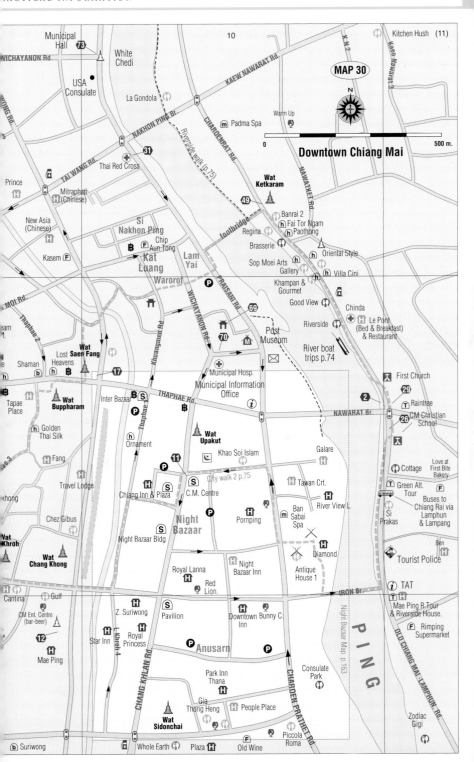

Downtown Chiang Mai

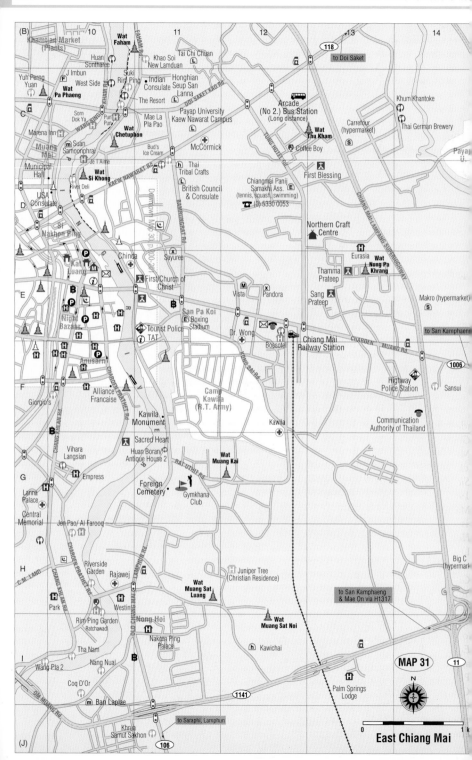

East Chiang Mai

MAP 31

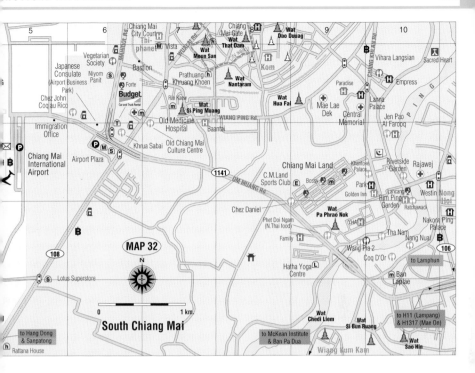

South Chiang Mai

FURTHER REFERENCE

nderson, Edward F. *Plants and Peoples of the Golden Triangle*. Silkworm Books, Chiang Mai, 1993.

ck, Carl. *Temples and Elephants: Travels in Siam in 1881-1882*. Oxford University Press, 1986 (first published by Sampson, Low, Marston, Searle & Rivington, London 1884)

isselier, Jean. & Beurdeley, Jean Michel. *The Heritage of Thai Sculpture*. Asia Books Co. Ltd. Bangkok, 1974.

wis, Elaine. & Lewis, Paul. *Peoples of the Golden Triangle*. Thames & Hudson, New York, 1984.

nth, Hans. *A Brief History of Lan Naa*. Silkworm Books, Chiang Mai, 1994.

ongpaichit, Pasuk & Baker, Chris. *Thailand: Economy & Politics*. Oxford U.Press, 1995

angwatthanakun, Songsak. & Cheesman, Patricia. *Lan Na Textiles: Yuan, Lue, Lao*. Centre for the Promotion of Arts and Culture, Chiang Mai University, 1988.

emchit, Sommai. & Doré, Amphay. *The Lan Na Twelve-Month Traditions*.

Chiang Mai, 1992.

Punjabhan, N., Wichienkeo A. & Na Nakhonphanom, Somchai. *The Charm of Lanna Woodcarving*. Rerngran Publishing, Bangkok, 1994.

Reynolds, Frank E. & Reynolds, Mani. B. (translators). *The Three Worlds According to King Ruang. A Thai Buddhist Cosmology*. The Institute of Buddhist Studies, Berkeley, 1982.

Shaw, J.C. *Northern Thai Ceramics*. 2nd Ed. Oxford University Press, 1989.

Skinner, William G. *Chinese Society in Thailand: An analytical history*. Cornell U.P. Ithaca 1957

Snodgrass, Adrian. *The Symbolism of the Stupa*. Cornell University, New York, 1985.

Wyatt, David. K. *A Short History of Thailand*. Silkworm Books, Chiang Mai, 1984.

Wyatt, David. K. *The Chiang Mai Chronicle*. Silkworm Books, Chiang Mai, 1995.

Vatikiotis, Michael. R.J. *Ethnic Pluralism in the Northern Thai Capital of Chiang Mai*. Phd. Thesis. University of Oxford, 1984

USEFUL THAI

THAI IS A TONAL LANGUAGE. These are marked as follows. High ´, low `, falling ^, rising ˇ. The middle tone has no mark. Visitors with atonal mother tongues will find it hard to hear the tones. To better pronounce the transliteration in this book, study the near sound equivalents listed below.

consonants

cheu (to meet)	ch	=	j as in jam,
chok	ch	=	ch as in chin
kuti (monk's house)	k	=	g as in garden
khun (you)	kh	=	c as in cup

phan (a thousand)	ph	=	p as in paper
thao rai (how much)	th	=	t as in time

vowels

i	=	as in 'tip', or as in 'need'
o	=	as in 'top', or as in 'poor'
u	=	as in 'good', or as in 'shoe'
a	=	as in 'come', or as in 'farm'
e	=	as in 'get'
eu / oe	=	as in 'word'

Obviously, it is better and more fun to ask a Thai to help say the words correctly. The Thai spellings should help you to do this.

Numbers

0 (๐)	Sǔn	ศูนย์
1 (๑)	nùng	หนึ่ง
2 (๒)	sǒng	สอง
3 (๓)	sǎm	สาม
4 (๔)	sìi	สี่
5 (๕)	hâ	ห้า
6 (๖)	hòk	หก
7 (๗)	chèt	เจ็ด
8 (๘)	pàet	แปด
9 (๙)	kâo	เก้า
10 (๑๐)	sìp	สิบ
11	sìp èt	สิบเอ็ด
12	sìp sǒng	สิบสอง
13	sìp sǎm	สิบสาม
20 (๒๐)	yi sìp	ยี่สิบ
21	yi sìp èt	ยี่สิบเอ็ด
25 (๒๕)	yi sìp hâ	ยี่สิบห้า
30	sǎm sìp	สามสิบ
40	si sìp	สี่สิบ
50	hâ sìp	ห้าสิบ
100 (๑๐๐)	nùng rói	หนึ่งร้อย
200	sǒng rói	สองร้อย
1,000	nùng phan	หนึ่งพัน
5,000	hâ phan	ห้าพัน
10,000	nùng mèun	หนึ่งหมื่น
100,000	nùng saěn	หนึ่งแสน
1,000,000	nùng lán	หนึ่งล้าน

Common Words

Monday	wan chan	วันจันทร์
Tuesday	wan angkhan	วันอังคาร
Wednesday	wan phút	วันพุธ
Thursday	wan pharúhàt	วันพฤหัส
Friday	wan sùk	วันศุกร์
Saturday	wan sǎo	วันเสาร์
Sunday	wan athít	วันอาทิตย์
today	wan ní	วันนี้
yesterday	mûa wan	เมื่อวาน
tomorrow	phrûng ní	พรุ่งนี้
this week	athít ni	อาทิตย์นี้
this month	duan ní	เดือนนี้
this year	pi ní	ปีนี้
next week	athít nâ	อาทิตย์หน้า
next month	duan nâ	เดือนหน้า
next year	pi nâ	ปีหน้า
toilet	hông nám	ห้องน้ำ
water	nám	น้ำ
hotel	rongraem	โรงแรม

Politeness particles are frequently used, particularly when asking or answering questions. They soften the words spoken and encourage a harmonious feeling in the mind of the Thai.

The particle for women:

    khá/khâ   คะ/ค่ะ

The tone of คะ is high when asking a question and low (ค่ะ) when answering.
For men: khráp   ครับ

Questions & Phrases

When?

    mûa rài (khá/khráp)   เมื่อไหร่ (คะ/ครับ)

How much?
    thâo rài (khá/khráp) เท่าไหร่ (คะ/ครับ)
Where
    thînǎi (khá/khráp) ที่ไหน (คะ/ครับ)
Where are you going?
    pai nǎi (khá/khráp) ไปไหน (คะ/ครับ)
Hello (and goodbye)
    sawàddi (khà/khráp) สวัสดี (ค่ะ/ครับ)
See you again
    cheu kan mài (") เจอกันใหม่ (ค่ะ/ครับ)
Good luck
    chôk di (") โชคดี (ค่ะ/ครับ)
Goodbye (formal)
    la kòn (") ลาก่อน (ค่ะ/ครับ)
Thank you
    khôp khun (") ขอบคุณ (ค่ะ/ครับ)

I'm enjoying myself
    sànúk (khà/khráp) สนุก (ค่ะ/ครับ)
Good
    di (khà/khráp) ดี (ค่ะ/ครับ)
No (use with politeness particle)
    mâi khà/khráp ไม่ (ค่ะ/ครับ)
No, I don't want it.
    mâi ao (khà/khráp) ไม่เอา (ค่ะ/ครับ)
I'm sorry!
    khǒ thôt (khà/khráp) ขอโทษ (ค่ะ/ครับ)
Not good
    mâi di (khà/khráp) ไม่ดี (ค่ะ/ครับ)
I don't understand
    mâi khâochai (khà/khráp) ไม่เข้าใจ (ค่ะ/ครับ)
Never mind
    mâi pen rai (khà/khráp) ไม่เป็นไร (ค่ะ/ครับ)

GLOSSARY

mphoe	district town		*makara*	mythical water beast
un	village		*mom*	mythical wolf-like guardian
angwat	province		*mondop (mandapa*)*	type of tower
ao	northern lord, prince or ruler		*muang*	northern Thai valley community
edi	(cetiya), stupa, pagoda		*naga*	mythical serpent
iang	northern Thai capital		*nam tok*	waterfall
o fa	garuda finial on temple roof		*phasin*	tube skirt
namma (thamma)*	Buddhist natural law		*prasat*	tower
i	mountain		*sangha*	the monkhood
ukkha (thukkha)*	unsatisfactoriness		*sala*	Thai hall or shelter
kham	royal hall		*singha*	mythical lion guardian
trai	scripture library		*Songkran*	Thai new year
ng	(hamsa) mythical gander		*sonthaeo*	pick-up minibus
ai	stream		*talaeo*	talisman to ward off evil spirits
yen	cool heart		*tambon*	village group
lae	decorative finial on roof		*tin chok*	decorative weaving style on hem of tube-skirt
mphaeng din	earthern rampart		*tung*	pennants
am muang	northern Thai language		*thewada (deva*)*	heavenly spirits
antok	low table, local dining style		*ubosot*	consecrated ceremonial hall
on muang	northern Thai people		*viharn (vihara*)*	ceremonial hall
athong	float offering		*wiang*	northern town
mphan	mythical human-beast creature		*wien tien*	circumambulation of chedi or *viharn*
ti	monks residence		*wan phra*	Buddhist holy day
e nam	river			
dha chat	penultimate incarnation of Buddha			

* Pali-English variant.

INDEX

CITY STREET LIST

Anusarn	ถนนอนุสาร	G4
Arak	ถนนอารักษ์	E3-4
Om Muang	ถนนอ้อมเมือง	E6-H7-J6
Bunruangrit	ถนนบุญเรืองฤทธิ์	E3-4
Bamrungburi	ถนนบำรุงบุรี	E4-F4
Bamrungrat	ถนนบำรุงราษฎร์	H3
Chaban	ถนนชัยบ้าน	F3-E4
Chaiyaphum	ถนนชัยภูมิ	F3
Chang Khlan	ถนนช้างคลาน	G4-6
Chang Moi	ถนนช้างม่อย	G3
Chang Phuak	ถนนช้างเผือก	F2-3
Charoen Muang	ถนนเจริญเมือง	H4-J4
Charoen Prathet	ถนนเจริญประเทศ	G4-H5-G6
Charoenrat	ถนนเจริญราษฎร์	G3-H3
Chiang Mai-Lamphun	ถนนเชียงใหม่–ลำพูน	H4-7
Chiang Mai-Lampang Super Highway	ถนนเชียงใหม่–ลำปาง ซุปเปอร์ไฮเวย์	C2-F1-J3
Chiang Mai Land	ถนนเชียงใหม่แลนด์	F6-G6
Chotana	ถนนโชตนา	E1
Faham	ถนนฟ้าฮ่าม	H1-2
Huai Kaew	ถนนห้วยแก้ว	B4-C2-E3
Inthawarorot	ถนนอินทวโรรส	E3-F3
Kaew Nawarat	ถนนแก้วนวรัฐ	G3-I2
Kamphaengdin	ถนนกำแพงดิน	G4-5
Koh Klang	ถนนเกาะกลาง	G7
Kotchasan	ถนนคชสาร	F4
Loi Khroh	ถนนลอยเคราะห์	F4-G4
Maninopharat	ถนนมณีนพรัตน์	E3-F3
Mun Muang	ถนนมูลเมือง	F3-4
Nantaram	ถนนนันทาราม	E5-F5
Nimmanhaemin	ถนนนิมมานเหมินทร์	C2-3
Prapokklao	ถนนพระปกเกล้า	F3-4
Praisani	ถนนไปรษณีย์	G3-4
Ratchadamnoen	ถนนราชดำเนิน	E4-F4
Ratchamankha	ถนนราชมรรคา	E4-F4
Ratchaphakhinai	ถนนราชภาคีนัย	F3-4
Ratwithi	ถนนราชวิถี	E3-F3
Sanam Kila	ถนนสนามกีฬา	F2-3
Samlan	ถนนสามล้าน	E4
Singharat	ถนนสิงหราช	E3
Sirimangkhlachan	ถนนศิริมังคลาจารย์	D2-3
Si Phum	ถนนศรีภูมิ	E3-F3
Sidonchai	ถนนศรีดอนไชย	G4
Suthep	ถนนสุเทพ	B3-D3
Suriwong	ถนนสุริวงค์	F5
Thaphae	ถนนท่าแพ	G4
Thiphanet	ถนนทิพยเนตร	E4-5
Thung Hotel	ถนนทุ่งโฮเต็ล	I2-4
Wang Sing Kham	ถนนวังสิงห์คำ	G1-2
Wualai	ถนนวัวลาย	F4-E5